THE
NATURAL SUPERIORITY
OF WOMEN

The
Natural Superiority
of Women

ASHLEY MONTAGU

Fifth Edition

ALTAMIRA
PRESS

A Division of
ROWMAN & LITTLEFIELD PUBLISHERS, INC.
Walnut Creek • *Lanham* • *New York* • *Oxford*

ALTAMIRA PRESS
A Division of Rowman & Littlefield Publishers, Inc.
1630 North Main Street, Suite 367
Walnut Creek, CA 94596
www.altamirapress.com

Rowman & Littlefield Publishers, Inc.
4720 Boston Way
Lanham, MD 20706

12 Hid's Copse Road
Cumnor Hill, Oxford OX2 9JJ, England

British Library Cataloguing in Publication Information Available

Library of Congress Cataloging-in-Publication Data

Montagu, Ashley, 1905–
   The natural superiority of women / by Ashley Montagu. —5th ed.
   p. cm.
   Includes bibliographical references and index.

   ISBN 0-7619-8981-1 (cloth : alk. paper)
   ISBN 0-7619-8982-X (pbk. : alk. paper)
   1. Women—Psychology. 2. Feminism—Psychological aspects. 3. Sex role. I. Title.
HQ1206.M65 1999
305.4—dc21   98-40173
                                                                CIP
Printed in the United States of America

⊖™ The paper used in this publication meets the minimum requirements of American
National Standard for Information Sciences—Permanence of Paper for Printed Library
Materials, ANSI/NISO Z39.48–1992.

Production and editorial services: Pattie Rechtman
Editorial management: Jennifer R. Collier
Cover design: Joanna Ebenstein

To Marjorie
With all my love

CONTENTS

About the Author

The times call for the social scientist who controls at a good level the many different sciences that deal with human nature. In this area Ashley Montagu is our and the world's best man.

— *The New York Times*

Born in England in 1905, Ashley Montagu was educated at the University of London, University of Florence, and Columbia University. After serving as a research worker in natural history at the British Museum, he became curator of physical anthropology at the Welcome Medical Historical Museum in London. He has taught anthropology at Harvard, Princeton, and the University of California. He has been director of research for the New Jersey Committee on Growth and Development, and for many years served as chairman of the Anisfield-Wolf Award Committee on Race Relations. He wrote, directed, and produced the film "One World or None," and was the rappporteur of the Scientific Committee which, in 1950, drew up the famous UNESCO "Statement on Race." He has been called "the most successful writer to a literate public since H. G. Wells." His hobbies are book collecting and gardening.

True Science teaches that the elevation of woman is the only sure road to the elevation of man.

—Lester F. Ward

If ever the world sees a time when women shall come together purely and simply for the benefit and good of mankind, it will be a power such as the world has never known.

—Matthew Arnold

If I were asked . . . to what the singular prosperity and growing strength of that people ought mainly to be attributed, I should reply: To the superiority of their women.

—*Democracy in America*, Pt.II, Bk. III, Ch. 12, 1840,
Alexis De Tocqueville

Adams owed more to the American woman than to all the American men he ever heard of, and felt not the smallest call to defend his sex who seemed able to take care of themselves; but from the point of view of sex he felt much curiosity to know how far the woman was right, and, in pursuing this inquiry, he caught the trick of affirming that the woman was the superior. Apart from truth, he owed her at least that compliment.

—*The Education of Henry Adams*, Ch. 30

What is better than wisdom? Woman.
And what is better than a good woman? No-thing.

—"The Tale of Melibeus," *Canterbury Tales*
Geoffrey Chaucer

The best half of creation's best.

—*The Angel in the House*
Coventry Patmore

The most interesting study of womankind is man.

—Ella Wheeler Wilcox

FOREWORD

BY SUSAN SPERLING

On a recent visit to a friend on the faculty of a prestigious midwestern university, I examined a curious letter I found on top of a stack of manuscripts in her guestroom. It had been sent to faculty and administrators and consisted of a long, literate, racist and antifeminist tract. It vilified blacks and Latinos as substandard in intelligence, Jews as morally degraded, and feminists as poisoning relations between men and women. The general tone of this anonymous document was *epater les progressives.* While further out in rightfield than some of the polemic on race and gender recently generated within the academy, some of its messages were quite resonant with the ideas of academics such as Murray, Hernnstein, and Dinesh de Sousa.

I read on in fascinated horror. The author of the tract soon fixed his hostile gaze on those seminal figures of twentieth-century anthropology, Franz Boas and his acolyte, Ashley Montagu. He indicted them both for, presumably, through their writings, provoking ethnic and racial intermixing. The author went on to uphold the very sort of nineteenth-century racism posing as science that Boas and Montagu were instrumental in unmasking. It is tempting to call such views as these marginal, but it would be a mistake to do so. Some of the ideas in this diatribe have increasingly important cachet in the United States of the late twentieth century. Witness what now floats on the ether of the internet and sits on the shelves of popular bookstores. The year 1994 saw the publication of both *The Bell Curve* and Phillipe Rushton's *Race and Evolution,*[1] the latter of which states that blacks are genetically inclined to greater libido, less intelligence, and less parental investment in their children. Rushton is no anonymous writer of diatribes, but a former Guggenheim Fellow and tenured faculty person, and a recipient of almost a million dollars from the racist Pioneer Fund. Biological reductionism and stereotyping also pervade some of the mainstream discourse on gender within the academy. A recent literature in the new discipline of "evolutionary psychology" posits innate differences in basic behaviors of men and women. According to some evolutionary psychologists, men are largely motivated by the drive to inseminate as many fertile women as possible. Women, on the other hand, are believed to attempt to hold on to high status male provisioners for themselves and their offspring.[2]

The twin constructs of race and gender were key formulations during anthropology's early years and continue to be in its central zone of contestation. The abhorrent tract I read in my friend's guestroom makes one correct point: Ashley Montagu has been in the thick of things for a long time, a central figure in the struggle for what constitutes the modern scientific study of human differences, versus retrograde repackaging of nineteenth-century racism, sexism, and eugenics. This struggle has often been misapprehended as one between the "politically correct" and the "politically incorrect." But it has much to do with correct science, which incorporates sophisticated research strategies from biology and social science into anthropology, as opposed to incorrect science. What is generated within the academy about race and gender has important implications for public under-standing of human differences, a perspective that Ashley Montagu has represented for decades. In a period in which the increasing emiseration of the poor, many of them women, is justified by neosocial Darwinism, scholarly and popular ideas about these issues are more than purely academic.

Seeded by the Enlightenment search for the "laws of nature," germinated within the social and political-economic environ-ments of nineteenth-century colonialism, anthropology has been formed by and formed Western taxonomies of male, female, self, and other. But the birth of anthropology as a modern discipline, some might say its delayed birth, took place in the middle of this century. Ashley Montagu was present at this birth and was one of its midwives. Although himself born early in this century, Montagu spans two centuries in his intellectual influences and formation as a scientist and popular intellectual. Two of his teachers, the British evolutionary anatomist Sir Arthur Keith and the American anthropologist Franz Boas, respectively represent nineteenth- and twentieth-century directions. To understand why Montagu's writings on gender and race are so important—and his work on race and gender *should* be examined as a dyad—it is important to view them in the broad sweep of twentieth-century academic and popular discourses on these issues.

Montagu wrote this book during a period crucial to the formulation of twentieth-century discourses on gender and race in anthropology and related disciplines, and reading his work offers insights into this history. A historically contextualized reading of *The Natural Superiority of Women* allows us to unravel some of the important threads of theory and practice in the study of difference at mid-century. Montagu's recognition of the complex relationships between culture and biology, his "insistence on the principle of multiple and interlocking causation," as Aldous Huxley wrote in his forward to Montagu's first edition of *Man's Most Dangerous Myth: The Fallacy of Race* (1942),[3] his apprehension of the social and political contexts of scientific studies of gender, and, finally, his deconstruction of the Western ideology of male dominance are important contributions to the history of gender studies. In subsequent editions of the book, Montagu engages a number of important feminist writers inside and out of the academy, and this most recent edition provides a fascinating discourse between the author of the original text and these later works on gender relations.

Race

It is useful to look at the arguments that Montagu makes regarding that other locus of "difference," race, because he developed many of his criticisms of scientistic sexism along the same lines as his deconstruction of racialist typologies. Montagu is explicit about the linkage between sexism and racism as parallel modes of oppression:

> The women of the nineteenth century—second class citizens within male-dominated societies—were treated in a manner not unlike that which is still the bitter experience of blacks in the United States and in many parts of the world. Traits mythically attributed to blacks today were for many generations saddled upon women. . . .

says Montagu in the forward to the fourth edition of this book,[4] and he reiterates this in *The Natural Superiority of Women.*

Montagu studied anthropology at University College and the London School of Economics in the early 1920s, where the received wisdom on the issue of race was still very much that of a hierarchy of primitive to more advanced human types exemplified by modern peoples. According to this central construct of nineteenth-century cultural evolutionism, living groups such as the Australian aborigines were thought to exemplify earlier stages of European evolution. This mode of analysis was also frequently applied to social and economic classes and to the sexes within Europe. The lower classes and women in general were thought by many, including Darwin, to represent more primitive levels of adaptation. An early teacher of Montagu's, Sir Arthur Keith, believed that racial animosities are part of "the primitive organization of the brain."[5] As a student of Franz Boas, Montagu came under the influence of a powerful critic of this kind of thinking, one who turned decisively away from the racialism of nineteenth-century physical anthropology. Boas's 1940 book *Race, Language and Culture*[6] drew attention to the many errors of nineteenth-century anthropometry, so elegantly unpacked by Stephen Jay Gould at a later date in *The Mismeasure of Man.*[7] These included the misuse of statistics, the arbitrariness of assigning varied individuals in human populations to groups based on "ideal types," and a fundamental misunderstanding of the complex relationship between biology and culture.

Sir Arthur Keith had said "Nature keeps her human orchard healthy by pruning and war is her pruning hook."[8] In distinct contrast to this Malthusian perspective, Boas wrote in 1941,

> It is also necessary to remember that in varying environment human forms are not absolutely stable, and many of the anatomical traits of the body are subject to a limited amount of change according to climate and conditions of life. . . . The stature in European populations has increased materially since the middle of the nineteenth century. War and starvation have left their effects upon the children growing up in the second decade of our century. . . . The importance of selection upon the character of a population is easily over-estimated. . . . The economic depression of our days shows

clearly how easily perfectly competent individuals may be brought into conditions of abject poverty and under stresses that only the most vigorous minds can withstand successfully. Equally unjustified is the opinion that war, the struggle between national groups, is a selective process which is necessary to keep mankind on the onward march."[9]

Boas, a German Jewish academic refugee to America in 1899, well understood the Malthusian and eugenic implications of such thinking, as well as its scientific invalidity. His ideas and research agendas influenced most of those who were important to the early twentieth-century reformulation of anthropology as distinct from nineteenth-century scientistic racism and ethnocentrism.

In the drafting of both the first and second UNESCO statements on race, Montagu applies some of the same analytical frameworks to race as he would to gender in *The Natural Superiority of Women*. The UNESCO statements on race[10] move the concept of race out of its nineteenth-century biologizing framework and firmly into the context of social construction: "For all practical social purposes, "race" is not so much a biological phenomenon as a social myth. According to present knowledge, there is not proof that the groups of mankind differ in their innate mental characteristics, whether in respect to intelligence or temperament."[11] Three individuals assumed primary authorship of the first statement on race, Ashley Montagu, Julian Huxley and Theodosius Dobzhansky. As authors of these "sacred texts of mid-century biological humanism,"[12] each contributed essential elements of the formulation of the statements. Dobzhansky and Huxley, along with the evolutionary geneticist Haldane (important in the drafting of the second statement) were architects of the modern evolutionary synthesis.

Montagu's contribution reflected a Boasian theme not much noted in discussions of Boas's unparalleled influence in American and twentieth-century anthropology. Boas is often characterized as responsible for a disjunction between biology and culture. But Boas was a physical anthropologist as well as a social scientist, as illustrated by his application of classic anthropometric techniques to prove that head measurements of immigrants to America in the early twentieth century were not inherited ethnic or racial "traits," but rather a result of impoverished environments.[13] Thus, Boas showed that socioeconomic class can influence biology. In his approach to race and gender, Montagu is an exemplar of this synthetic tradition, combining insights from biological and cultural studies, and recognizing that not only culture but also biology are contingent phenomena. Montagu writes,

> It gradually became clear to me that the most important setting of human evolution is the human social environment and that the adaptive responses to the challenges of different environments can influence evolutionary changes through the media of mutation, natural selection, social selection, genetic drift, and hybridization.[14]

Like his teacher Boas, he was committed to the insight that "educability" and behavioral plasticity are hallmarks of the human species, and that cooperation rather than violence, and progress in the achievement of human dignity are possible. A central assertion of the UNESCO statements is the mental equality of races, and Montagu goes on to apply some of the same reasoning to his deconstruction of the assertion of male superiority over women in cognitive ability.

The 1950 UNESCO statement on race reads: "with respect to most, if not all, measurable characteristics, the differences among individuals belonging to the same race are greater than the differences that occur between the observed averages for two or more races within the same major group."[15] In contrast to the racial typologies of the eighteenth- and nineteenth-century west, this approach strips the category "race" of essentialist biological meaning, and allows us to inquire how the categories of race and gender have been historically constructed. The historian of science Donna Haraway has pointed out how essential the modern synthesis was to anti-racism and feminism in the post-world war II period:

> The "plain evidence" of the eyes, so relied upon in typological approaches to race and sex, has been forced to give way, at least in important part, to a biology constructed from dynamic fields of difference, where cuts into the field come to be understood as the historical responsibility of the holder of the analytical knife.[16]

The UNESCO statements were critical moments in the formulation of the scientific and political meanings of race that would irrevocably change the direction of studies of race by twentieth-century anthropologists. Some recent discussions of this formative period in modern physical anthropology have claimed erroneously that Montagu and others made race "off limits" as a field of inquiry for political reasons.[17] While Montagu and Dobzhansky were clearly very aware of the political implications of the statements (and their importance as a response to racist scientism of the past, including that used in Germany to justify the Holocaust), the statements also reflected the growing body of scientific evidence on variation in population genetics. This is not to imply that typological racialism (or sexism) in science is now dead. On the contrary, the last decade has seen a resurgence of racial and gender typologies, often loosely based upon sociobiological assertions, more about which later. But the new approach crafted by Montagu, Dobzhansky, and others opened the arena for increasingly effective contestation of nineteenth-century racist science, as well as new ways to examine popular and academic received wisdom about gendered roles and abilities.

Gender and Evolutionary Theory

Montagu's vision in this book of the role of gender in the human past is in many ways a discourse with a century of anthropological theory. The issue of male dominance was a central concern in the Victorian evolutionary debate. Darwin and other evolutionists had asserted that it was both universal and "natural." This assertion is congruent with many aspects of popular thought on gender in nineteenth-century Europe, and with Victorian moral precepts on the relationships between the sexes.[18] As noted by Frederick Engels, Bertrand Russell and others, Darwinism was both an expression of Victorian individualism and liberalism, and broadly used to justify these theories as natural law. In *The Origin of Species*,[19] Darwin discussed sexual selection as involving active males and passive females. In *The Descent of Man* he wrote that "woman seems to differ from man in mental disposition, chiefly in her greater tenderness and less selfishness" and "Man is the rival of other men, he delights in competition, and this leads to ambition which passes too easily into selfishness," and in a famous (or infamous!) passage,

> The chief distinction in the intellectual powers of the two sexes
> is shown by man's attaining to a higher eminence, in whatever

he takes up, than can woman—whether requiring deep thought, reason, or imagination, or merely the use of the senses and hands. If two lists were made of the most eminent men and women in poetry, painting, sculpture, music (inclusive both of composition and performance), history, science, and philosophy, with half a dozen names under each subject, the two lists would not bear comparison. We may also infer . . . that if men are capable of a decided pre-eminence over women in many subjects, the average of mental power in man must be above that of women . . . (men have had) to defend their females, as well as their young, from enemies of all kinds, and to hunt for their joint subsistence. But to avoid enemies or to attack them with success, to capture wild animals and to fashion weapons requires the aid of the higher mental faculties, namely, observation, reason, invention, or imagination. These various faculties will thus have been continually put to the test and selected during manhood.[20]

The Natural Superiority of Women may be read as a multilayered argument against this passage in Darwin, taking us on a century-long time travel in which Montagu engages many of the chief arguments against this view of women's "natural" inferiority. During Darwin's lifetime, feminists Eliza Burt Gamble and Antoinette Brown Blackwell indicted the sexist bias in Darwin's work, their ideas receiving little attention among scientists.[21] Important twentieth-century works in human and animal ethology followed this model of active male and passive female (a model also embedded in Geddes' and Thomson's influential *The Evolution of Sex,* written in 1890).[22] To the "Man the Hunter" model of the 1960s and 1970s, may be added such studies as Wickler's (1973) work on algae, showing active males and passive females, Geist's on mountain sheep (1971) and Williams' text on the evolution of human behavior, *Sex and Evolution* (1975), standard references of the period.[23] As a number of feminist anthropologists have pointed out, both Darwinism and the androcentric evolutionary literature of the 1970s occurred coincident with the first and second waves of Western feminism, and both were popularized as in some cases explicit rebuttals to claims for gender equality.[24]

Montagu's response to Darwinian sexism, past and present, is complex. On the one hand, he staunchly denies and effectively deconstructs the idea of women's passive role in evolution and hence inferior cognitive and other abilities. On the other hand, his belief that women are less competitive and more naturally nurturant essentializes gender in ways that resonate strongly with nineteenth-century concepts. This bridging of the Victorian and modern is one of the fascinating things about Montagu: At the same time that we find him in a discourse with modern feminists such as Ervin-Tripp, Greer, Gimbutas, and Heilbrun, he is also responding to late Victorians such as Geddes and Thomson, some of whose ideas about essential qualities of male and female biology he echoes. *The Natural Superiority of Women* is in some ways a late Victorian treatise, in the very best sense. Like such works, it takes on large questions, drawing from biological and cultural studies, and thus making use of anthropology's holistic forte. This integrative approach, characteristic of earlier phases of the discipline, has been largely abandoned as the field experienced radical fragmentation in the last decades of the twentieth century.

Montagu is wonderfully prescient, pointing us in the direction of modernity and postmodernity in some key areas of race and gender studies. *The Natural Superiority of Women* also reflects essentializing visions of women inherited from the Victorian period, while the author at the same time deconstructs key aspects of Western patriarchal ideology. Montagu endorses an essentialist theory of women's role as mothers as preeminent. Nowhere is this more forcefully illustrated than in his ambivalence towards the modern women's movement, which he embraces as doing "magnificent work," while indicting "extremists" in the movement who attack as sexist those claiming the primacy of needs for female nurturance in the early years of childhood. At the same time, Montagu contests key aspects of Western patriarchal ideology using data from physical anthropology, cultural anthropology, cognitive and developmental psychology, and physiology. To follow the various threads that make up the dense weave of these nineteenth- and twentieth-century gender studies requires an examination of "contradictions, tensions, and paradoxes"[25] from which patterns emerge.

In the area of evolutionary studies, some of the themes played in the UNESCO statements are reflected in the work of Sherwood Washburn, the key formulator of the "new physical anthropology" at mid-century. Washburn wove together the humanism of the

U.N. statements with important elements of the new synthesis, translating "population" into social group and emphasizing the universal origin of human behavior and culture. This post-World War II "biological humanism" laid the groundwork for the development of a theory of human origins that explains the universal nature of human adaptations at the time of origin, including gender differences.[26] By taking the study of populations to the level of social group, and through his encouragement of generations of students in primate field studies, Washburn set much of the research agenda for decades of physical anthropology, joining functional comparative anatomy to primate field studies.

Primate Studies of Gender

It is from Washburn and his students' work that the model of Man the Hunter arose, around an explicit analogy to the behavior of Savannah baboons. According to this model, key elements of human culture are derived from our species' hunting past, in which males were presumably responsible for tool-making and cooperation.[27] Because Montagu explicitly rejects the model Man the Hunter in his analysis of the origins of human culture, it is useful to travel down the primatological paths that led to the wide dissemination of the image. Modern Western primate studies arose largely in decolonized Africa and other Third World sites. Soon thereafter, anthropological primatologists and their advocates in other disciplines began to fit data about monkeys and apes into models of human evolution. The template had been set earlier in the century by Robert M. Yerkes and Clarence Ray Carpenter, both of whom worked with nonhuman primates to examine human evolutionary issues. Earlier in the century, before the advent of commercial plane travel and antibiotics, both essential to the ability of Western scientists to undertake large-scale field studies (Washburn, personal communication), Robert Yerkes and his colleagues had undertaken experiments with captive apes on issues of gendered behavior. Yerkes, working with caged chimpanzees, set up a series of food-chute experiments in which females and males were offered food items through a chute leading to their cage. He believed that females traded sexual access to males in exchange for food, and that this indicated evolutionary behavioral adaptations. Yerkes believed that females and males were equally intelligent, but had distinct psychobiological and temperamental differences.[28]

After the Second World War, naturalistic field studies of primates proliferated in the a number of Western societies, including the United States.[29] In the period since World War II, field and laboratory studies of primates have produced a large body of data on the behavior of diverse species. Explaining gender differences in our species' evolution has been a major focus of models of primate evolution in the post war period, which have often proposed that changes in reproductive behavior is a central factor in the hominid transition. In the 1960s data from a variety of field studies, particularly those of savannah baboons and the chimpanzees of the Gombe Reserve in Tanzania, were incorporated into structural-functionalist models for human evolution, centering on the sexual division of labor, the origin of the family, and the origins of human gendered behavior. In much of the academic and popular evolutionary literature of the 1960s and 1970s, an analogy was made between the savannah baboon troop and early hominids. The message in these accounts of early hominid life is about aggression and territoriality as biologically determined hominid traits, male hunting as the engine of the hominid transition, and the dominance hierarchies of males as functioning to maintain social order and cooperation.

Linda Marie Fedigan has reviewed many of the evolutionary reconstructions by primatologists of this period.[30] She points out that the "baboonization" of early human life in such models rested on a savannah ecological analogy: Since protohominids evolved on the African savanna, presumably they would have shared certain selective pressure with modern baboon troops, particularly for predator protection by large males. There is now evidence that the earliest phases of human evolution may not have occurred in savanna paleoenvironments, and that, in any case, our species is genetically magnitudes more closely related to forest-living apes than to baboons.[31] Washburn, his student Irven DeVore, and other early post-war period baboon researchers had viewed male dominance as functioning to organize troop members hierarchically and to control overt aggression. Fedigan argues that the other primary model for protohominid evolution, that of the chimpanzees studied by Jane Goodall at the Gombe Reserve in Tanzania, was far more sensible.[32]

Here the analogy rested on the immensely closer phylogenetic relationship between chimps and human with humans and chimps sharing about 98% of their genes, reflecting their recent common ancestor. This model emphasized the mother-offspring bond, sharing within the matrilocal family, the immigration of young females to new groups, birth spacing, and temporary sex bonding. It is to this chimpanzee behavioral model that the first wave of feminist authors, in particular the constructors of the "woman the gatherer" model, would turn for primatological evidence of the social centrality of females in early hominid evolution.[33]

The savanna baboon model was compatible with, and tended to bolster, a Hobbesian view of human society, while the chimpanzee model originally tended to reflect a more benign view, stressing the mother-infant pair and a more flexible, less hierarchical social structure. But many of the assumptions underlying the early use of ape and baboon behavioral data in models for hominid evolution were equivalent: Ape and monkey behavior were the microcosms of human social behavior and political life, including the politics of gender. Fedigan points out the "baboonization" of protohominids became so common that by the early to mid-1970s not a single introductory text in human evolution omitted reference to it. As Rowell[34] and other critics of this model stressed, many of the generalizations and assumptions about the functions of male dominance made by early baboon researchers and their popularizers were unsubstantiated by data from other field sites. Rowell's study of the troop movements of forest baboons, for instance, indicated that the direction of daily foraging routes was determined by a core of mature females rather than by the dominant males. As feminist scholars such as Sandra Harding and Donna Haraway note,[35] women primatologists often have had a different vision of group structure and behavior because they attended to female actors in ways that male primatologists did not.[36] This focus on female behavior in baboons and a variety of other species became fuel for the critical deconstruction of the baboon model during the 1970s. In addition, a number of studies questioned the assumption that male dominance conferred a reproductive advantage on particular males, thus contributing to selection for male aggression.

The period between the mid-1950s and the mid-1970s saw a tremendous emphasis on the baboon model and Man the Hunter hypothesis for human evolution. Haraway has pointed out the deep postwar anxieties that fueled this image, anxieties about the fate of civilization, social stability, the stress of urban environments and the potential instability of the modern family.[37] Popular books of this period, including Robert Ardry's *African Genesis* (1961), *The Territorial Imperative* (1966), *The Social Contract* (1970), and *The Hunting Hypothesis* (1976); Lionel Tiger and Robin Fox's *The Imperial Animal* (1971); Desmond Morris's *The Naked Ape* (1967); and Konrad Lorenz's *On Aggression* (1966), brought these images of male aggression, dominance and social control to a wide readership.[38] During this period, a number of popular books contested these images of territorial and aggressive males and passive females as the ordering force of hominid society. Jane Goodall's *In The Shadow of Man* (1971), Elaine Morgan's *The Descent of Woman* (1972), and Evelyn Reed's *Woman's Evolution* (1975) challenged the zeitgeist of male dominance and hunting ability as the starting point of a heavily gendered account of the hominid transition.[39] It is to these contestations of the primacy of male agency as central to the hominid transition that Ashley Montagu turns in his discussion of the human past. He indicts the "putdown" of women as implicit in the Man the Hunter model and cites some of the important texts contesting the model, such as Dahlberg's edited volume *Woman the Gatherer* (1981), Nancy Tanner's *On Becoming Human* (1981), and Richard Lee's work on the San of the Kalahari (1979, 1974).[40] Montagu argues for the importance of women's gathering of up to 80% of the food consumed by modern food foragers, and against the obfuscation of the significance of their economic and social roles in the androcentric evolutionary models of the 1960s and 1970s.

Cultural Anthropology of Gender

The Natural Superiority of Women also attempts to make sense of the widespread subordination of women in many of the world's complex societies. To place this aspect of the book in context, it is useful to look back at the nonlinear pathways taken by feminist scholars in cultural anthropology who have attempted to understand the causes of the existence of women's subordination in many cultures studied by twentieth-century anthropologists. Early in *The Natural Superiority of Women*, Montagu takes up the question of whether male dominance is a universal, biologically determined feature of human life or culturally determined in particular political, economic, and historical settings, contexts that he asserts have only existed for a relatively narrow time frame in our species' history. How he solves this conundrum reveals much about his intellectual roots and how they have branched in the soil of twentieth-century gender discourses.

A key concern of the mid-Victorian debate about gender was whether female subordination was universal or "natural." Bachofen asserted that human cultures had undergone a matriarchal phase in which women ruled over men and were later deposed.[41] Civilized women, it was proposed by many Victorians, were less subordinated than "indigenous" women. Anthropologist Micaela di Leonardo has pointed out the ways in which "assertions of male lust, female purity or licentiousness, male anxiety of paternity, and female capacities for moral uplift were deeply woven into these accounts and found their way into the evolutionary schemata of those late Victorians Marx and Freud."[42]

In the early 1970s feminist anthropology (or "the anthropology of women," as it was then called) was part of the larger political and academic ferment in the United States growing out of the 1960s, including the civil rights and antiwar movements, feminism, and environmentalism. Marxist theory underwent a revival in the post-McCarthy academy, Kuhn's influential book *The Structure of Scientific Revolutions* provided persuasive evidence for a historically and socially contextualized science (vs. "timeless" scientific authority), and a generation of predominantly white, middle-class and college-educated women began to limn the links between politics and knowledge and to question the received wisdom of classic social science work on gender formation and relations.[43]

Despite the high profile of a small number of women in the field, most notably Margaret Mead and Ruth Benedict, women anthropologists have had significantly lower academic status for most of the twentieth century.[44] Most of the ethnographic work considered foundational to the discipline before the 1970s was done by men. Male ethnographies most often focus on male activities, perspectives and structures of power and authority;

male anthropologists have had more access to and interest in the lives of men, among other reasons. In some cases, wives in the field with anthropologist husbands studied women and wrote "women's ethnographies," such as Elizabeth Fernea's *Guests of the Sheik*.[45] By the early 1970s gender was being written into anthropology as exemplified by two important anthologies of feminist anthropology published in the middle of the decade: Rayna Rapp Reiter's *Toward an Anthropology of Women* (1975)[46] and Michelle Rosaldo and Louise Lamphere's *Women, Culture, and Society* (1974).[47] These works included new data and theoretical approaches. Women's kinship struggles in the distribution of power were noted by Jane Collier; Louise Lamphere, who surveyed the political ramifications of women's networks cross-culturally; and Sylvia Yanagisako. Annette Weiner and Jane Goodale returned to the sites of two classic male ethnographies to reconsider the lives of women. Both showed women's power in kinship relations and prestige. A number of studies of peasant populations emphasized the significance of women's economic roles.[48]

Eleanor Leacock used ethnohistorical evidence to rework Engels' theory linking the rise of private property to woman's subordination.[49] She argued for precolonial, pre-state egalitarian societies, as does Montagu in *The Natural Superiority of Women*. In doing so, Montagu refers to the work of archaeologist Marija Gimbutas and her popularizers, suggesting widespread matricentric cultures in Europe and elsewhere until their conquest by warrior-based groups.[50] Rosaldo, Chodorow, and Ortner substantially reworked Weberian, Freudian, and Levi-Straussian theoretical frameworks, respectively.[51] Gayle Rubin's "sex-Gender system" reoriented theoretical issues in Freud, Marx, Levi-Strauss, and Lacan.[52] In the introduction to her important edited volume, *Gender at the Crossroads of Knowledge: Feminist Anthropology in the Postmodern Era*, di Leonardo describes as the "conundrum of ethnographic liberalism,"[53] the problem faced by feminists in taking a cultural relativist approach to their data, and at the same time explaining the seeming near-universality of female subordination over two decades of ethnographic work. One approach has been the "indigenous women better off model" based on the assertion that women outside of the industrialized west enjoy a higher status. Working within this framework, some feminist ethnographies have noted the fact that peasant women in many groups exercise considerable power and influence. One advantage of this perspective, di Leonardo notes, is the way in which it fits with ethnographic liberalism's advocacy stance, functioning to *epater* complaisant westerners. At the same time, she points out, it was sometimes simply true.

Another approach has been the return to Marxist evolutionary models, such as the one proposed by Engels in *The Origin of the Family, Private Property, and the State* (1884).[54] Engels had based his model heavily on L. H. Morgan's research on kinship terminology, which links different systems to evolutionary stages of human culture. These approaches identify particular modes of production to gender relations, claiming an originally egalitarian social structure that becomes stratified with the rise of private property. These studies reversed the Victorian ideology of Western colonialism's "uplifting" impact upon women, claiming a worsening effect after contact with the West.[55] An important feminist rereading of structuralism, particularly Levi-Strauss's analyses of symbolic structures of human cognition, is reflected in the work of Sherry Ortner.[56] Ortner's influential and controversial theory claimed an association between women and nature and men and culture as a universal symbolic cognitive model, and links this to women's subordination. An entire book of feminist critique takes up the problems posed by her theory.[57] Other important approaches to symbolic structures include Michelle Rosaldo's separation of domestic and public domains, in which she proposed that societies with rigid separations between these domains tend to devalue the private and thus women.[58] Chodorow's Freudian revisionism looked at the role of mothers as by its very nature engendering universal male resentment of female authority, male dominance, and weak female ego boundaries in daughters.[59] Other ethnographies offered data without proffering larger theoretical points, such as Margery Wolf's 1974 Taiwan ethnography *The House of Lim* or Liz Dalby's ethnography of Japanese geishas,[60] which document avenues of authority and power among women informants.

Each of these approaches to the relationship between gender and culture has received substantial critical attention. For instance, it has often been noted that the evolutionary Marxist explanations use living cultures as exemplars of the past, thereby employing the Victorian comparative method discarded by many in the twentieth century. There are also numerous examples of nonegalitarian small-scale societies, among groups in Papua New Guinea for example. In this regard, Rapp (1979) has shown that changes brought about by capitalist production relations, or even the colonialism that preceded them, are not automatically detrimental to women. Jordanova and Bloch have noted that Ortner's symbolic associations model is not universal, that the oppositional categories nature/culture have a specifically Western, enlightenment history.[61] In contrast to the grand theoretical visions, di Leonardo suggests strongly that the most significant labor of feminist anthropology to date may consist of the careful attempts to understand the particular meanings of gender in specific cultural, political-economic and historical contexts.

This most recent edition of *The Natural Superiority of Women* builds upon a number of these perspectives in feminist anthropology. Montagu makes good use of the revised view of women's power in a number of non-Western cultures, pointing out the Western lack of familiarity with the reality of women's activities in many other settings, such as his use of ethnographic data from the Agta people of Luzon, Philippines. In offering explanations for the widespread observation of female subordination in many complex societies, he cites the archaeologist Gimbutas' theory that female subordination in Europe and the Near east is a relatively recent phenomenon, only about seven thousand years old, and imposed by warfare bringing about a shift from matricentric to androcentric culture.

Here, again, we can see Montagu's bridging of late Victorian and modern anthropology. Montagu uses modern foraging societies as examples of what human life may have been like in prehistory. This has been a popular turn in evolutionary analysis, since most of our history as a species has been spent as food foragers. In Montagu's (and many other influential modern social scientists') embrace of the San and other food foragers as models of what gender relationships might have been like for early hominids there is a persistence of same cultural evolutionary schemes of the nineteenth century that he explicitly indicts. Recent revisionist ethnographies of the San speakers of the Kalahari illustrate the problem with generalizing about the past from our often flawed visions of food foragers. For instance, in Edwin Wilmsen's study of the San, he suggests that "their bodies express their structural position as an ethnically encoded underclass in the political economy of the Kalahari,"[62] and that they have a long history of herding, farming, domestic service and begging, even as laborers in African mines, as well as food foraging. In his use of the San as models of food foraging society, Montagu essentializes them, a move criticized in some recent feminist anthropology.

Despite the hopeful liberalism of Montagu's interpretation on this issue, we are left with the unruly facts of groups as diverse and historically separate as cultural communities in Highland New Guinea and the Amazon basin which have developed their own "brands" of institutionalized female subordination. Hence, unilineal models are insufficient to explain these widespread cultural forms. Perhaps in response to this fact, Montagu posits a revision of Freudian arguments that universalize male jealousy of female reproductive processes, in a similar vein to some psychological anthropologists such as Melford Spiro. Spiro has recently analyzed a variety of cross-cultural myths of female danger and pollution as universal responses of males to the reproductive role and power of mothers.[63]

Other feminists have questioned essentialist visions of the family with great currency in the modern west. In their seminal essay "Is there a Family?", Collier, Rosaldo, and Yanagisako view the family "as not a concrete institution designed to fulfill universal human needs, but as an ideological construct associated with the modern state."[64] They deconstruct Malinowski's theory of the universality of the family (itself an attempt to overturn the nineteenth-century evolutionary model of "primitive promiscuity" as the earliest stage of human culture). Malinowski believed that essential features of the family exist in all cultures, flowing form the universal need of the human infant for prolonged nurturance. Collier et al. point out that this bounded unit is not really defined as such in many cultures. For instance, among the Zincantecos of southern Mexico there is no similar term for parents and children to the English word "family," the basic social unit is defined as "the House," which may include from one to twenty people:

The Malinowskian view of The Family as a universal institution—which maps the "functions" of nurturance onto a
collectivity of specific persons (presumably nuclear relations)
associated with specific spaces (the home) and specific affective
bonds (love), corresponds to that assumed by most contemporary writers on the subject. But a consideration of available
ethnographic evidence suggests that the recent view is a good
deal more problematic than a naive observer might think.[65]

Collier, Rosaldo, and Yaginasako point out that when anti-
feminists attack the ERA, it is often on the grounds that women's
equality has encouraged the loss of nurturant bonds within the
family. Because this is where we are used to receiving nurturance, they write, it is a functionalist error to assume that this
is the only site and constellation of personae that can provide
nurturance. Family and work are conceived a oppositional
realms; the latter where cutthroat capitalism holds sway and
the former becoming everything oppositional to that. This
taxonomy not only represents real relationships between people,
but to some degree helps shape them.

Thus, the ideal of the postindustrial Western family becomes

an ideological construct with moral implications. . . . This
ideology also exploits women's weariness with the incom-
patibility of postindustrial work and family demands, as well
as their anxiety over the asymmetrical terms of the heterosexual
courtship and marriage market and of women's vulnerability
to divorce-induced poverty.[66]

Montagu's approach to the modern Western family is sometimes
ambiguous. On the one hand, he thoroughly rejects the idea of
superior male authority within the family, at the same time
embracing the concept of an essentialized, morally superior
woman as the civilizing influence in family life. Here, again, we
see him bridging essentialist visions of women reified in the west
over the last centuries and a progressive egalitarian view of power
and authority within family life.

But the most sophisticated feminist theory in anthropology
is moving steadily in another direction from these universalizing
discourses inherited from the Victorian period—merging
feminism and political economy, minus the Victorian evolutionary stagism of earlier Marxist theory. This suggests a

comparative ethnography that abandons the search for the universal "key" to male dominance over women in favor of assessing the full range of human gender arrangements and their connection to human biology, specifically contingent histories of change and its political economic correlates, including colonization and decolonization, and warfare. Such a framework suggests that although San speakers of the Kalahari cannot be essentialized as egalitarian food foragers similar to our earlier stages as a species, their recent history of forced relocation by the former apartheid government of South Africa (which brought about a rise in interpersonal violence, including male violence against women) can teach us something important about the contexts of violence against women. We may learn much about gendered violence from these shifting, historically, politically and economically complex contingent processes as they unfold in human communities.

Gender, IQ, and Cognition

In its treatment of the question of whether there are cognitive differences between the sexes, *The Natural Superiority of Women* mines another rich area of modern social science debate. Montagu's discussion of intelligence—specifically the question of whether innate versus socialized differences in cognitive ability and intellectual performance exist between the sexes, embraces the progressive agenda of social constructionism, which asserts that much that has been previously viewed as ineradicable, biologically based difference is, in fact, culturally constructed. Here he works with the nuanced palate of late twentieth-century data and theory when he writes,

> The principal error committed by the intelligence testers has been the assumption that their tests yield a quantitative measure of the biological determinant of intelligence. Evidence today reveals that these tests measure, if they measure any-thing, the combined effects of socioeconomic and schooling combined with genetic factors passed through the alembic of a unique personality. While there is no known method of teasing out of this amalgam what is due to biological factors and what is due to genes plus the individual history of the person, we do know that when the environmental factors are improved IQs go up, and that when they are depressed IQs go

down. What, then, do they measure? No one really knows what intelligence is.[67]

The topic of comparative male and female intelligence was legitimized by Darwinian evolutionary writings because of their emphasis on the importance in natural selection of variation. As Stephen Jay Gould illuminates in his exhaustive deconstruction of racist anthropometry in *The Mismeasure of Man*,[68] intelligence was studied by important Victorian phrenologists and neuroanatomists, such as George Romanes, who believed that brain size and intelligence were secondary sexual characteristics. In 1910 Helen Thompson Woolley presented the first methodological critique of work in the psychology of gender differences, asserting that,

> There is perhaps no field aspiring to be scientific where flagrant personal bias, logic martyred to the cause of supporting prejudice, unfounded assertions, and even sentimental rot and drivel have run riot to such an extent as here. Up until this period, the kinds of studies upon which assertions of gender differences in ability were based included such tests as rate and endurance in tapping on a telegraph key, tests of handwriting and association. In the case of handwriting, women were judged to be more conventional and men more individual. In tests of association, women and men were asked to write a number of associations when presented with a word. In one study of association women were judged to show more "concrete forms of response, a more subjective attitude, and more indecision."[69]

There was very little research using psychological methods.

These kinds of studies were largely replaced by standardized IQ tests during the next decades, during which the mental testing movement came to predominate in studies of all kinds of presumed cognitive differences, including those alleged between races and the sexes. As J. S. Hyde points out in an essay on the psychology of gender differences,[70] the original IQ test had been developed by Binet in France with politically "benign" and practical goals. Binet had been commissioned by the French Minister of Public Instruction to identify children who might benefit from special education. Stanford psychologist Lewis Terman published the first American version in 1916. Neither Terman nor Binet believed that there were patterns of gender difference in performance on the Stanford-Binet. Terman published comments to the effect that girls did as well as boys on the test, and that women's comparative lack of professional advancement was due to social causes not innate differences in intellectual ability. The tests were, in fact, constructed to balance items that would advantage either sex, reflecting this ideological commitment to gender equality in ability.

The next phase in the testing movement occurred between the 1930s and 1940s, when there was a shift in focus to a method known as factor analysis in intelligence testing. L. L. Thurstone, for instance, developed the Primary Mental Abilities Test (PMA), which is based on factor analysis applied to seven areas of variation in ability, including mathematical ability, spatial ability, and verbal ability. Researchers began to use this style of analysis and to apply it to research on gender differences in these areas. By the 1930s there were numerous textbooks in differential psychology that reviewed a fairly large body of data on presumed group differences in abilities by gender, race, class, and age. Anastasi and Tyler drew similar conclusions: that women were superior in verbal abilities across the lifespan, and that men excelled in spatial relations tests, but that this difference emerged later than differences in verbal skills.[71] Another set of differences believed to emerge later in men were mathematical skills requiring reason rather than computation. These perspectives have dominated the field of psychology of gender differences for many years. In their important and comprehensive review of studies of gender differences, the psychologists Eleanor Maccoby and Carol Jacklin reviewed thousands of studies on gender differences in cognition, personality and behavior.[72] They concluded that much research was methodologically flawed and they on this basis dismissed conclusions about differences in the areas of achievement motivation, self-esteem, and higher-level cognitive tasks. They agreed that gender differences were well-supported by research in four areas: girl's greater verbal ability, boys greater mathematical and visual-spatial abilities and greater aggression. Gender differences in these areas have been reified and widely taught to many generations of undergraduates in introductory psychology classes.

In 1979 Jeanne Block published a critique of Maccoby and Jacklin's work, pointing out significant problems in their method of assessing data.[73] By the 1980s a new statistical approach was applied to the analysis of gender differences in a wide range of studies. Called meta-analysis, it uses sophisticated quantitative methods to combine evidence from different research studies. This method has, among other things, allowed researchers to take into account intra-sex variability, to average the results of studies with greater reliability, and to indicate the magnitude of gender differences. Hyde applied meta-analysis to the studies reviewed by Maccoby and Jacklin in 1981 and found that the differences reified by these authors were not as significant as thought. She also found that the differences within the sexes are greater than those between the sexes. The general conclusions emerging from modern metaanalysis of cognitive abilities are, as Montagu noted in the early 1950s, not large. In analyses of social behaviors, such as aggression and helping, whether such differences are found depends upon context and methodology.[74]

But the vision of race, gender, and class typologies of aptitudes persists, and in fact has had a significant resurgence in the 1990s. In 1994 Hernnstein and Murray published *The Bell Curve: Intelligence and Class Structure in American Life*, which attempts to justify race and class inequality by attributing it to innate differences in intelligence between groups. This claim has been repeatedly made over the course of the last century, to be refuted as "unfounded race, class, and gender prejudice," as Adolph Reed, Jr. points out in his review of the Murray and Hernnstein book in *The Nation*.[75] Hernnstein and Murray claim that rigid IQ stratification exists in every sphere of social life, winnowing out the "haves" from the "have nots." They propose a kind of brave new world in which people are slotted for the places that best fit their intelligence. In the book, they claim that Sir Cyril Burt, William Shockley, Arthur Jensen, and others who have asserted group differences in heritable aspects of intelligence, were maligned and persecuted by politically motivated ideologues.

That many of the early psychometricians had political and social agendas is clear. Daniel Kevles's *In the Name of Eugenics*[76] documents extensively the involvement of earlier psychometricians, including some of the founding fathers of modern psychometry, with the eugenics movement before World War II. Hernnstein and Murray neglected the work of many in this area of research, including Harvard psychologist Howard Gardner,[77] whose arguments for multiple fields of intelligence Montagu cites enthusiastically. Hernnstein and Murray write,

> The broad envelope of possibilities suggests that senior business executives soak up a large portion of the top IQ decile who are not engaged in the dozen or so high IQ professions. . . A high proportion of people in those positions graduated from college, one screen. They have risen in the corporate hierarchy over the course of their careers, which is probably another screen for IQ. What is their mean IQ? There is no precise answer. Studies suggest that the mean for . . . all white collar professionals is around 107, but that category is far broader than the one we have in mind. Moreover, the mean IQ of four year college graduates in general was estimated at about 115 in 1972, and senior executives probably have a mean above that average.[78]

Putting aside the question of whether such reasoning constitutes "science," the implications for non-whites and women here are obvious, as the ranks of senior business executives are still largely filled by white men. Hernnstein and Murray's scientistic racism and sexism has as serious implications for white women as it does for women and men of color. That these authors could propose such a simplistic and unsupported social Darwinist argument in 1994, and be taken seriously, speaks to the persistence and power of this retrograde ideology well into the end of the twentieth century.

As geneticist Richard Lewontin has pointed out, the relationship between genes and complex behaviors such as intellectual performance is not a simple one. Control does not flow from the gene outwards only, but development involves an interaction between the growing organism, its genotype and the environments in which it develops from conception on.[79] This epigenetic view of development reflects the consensus among modern geneticists, so often neglected in the popular literature of group "difference," whether speaking about race or gender. Ashley Montagu spoke to the complexity of biological and environmental interactions, including cultural experience, in the formation of adult human beings, long before these perspectives were widely understood or appreciated, as in his mid-century opus on race "The most important setting of human evolution is the human social environment."[80] Since the publication of *Man's Most*

Dangerous Myth, he has continued to reflect this perspective of complexity in behavioral and biological interactions in human evolution and individual development in his large corpus of works on these issues.

Many other contemporary examples of Victorian scientistic sexism and racism thrive in the contemporary political arena. Women's reproductive and economic rights, the rights of recent immigrants in U.S. society, as well as the rights of African Americans to economic and political justice are debated in the context of a retrograde shift to the political right in American life. Hernnstein and Murray's warning in *The Bell Curve* of the "dysgenic" effects for the nation of the relatively greater number of children of "low-IQ women" and the "shifting ethnic makeup" resulting from immigration of presumably low IQ, high fertility populations will "lower the average American IQ by 0.8 points per generation."[81] It is ironic, and disturbingly so, that four decades after the egalitarian UNESCO statements and books such as Montagu's on race and gender, such a return to discredited social Darwinism and eugenics dominates the popular discourse on these issues.

Recent Trends

Montagu's writings on race and gender have stood for at least half a century in opposition to the kind of corrupt scientism found in *The Bell Curve* and similar works. *The Natural Superiority of Women* is, in many respects, a palimpsest of many twentieth-century scientific, humanistic, and progressive approaches to the issue of gender. At the same time, Montagu's roots in late Victorian and early twentieth-century science are reflected in his engagement with the ideas of the evolutionary theorists Patrick Geddes and J. Arthur Thomson, the sexologist Havelock Ellis, whose classic work in late Victorian sexology *Man and Woman* (1898) Montagu liberally cites.[82]

The important bridge that Montagu provides between late nineteenth century and current evolutionary discourses can be traversed in his discussion of neoteny, the concept that humans retain characteristics of the young into adulthood. Montagu's compelling book on this subject, *Growing Young* (1981) presents his own thoughts on this important subject, and those of others from Havelock Ellis to Stephen Jay Gould, who, like Montagu, convincingly argue that neoteny has been strongly selected over the course of human evolution. The Victorian influence can also be felt in Montagu's often essentializing visions of womanhood, some of which are worthy of the Victorian "angel of the hearth" portrait tradition. He writes,

> Because women are unselfish, forbearing, self-sacrificing, and maternal, they possess a deeper understanding than men of what it means to be human. . . It is the function of women to teach men how to be human . . . it is in this that women can realize their power for good in the world and make their greatest gains.

While not entirely different from some modern essentialism within women's studies (i.e., Carol Gilligan's assertion that girls and boys develop fundamentally different perspectives on issues of moral responsibility),[83] it is at odds with much of late twentieth-century feminism, which has separated itself from these fixed images of gender. Women, when given the opportunity, seem to do a pretty good job of being "men"; that is, competitive and assertive in the postindustrial workplace. Montagu's attachment to this philosophy of maternalism leads him to his one scathing criticism of the modern women's movement.

> The Women's Liberation Movement has done magnificent work, but as in all movements there are some extremists in it who argue that those who plead the need of motherhood, who emphasize the importance of mothering in the first few years of the child, are nothing but male chauvinist pigs who are engaged in a conspiracy to perpetuate the servitude of the female.

Here, I think, he sets up a straw woman: few feminists of my acquaintance have ever suggested that the "need of motherhood" should be trashed. On the contrary, it is modern feminist activists who have most consistently fought for the rights of mothers in a society in which too much lip service and too little actual economic support honors this reification of abstract versus real mothers or their children. It is fascinating that, in his dialogue with feminists Greer, Heilbrun, Gimbutas, and others, Montagu stretches to bridge these earlier visions and late twentieth-century feminism.

Modern trends in gender studies are sharply divergent, with sophisticated, nonreductionist research strategies often failing to gain a public hearing, while a regressive biological reductionism dominate the airwaves and bookstores. Montagu's commitment to the role of the anthropologist as public communicator about this issue has been crucial. Biologically oriented feminists in and out of the academy continue to show the complex interactions between culture and biology, an idea that Montagu introduces repeatedly in the book, with its insistence on "multiple and interlocking causation." In these accounts there is an explicit recognition of the social and political context of science. Recent work in cross-cultural studies of reproduction over women's life cycles reveals the way that biological events such as menarche and menopause are affected by cultural practices. Rather than a universal ovary and female body, we learn of a flexible, responsive body that develops epigentically in relationship to a variety of cultural practices. These practices are part of the larger ecology, including subsistence methods, the division of labor, reproductive rules and practices, social stratifications, diet, politics and history.[84] Ashley Montagu speaks to this when he distinguishes between what he calls "first nature" and "second nature," the latter being the effects of culture upon biology.

Over the last decade, as in so many fields, much feminist research has shifted attention to discourse analysis, from the issue of power to that of the representation of power. Feminists in the cultural constructionist realms of the social sciences and humanities have shown the ways in which the idea of polarized gender is itself a historically-based Western construct.[85] Cultural anthropologists, particularly those engaged in a decade of work in Gay/Lesbian studies, have revealed the more nuanced understandings of what constitutes the continuum of gendered roles and behaviors available in some other cultures, an area that Montagu does not specifically engage in this book.[86] But essentialist visions of male and female have made a huge comeback with some of the popularizations of sociobiology since the mid-1970s. Sociobiology universalizes gender strategies, reducing them to essential characteristics of all males and all females. Males, from insects to humans, are presumably always seeking ways to inseminate multiple fertile partners while females, according the sociobiologists, seek to maximize their larger investment in fewer progeny through attracting and keeping high status male provisioners. This approach blurs the substantial differences in patterns of sexuality, reproduction, and marriage cross-culturally, not to mention the immense variation in interspecific reproductive patterns. Unfortunately the debate about sociobiology has often been construed as one between reductionists in the biological and evolutionary sciences who contend that genetic mechanisms selected over phylogenetic history control important human behaviors, and feminists and other cultural constructionists who deny that biology has any important role in human experience.[87] This is far from true: Within modern biology there is an increasing appreciation for the importance of developmental environments in shaping behavior and structure. Many social scientists are interested in the ways in which biology interacts with culture in different settings. The question is one of what constitutes good science, not whether biology or experience are important in the development of human beings.

Sociobiology, having declared genes *uber alles*, is a regression to earlier reductionist modes of understanding behavior, with individual and cultural variation treated a merely a thin veneer over the basic biogram of genetic competition or "kin-selection." Most often, these ideas have been used to forward conservative social agendas. A more reformist perspective among sociobiologists has recently suggested that social institutions may attempt to mitigate extremes of behavior, but must always work within the basic fixed genetic "program." It is no coincidence that sociobiology and the second wave of Western feminism were simultaneous occurrences. Early sociobiologists clearly envisioned their new model as "disproving" feminism. The sociobiologist van den Berghe wrote: "Neither the National Organization for Women nor the Equal Rights Amendment will change the biological bedrock of asymmetrical parental investment."[88] Philip Kitcher, a preeminent critic of sociobiology, points out,

> Sometimes the expression is tinged with regretful sympathy for ideals of social justice (Wilson) at other times with a zeal to *epater les feministes (van den Berghe)* . . . [it] is far from clear that sociobiologists appreciate the political implications

of the views they promulgate. These implications become clear when a *New York Times* series on equal rights for women concludes with a serious discussion of the limits that biology might set to women's aspirations and when the new right in Britain and France announces its enthusiasm for the project of human sociobiology.[89]

In recent years, modern evolutionary science has diverged along these two distinctly different paths. Reputable studies in primatology, genetics, and developmental biology have revealed the exquisitely contingent nature of much biological and social development in our own and other species. At the same time, narrow biological determinism—a kind of genetic fundamentalism related to nineteenth-century sexism—has persisted in popular and academic settings. Recent theorists in a new branch of evolutionary study dubbed "evolutionary psychology" use sociobiology to analyze human marriage and sexual practices. According to the new crop of evolutionary psychologists, because males ejaculate so many millions of sperm over the life cycle, whereas females ovulate far fewer eggs over a lifetime (and in addition must invest heavily in the nurturance of dependent offspring) it pays men to inseminate as many women as possible. Women presumably do better by choosing their inseminators with great care and cunning, since they have fewer shots at the genetic jackpot. Evolutionary psychologists assert that observations in our own and other human societies empirically support the conclusion that gendered sexual behaviors are fixed by biology.[90] Historian Thomas Laqueur has limned the fluctuating concepts of male and female sexuality in his book *Making Sex; Body and Gender from the Greeks to Freud.*[91] Studies such as these show the immense amount of variation in what is associated with womanhood and manhood cross-culturally.

In contrast to some of these recent reductionist trends, Ashley Montagu has always stood for a nonreductionist progressive and humanistic natural science. He knows that other things shape behavior beside genes, and shape it in important ways. He also tells us that little in human life is fixed and unchangeable. As biologist Susan Oyama has pointed out, the human world has never existed before and its conditions are constantly changing.[92] *The Natural Superiority of Women* is an important signpost on the road to this more robust vision of what it is to be human. In his brilliance, resilience and persistence, Ashley Montagu continues to show us how the toolkits of biological and cultural anthropology can be used to build understanding of the human condition. Contemplated in this light, his work is an inspiration.

Preface to the Fifth Edition

Since the fourth edition of this book was published in 1992, much new information bearing on the natural superiority of women has become available. The new findings unexceptionally support and confirm the conclusions reached in this book. These conclusions are based on incontrovertible evidence, evidence that can be confirmed by anyone who will take the trouble to examine it. The facts cannot be argued away. At most it is their interpretation that may be questioned. Here in the light of the findings of science I have attempted to offer the most highly probable explanation of the meaning of the facts. I do not think that these explanations can be seriously challenged. Nor since May 1952, when the book was first published has there been a serious challenge to any of its conclusions. It is necessary to make this unequivocally clear. This is not a work based on the author's opinions. What I am trying to say in this book is that the evidence for the natural superiority of women set out in it represents the actuality of nature. Anyone who desires to argue with the facts of nature should not be intimidated by such a statement. On the contrary, they should be encouraged to doubt and to question, for most people have a way of mistaking their prejudices for the laws of nature. I do not claim to be exempt from this particular frailty. None of us is. The facts set out in this book, however, are either true or false. If it can be shown that any of them are questionable, I would welcome the evidence.

I have endeavored to leave the book essentially as it was written, except that I have brought it up to date, with the latest findings and figures available up to the time of publication. I have also added a certain amount of new material. The results of recent research have in many places enabled me to present the earlier data in reinforced form.

If, for millennia, women have been the "inferior race" of the masculine world, their legitimate claims to being valued at their true worth can no longer be dismissed with a contemptuous shrug or with mordant humor consigned to the collection of more cranky notions entertained by women and their defenders. Prejudice and ignorance have too long complicated the relations between the sexes. The times call for greater understanding based on knowledge. I have in this book, attempted to provide both.

In 1968, for the preface to the second edition of this book, I wrote that "the liberation of women will also mean the liberation of men." While the language and focus of the women's movement may have changed since then, its strength and indeed its diversity continue to constitute a happy augury for the future. Toward that end this book is once again offered as a modest contribution.

Princeton, New Jersey
January, 1999

Preface to the First Edition

I have been thinking about the theme of this book for some thirty years. For an equal number of years, I have discussed it, on and off, with various friends. However, it was not until I talked about my ideas with Norman Cousins, editor of the *Saturday Review,* that, upon his urging, I set them down in an article bearing the same title as this book. This was published in the March 1, 1952, issue of the *Saturday Review.* The response to that article was extraordinary and gratifying. The *Saturday Evening Post* asked to reprint it, and it appeared in July 1952 in its pages.

Because it was Norman Cousins who suggested the writing of this book, it is a very real pleasure to be able to express my thanks to him both for his interest and for his enthusiasm. I am also obliged to Mr. Jack Cominsky, publisher of the *Saturday Review,* for many courtesies. Thanks are also due to Mrs. Marjorie Child Husted for her continued interest in this volume, It has been a pleasure to work with Mr. George Platt Brett, Jr., president of the Macmillan Company, and with my gentle editor, Miss Eleanor Daniels. To my wife I owe deepest thanks for her helpful readings of the manuscript and for being all that a naturally superior person should be.

1952

Prologue

The idea of "superiority" has quite rightly troubled many people, especially women. Genuinely superior persons don't think of themselves as such, and refuse any attempt to describe them as being so. It is only those people who are insecure about themselves who feel compelled to announce their view of themselves to the world. This is the well-known inferiority complex, defined as the repressed fear and resentment of being inferior. We have, indeed, had altogether too much of such things as "superior races" and "inferior races," for there are, in fact, no such entities. Such terms represent the expression of myths the function of which is to keep people, as the expression goes, "in their proper place." Racism is the most blatant expression of that policy. Long ago I wrote in my book *Man's Most Dangerous Myth: The Fallacy of Race,* "If some groups of humanity are culturally more advanced than others, it is because their opportunities have been greater, and not because of some supposed innate superiority. No group of human beings is of less value in the scale of humanity than any other, for all groups of human beings possess the potentialities for development which, under the proper environmental stimulation, would enable them to contribute maximally to the achievement of humanity."

In the world of humanity, of humankind, it is not so much groups, whether they be called national, "racial," ethnic, or sexual, that matter, as the person, the human being. Educability is the outstanding characteristic of the human species, and the variability both in physical and mental traits is so great that no two persons (with the possible exception of some so-called identical twins) will ever be alike. It is in the combination of these traits that the great riches of humanity lies. The strength of America is rooted in its diversity, and it is because you are different from me that you are precious to me. Not only are human beings capable of doing the things that humans have anywhere done, but also, in response to the challenges of the environment, continually to create and invent anew. From this the principle follows that every human being, regardless of group membership, has the right to fulfill his or her potentialities to the optimum.

Anyone who stands in the way of another's development, and compounds the wrong by denying or limiting their political or social rights, commits the greatest of all offenses against humanity. Yet this is the kind of malefaction that civilized peoples have committed not alone against other peoples, but have unrestrainedly felt free to commit against distinguishable groups within their own people. This is precisely how civilized men have been behaving toward women for millennia with the aid of the myth of masculine superiority. The Hellenic Greeks went so far as to deny biological maternity to the so-called mother of a child. As Aeschylus (525–456 B.C.) wrote in the *Eumenides,* "She who is called the mother of the child / Is not its parent, but the nurse of seed / Implanted in the beginning."

In the present book the mythology of female inferiority is challenged and dismantled on the basis of the scientific facts. My many years of work and research as a biological and social anthropologist have made it abundantly clear to me that from an evolutionary and biological standpoint, the female is more advanced and constitutionally more richly endowed than the male. It seemed to me important to make facts clear. Those are the provable facts. Women, as biological organisms, are superior to men. If anyone has any evidence to the contrary, let them state it. The scientific attitude of mind is not one of either belief or disbelief, but of a desire to discover what is and to state it, no matter what traditional beliefs may be challenged or outraged in the process.

To return to the term *superiority,* I do not think it is the label under which women will want to travel. It is enough to know what the biological facts are concerning the endowments of male and female, and where precisely the term superiority belongs. That is why the term must remain, in this book at least, for there is no substitute for it, even though it is something that every woman already knows, but will rarely speak of. Anna Quindlen in one of her delightful columns in the *New York Times,* unequivocally declared her belief in the inherent superiority of women; refering to a friend who said to her, "Have you ever noticed that what passes for a terrific man would only be an adequate woman?" "A Roman candle went off in my head," wrote Ms. Quindlen, adding that her friend was "absolutely right,"[1] That is essentially the fact presented in this book.

This book is designed to bring the sexes closer together, not to declare the supremacy of one to the other. If in these pages the natural superiority of women is emphasized, it is because the fact has thus far received far too little attention, and the time is long overdue that both men and women become aware of it and fully understand its meaning. sNatural superiority does not imply social inequality; on the other hand, the plea of this book is for more mutual love and understanding and complete social equality of the sexes. The plea is for the recovery of a sense of values that will enhance the appreciation of the sexes for each other. As Tennyson wrote long ago, "The woman's cause is man's. They rise or fall together." The idea that women are biologically superior to men will probably be new to most people. There have been several books in the past that have made such a claim, but these use grounds very different from those discussed in the present study. These works came to my attention some time after the publication of my own ideas on the subject. Scott Nearing wrote me that many years ago he and Nellie Seeds published a book entitled *Women and Social Progress* in which certain similar claims were made for women. It has also been pointed out to me that in 1917, H. L. Mencken published a book entitled *In Defense of Women,* maintaining similar views. Also, Mr. Samuel Chugerman has drawn my attention to the fact that the founder of American sociology, Lester F. Ward (1841–1913), "the American Aristotle," in several of his books set out his gynacocentric theory of the priority and superiority of the female. Ward had the great advantage of being a distinguished natural scientist who in the latter part of his life became a social scientist. Ward's ideas, late in coming to my attention, gratifyingly bring strong support to my own.

1

The Natural Superiority of Women

"Superiority: The quality or condition of being higher, greater, or better in some respect, or of having some attribute in a higher degree, than something else," the *Oxford English Dictionary*.

"Natural: Inherent in the very constitution of a person or thing," the *Oxford English Dictionary*.

"Oh, no!" I can hear you say, "Not superior, but equal, partners, complementary, different, but not superior. What an idea!" Men will mostly smile, while women, alarmed, will rush to the defense of men, as women always have and always will. I hope that what I have to say in this book will make women even more willing to do so, for men need their help more than they sometimes seem to know.

Certainly there have been those who have cogently, if not altogether convincingly, argued that women are as good as men; but I do not know, nor have I read, of anyone who has provided the evidence that women are more richly endowed than, or superior to, men. The case has been argued, and often stated, but how, indeed, could one successfully argue such a case in the face of all the evidence to the contrary? Is it not a fact that by far the largest number of geniuses, painters, poets, philosophers, scientists, and so on, have been men, and that women have made, numerically, by comparison, a very poor showing? Clearly the superiority is with men. Where are the Leonardos, the Van Goghs, the Michelangelos, the Shakespeares, the Donnes, the Galileos, the Newtons, the Einsteins, the Freuds, the Mozarts, the Bachs, the Kants, and the Humes of the feminine world? In fields in which women have excelled, in poetry and the novel, how many female poets and novelists of truly first rank have there been? Haven't well-bred young women for centuries been educated in music? And how many among them have been great composers or instrumentalists? Possibly there is a clue here in answer to the question asked. May it not be that women are just about to emerge from the period of subjection during which they were the menials of the masculine world, a world, in which the opportunities and encouragements were simply not available to women? Or in a profounder sense may we not say with Oscar Wilde that "owing to their imperfect education, the only works we have had from women are works of genius."

Today almost everywhere, in spite of remaining discriminations, women are achieving what was once considered beyond their capacity: The Nobel Prize in literature has gone to Selma Lagerlof (1909), Grazia Deledda (1926), Sigrid Undset (1928), Pearl S. Buck (1938), Gabriela Mistral (1945), Nelly Sachs (1966), Nadine Gordimer (1991), Toni Morrison (1993), and Wislawa Symborska (1996). The Nobel Peace Prize has been awarded to Bertha von Suttner (1905), Jane Addams (1931), Emily G. Balch (1946), Mairead Corrigan (1976), Betty Williams (1976), Mother Teresa (1979), Daw Aung San Suu Kyi (1991), Rigoberta Menchu Tum (1992) and Jody Williams (1997).

Not long ago it was inconceivable that any woman would ever have brains enough to attain great distinction in science. Marie Curie, the first scientist to receive a Nobel Peace prize twice—in 1903, when she shared the prize in physics, and 1911, for her work in chemistry—was regarded as a sort of rare mutation. But Mme Curie no longer remains the only woman scientist to receive a Nobel Prize: In chemistry, her daughter Irene Joliot-Curie shared the prize in 1935; Dorothy Crowfoot Hodgkin received it in 1964. Maria Goeppert Mayer shared the physics prize in 1963. In physiology or medicine, Gerty R. Cori shared the prize in 1947, Rosalyn S. Yalow in 1977, Barbara McClintock won it in 1983, Rita Levi-Montalcini shared it in 1986, Gertrude B. Elion in 1988, and Christiane Nusslein-Volhard in 1995.

Women scientists such as Lise Meitner of u-238 fame are no longer extraordinary exceptions; nor are women members of distinguished scientific societies exceptions: The first woman was elected to the National Academy of Sciences in 1925 and since then many others have been elected as members. In 1962, Marguerite Perey, discoverer of Francium, the eighty-seventh element, became the first woman elected to the French Academy of Sciences.

Among instrumentalists there have been such accomplished artists as Myra Hess, Wanda Landowska, and Midori.

As an artist Mary Cassatt was every bit as good as her great French artist friends, Degas and Manet, considered her to be, but it took the rest of the world more than half a century to grudgingly acknowledge it. The truth is that in painting and sculpture, as in virtually everything else relating to creativity and achievement, women have for the most part been written out of history. Germaine Greer has written a brilliant and thoroughly sound answer to the question, Why has there been no female Leonardo, Rembrandt, or other painter of genius? Her book *The Obstacle Race* is beautifully illustrated with the works of outstanding women painters. From these illustrations readers may judge for themselves how admirable so many of these women painters really were. Why there have been so few women artists of the first rank, Greer forcibly shows, were the consequences of the obstacles they faced in the form of family demands and childbirth, the effects of female submissiveness and erotic entanglements with adored male masters, the disturbances of patronizing overpraise, the humiliations of sexual innuendo, the limitations of working on a small scale, and finally, the oblivion of neglect and misattribution.[1] A tragic case in point is that of the French sculptor of genius, Camille Claudel, of whom more later (chap. 10).

However, it is not going to be any part of this book to show that women are about to emerge as superior scientists, musicians, painters, sculptors, or the like. I believe that in these fields they will manifest abilities at least as good as those of men, and possibly even better. Not perhaps, in the immediate future, will they emerge in greater numbers, largely because the motivations and aspirations of many women will continue to be in conflict with family life and its absorbing long-term demands. In the long run, given the same incentives, opportunities, and encouragements as males, there is every reason to believe that the laurels of genius will adorn the brows of women as comfortably and frequently as they will those of men. At this point, in something more than a parenthesis, it should be said that there is a genius of the heart which is vastly more valuable than the accomplishment of any other form of genius—but of that, more later. We do not know where the winds of genius may blow, but what we do know is that everyone possesses the genius and the spirit to transcend the daily circumstances of life, and to transform them to achieve new planes of meaning and creativity. What must be remarked here is that women are just beginning to emerge from their long-fettered period of subjection and the diehard discrimination against them. It is of interest to recall, as illustrative of the prevailing traditional attitudes toward women that the entire article on "Women" in the first edition of the *Encyclopedia Britannica,* published in 1771, consisted of six words: "the female of man. See Homo."

In the politics of sex most men have been Tories, and still continue to be so. If there is any man who without blushing can contemplate the history of his sex's conduct toward women, let it in charity be set down to the fact that he very likely does not consider himself responsible for the errors of his predecessors. Thus absolved from all responsibility for the past, it may be hoped that he will be willing to reexamine some of his inherited beliefs concerning the nature and place of women in the modern world and in the future. And although it may sometimes appear that civilization has a natural resistance against improving itself, there is some evidence that it is still possible for men living in an irrational world to behave rationally, with intelligence and a sense of responsibility.

On occasion men have claimed that they were attempting to escape from the domination of women, when in fact they were fleeing from their own self-doubts and an incapacity to master themselves. Women have always been a convenient screen upon which men have projected their weaknesses and ambivalence. For many men today, attitudes toward women remain very much what they were during the nineteenth century. The women of the nineteenth century—second-class citizens within male-dominated societies—were treated in a manner not unlike that which was the bitter experience of blacks in the United States and in many parts of the world. Nineteenth-century scientists and thinkers, with rare exceptions, were busily engaged in proving that women were inferior to men. Women, it was alleged, had smaller brains than men, were much less intelligent, became more emotional and unstable in stressful situations, were flighty, weakly creatures, and so drearily on.[2] In a crisis, it was asserted, one could always depend upon women to swoon or become otherwise helpless; they were hysterical and sickly creatures who suffered from the "vapors," with little judgment and less sense; they could not be entrusted with the handling of money; and as for the world outside, there they could be employed only at the most menial and routine tasks, as servants, nannies, or if they were adequately trained, as governesses.

It is not that Victorian men were misogynists by biological heredity, but they certainly were by social heredity. Before all else they were the inheritors of an intellectual and cultural climate into which they, as well as women, were thoroughly locked; a tradition in which the inferiority of women was a hoary-headed ancient belief that everyone took for granted, a fact of nature beyond question. But this "fact" of nature was, in fact, a prejudice, a myth.

What is a prejudice? What is a myth? A prejudice is a pre-judgment having no factual validity, a judgment or opinion held before the facts are known. What, then, is a fact? A fact is a datum of experience that has been repeatedly tested and confirmed by independent investigators, the current best fit between reality and our method of confirming it. The greatest enemy of truth is not error, but prejudice. A rigorous thinker or scientist is one who believes in proof without certainty, unlike most other people who tend to believe in certainty without proof. It is the nature of myth to elaborate, but never to prove.

Since most people who have been to school or college have been taught *what* to think rather than *how* to think, they are consequently at the mercy of any juggler who chooses to reinforce their prejudices or create new ones for them to believe. Hitler, for example, was such a one so that he easily persuaded his following, a whole nation, to believe that familiar myths were actual facts. In his case, he was quite aware of what he was doing. Concerning women, most nineteenth-century scientists seem to have been quite unaware that when engaged in the appraisal of women they were doing so with prejudiced minds, for what they were really doing was reinforcing the myths of their predecessors.

Let us say a little more about myths. It is important for us to understand what a myth is, for not even the best of us is any more free of myths than we are of prejudices—and each can be dangerous and destructive. What, then, is a myth?

A myth is usually a traditional belief, of unproven reality, which serves to explain some phenomenon of nature, creation, humankind, the supernatural, religion, persons, social conditions, and the like. Myths are often expedient fictions. What, then, are the functions of myth? Myths perform the double function of serving as *models of* and *models for* cultural attitudes and behavior. In this way they reflect the beliefs of and provide sanction for the actions of society, while at the same time furnishing the forms upon which belief and conduct are modeled. Built as they are into the structure of social relationships, they predetermine the categories of perception, fusing as they do what is unsoundly perceived with the imaginary. The danger of myths is that they tend to be reified as something that has a substantial existence, that is, turned into a truth, a reality. Such myths act as a force of daily life and of history, whereas in fact they are nothing but ideas, abstractions, which are erroneously treated as realities, in short social constructions. Racism is such a myth. It is interesting to note that everything derogatory that has ever been said by whites about blacks has been said by men about women. Indeed, women have been the scapegoats of the masculine world for a very long time.

It has been said that myths are not accountable to reality. But what is reality? Do our separate individual fictions add up to a joint reality? In many cases, and in many religions, for example, they do, and as such they are inarguable, but when it is possible to put them to the test of probability or the measure of the facts, it is another story. Facts seen through the distorting glass of prejudice take on a thoroughly warped significance, and far from being recognized for what they are, myths or prejudices, become "truths." The danger of such myths is that they too often fuse the false and imaginary into a blend that becomes a reality itself.

It was entirely by the skillful use of the hideously effective myth of racism that Adolf Hitler won over the German people, which directly led to World War II and the crimes against and death of many millions of human beings—the Holocaust. The losses to humanity have been incalculable, and will go on reverberating until the last syllable of recorded time. Seen from such a viewpoint the judgment of history is that any act of bigotry against any individual or group is a crime for which the guilty should be brought to justice. This is essentially what the Nuremberg trials were about. Myths tend to bring about what they describe, and thus tend to become "realities." Such realities are often more real to their believers than the truths which would show them to be unreal.[3]

It took World War I to make a dent in the myth of women's inferiority and begin the disintegration of some entrenched beliefs concerning female employability. During that horrible slaughter of over two hundred million human beings, a nightmare which seemed never ending, revolutionary changes were taking place on the home front. Women, for the first time, were enlisted to replace men in occupations that were formerly the exclusive male preserves.[4] Women became bus drivers, train engineers, truck drivers, ticket collectors, factory workers, farm workers, laborers, supervisors, executive officers, armed services personnel, and a great many other things which almost everyone had believed were beyond female capacity. At first it was claimed the women didn't do as well as men; then it was grudgingly admitted that they weren't so bad; and by the time the war was over many employers were reluctant to exchange their women employees for men! But the truth was out: Women do as at least as well as men in most of the fields that had been considered forever closed to them because of their supposed natural incapacities. In many fields, particularly where delicate precision work was involved, women had proved themselves superior to men.

As if releasing themselves from their fetters, women asserted their newfound freedoms in their clothing: the feminine silhouette was made to appear flat and as sexless as possible; unashamedly skirts were raised to show the whole leg (above the ankle); and that "glory to woman," long hair, was cut short in a manlike bob.

Notably, in 1873, Abba Goold Woolson, in her book *Woman in American Society,* presciently wrote of women's long hair, having by males been "declared a glory to women, she heaps upon her head such a mass of heavy, cumbersome braids, and skewers them on with such a weight of metal hair pins, she can dream of heaven only as place where it will be permitted her to wear short hair." Forty-five years later, after World War I, women fully achieved that heaven. Meanwhile they also had taken to smoking in public and dancing in mushrooming dance halls, in spite of admonitions to the effect that "dancing was the source of all evil." Somehow the "new woman" not only managed to survive, but to prosper. I lived through the period and saw it all happen— the development by women of a new attitude to life, the repudiation of the age-old androcracy, the government of women by men.

World War I saw the beginning of the erosion of a woman's bourgeois image as prostitute-parasite. With the emergence of new technology there was further attrition of the long-entrenched view that women were incapable of the strenuous work that was the exclusive domain of men. The period from 1918 to 1939 was essentially one of consolidation of gains, so that by the time World War II was created by a handful of men, the so-called "leaders of the world," there was no reluctance on the part of anyone in calling upon women to serve in civilian roles that were formerly considered to be exclusively male. The Korean War (1950–1953) and the Vietnam War (1954–1975) further enlarged women's opportunities to prove themselves, not merely as "Rosie the Riveter," but in almost every male-dominated occupation. Ethel Merman sang in *Annie Get Your Gun* (1964), anything men could do she could do better. The added significance here is that the words and music were written by a man, who was a sensitive observer and commentator on the human scene, Irving Berlin.

Women have some distance yet to travel before they achieve full emancipation. When men speak of human rights they usually mean the rights of men—men who will attend to the rights of everyone else. Unfortunately, today most countries remain delinquent in attending to the rights of women; and I am not speaking simply of political rights: I mean all the rights to which human beings, by virtue of their humanity, should be entitled. Since I have mentioned political rights, consider how appalling it is that as late as 1945, when the U.N. Charter was signed, only thirty-six countries in the whole world accorded women full political rights. Today men are still speaking of "mankind" when they should be speaking of "humankind."

In the United States, in so many ways one of the most progressive lands in the world, the only right truly guaranteed to women is the right to vote, and this by the Nineteenth Amendment to the Constitution, passed in 1919 largely through the work of Susan B. Anthony and Elizabeth Cady Stanton. Yet many other rights are not constitutionally guaranteed to women; these are states' rights which are at the disposition of legislatures, and may be changed as the wind listeth. Since most of the "wind" is under the control of male legislators, change will continue to proceed at a slow exhalation. A proposed Equal Rights Amendment (ERA) to the Constitution has, on several occasions, been an election-year promise by both the Democratic and the Republican parties at different times, but it has yet to be enacted into law. The proposed amendment reads: "Equality under the law shall not be denied or abridged by the United States nor by any state on account of sex." Even at this late date this proposed amendment has not become part of the United States Constitution. In 1948 a Senate Judiciary Subcommittee recommended, by a vote of seven to one, that the amendment "do pass," but no further action was taken. In 1972 the amendment was passed by Congress and went to the states for ratification, but failed to secure approval by the necessary minimum of thirty-eight states within ten years required for enactment. The most formidable opposition to the ERA came from conservative majorities in state legislatures. The most militant opposition has been that of STOP ERA, organized in 1972 under Phyllis Schlafly, editor of an influential conservative newsletter.

Apart from the right to vote, in some ways American women have no more constitutional rights than they had in 1789; in other words, medieval English common law is the law that still largely governs women and places upon them the stigma of inferiority and bondage. Constitutional and legal recognition of the equality of the sexes would be an important step in the right direction, but it can become part of the U.S. Constitution only if a sufficient number of citizens are in favor of it and are themselves effectively heard. The Family Medical Leave Act of 1993 is an important step in the right direction, as are the Violence Against

Women Act of 1994, and the Gender Equity in Education Act signed into law that same year. And, by 1993 all fifty states had revised their laws so that under certain conditions husbands could be prosecuted for sexually assaulting their wives. However, legal equality does not mean that the relationships between the sexes will become automatically and harmoniously balanced. Such recognition is helping; but the basic age-old problems between the sexes can no more be solved by constitutional amendment than have the much younger racial and religious problems. These difficulties are all problems in human relations and until they are solved, human beings will in large numbers continue to behave unintelligently and ineffectually.

What, then, is the solution? It lies in a revaluation of our values; in a complete revaluation and reorganization of what today passes for education, but represents nothing more than *instruction,* a very different thing. Instruction is really just a training in techniques and skills, the three Rs. Such training is, of course, indispensably necessary, but it is only a limited part of what should be understood by *education.* The very word is derived from the Latin *educare,* meaning to nourish and to cause to grow. And what is it that one should nourish and cause to grow? It has taken us late into the twentieth century to at last discover the answer to that question. It is: the basic behavioral needs of the child, the needs for growth and development as a physically and mentally healthy person, a whole person, one who is able to love, to work, to play, and to think soundly. These are the four great chords of mental health, and that is what education should be about.

The basic behavioral needs are complementary to our basic physical needs, the latter are the needs for food, oxygen, water, shelter, respiration, activity, rest, sleep, bowel and bladder elimination, and the avoidance of dangerous and noxious stimuli. These physical needs must be satisfied if the organism is to survive. What has not been recognized is that there also exists a set of complementary basic emotional needs, *the basic behavioral needs* are the need for love, sensitivity, friendship, stimulation, curiosity, wonder, thinking, work, enthusiasm, imagination, creativity, song, dance exploration, experiment, learning, and many others. It is the nourishment and encouragement of these behavioral basic needs that should be the primary concern of all education, for our very survival depends upon our response to the supreme challenge, civilization: the race between education and catastrophe.[5]

It is quite evident that because we have failed to understand the true meaning of education, we have become the most self-endangered species on this earth. Education should consist in satisfying the basic behavioral needs of the child. In addition, education should imply the encouragement, cultivation, and development of humane attributes and abilities. This, of course, implies a complete change of the prevailing educational system toward the recognition of the true worth of the child as a loving, brave, cooperative, independent thinker. There are already a number of private schools that have done just this, as well as a few public schools. The results are spectacularly good. In the recognition of the value of such schools, women have an important role to play.

Women have long been conditioned to believe that they are inferior to men, and though reluctant to do so have, like slaves, been forced to act as if they subscribed to what everyone believed to be the natural dispensature of nature. Because Scripture asserts it, and because men proverbially occupy the superior positions in almost all societies, male superiority has long been taken to be the natural dispensator of nature. Women's place is in the home, and man's place is in the counting house and on the board of directors. Women should not meddle in men's affairs, and so on. And yet change is occurring. Women have entered the counting houses and are seated as members of the boards of directors of large corporations. In the United States, women have become members of Congress and have attained cabinet rank; in many other parts of the world, in even greater numbers, women have attained similar positions. They have participated in peace conferences, in the General Assembly of the United Nations, and in international organizations of many different kinds. "Nevertheless," I wrote in this book's 1953 edition, "it is still inconceivable to many persons that there should ever be a woman president or prime minister. And yet that day, too, will come"

And, indeed, it has. The world does move. In September of that very same year, 1953, the Eighth Assembly of the United Nations elected its first woman president, Vijaya Laksmi Pandit of India. In 1960 Sirimavo Bandaranaike became prime minister of Sri Lanka (formerly Ceylon), the first woman in the world to hold such office. In January 1966 Indira Gandhi was sworn in as prime minister of India. In March 1969 Golda Meir was elected prime minister of Israel. These notable pioneers have been followed by other women serving as president, prime minister, and other offices around the world. Benazir Bhutto, the prime minister of Pakistan in 1988–1990 and again in 1993–1996, was the first woman prime minister of a Muslim country. Among other notable women leaders has been Kim Campbell, elected prime minister of Canada in 1993, the first woman political ruler in North America. That same year Agathe Uwilingiyimana became the first woman to serve as prime minister of Rwanda, and the following year was assassinated while in office. In November 1990 Mary Robinson was the first woman elected president of Ireland, an office held by Mary McAleese since 1997; McAleese is the first woman president to have succeeded another one. In addition to Ireland, women currently hold the highest offices in Sri Lanka (president and prime minister), Bangladesh, Guyana, San Marino, and New Zealand, where Jenny Shipley is the first New Zealand woman to hold the office of prime minister.

So much for the highest offices of many lands. It is an important beginning, but a small one. When one has enumerated all the advances that have been made, the truth remains that women are grossly underrepresented in the houses of parliament and legislatures of all lands. This constitutes a great loss to humanity, for as Matthew Arnold said more than hundred years ago, "If ever the world sees a time when women shall come together purely and simply for the benefit and good of mankind, it will be a power such as the world has never known."

It is curious, is it not, that so many who really accept the reality of a queen as ruler still have some hesitation accepting the idea of a woman president? Queen Elizabeth I of England has been a heroine of the English-speaking world for five centuries, and Queen Elizabeth II of England has been one of the most popular figures of the English-speaking world. Margreth II of Denmark, the first Danish queen in five centuries, has ruled since 1972. Queen Beatrix of the Netherlands has been equally popular, as was her mother Queen Juliana and grandmother Queen Wilhelmina. Queen Jadwiga (1373–99) of Poland is remembered as one of its greatest rulers and one of the truly inspired peacemakers of history. In an age of bloodshed and cruelty, she consistently tried to settle internal and international conflicts and resist aggression by diplomacy, arbitration, negotiation, and appeals to reason and justice. Believing in education as a basis for enlightenment, she left her jewels to endow the University of Krakow. Queen Elizabeth I and Queen Victoria rank among the most notable English monarchs, and both their reigns coincided with a rise in prestige and prosperity such as England had never before experienced. It is important to observe that today in the United States there is probably a higher proportion of the population that would vote for a woman president than there has been at any other time in our history, and that is a healthy sign.

Having successfully freed herself from her thralldom to man, woman has now to emancipate herself from the myth of inferiority and to realize her potentials to the fullest. That seems a consummation well on its way to fulfillment.

It was asked earlier: Can one argue the natural superiority of woman in the face of all the evidence to the contrary? The evidence to the contrary merits our serious attention, and that it shall receive. What has, up to now, usually been omitted from discussions of this sort is the evidence in the pages which follow. Let me make it quite clear at the outset that the evidence does not consist of my opinions or speculations, but of the verifiable facts of science. As Mark Twain remarked, supposing is good, but finding out is better.

As we shall see, the findings of modern science controvert the age-old belief in feminine inferiority. It is not only possible to show that most of the things that have been said about women to their disadvantage are false; it is also possible to show that women are naturally biologically more richly endowed with genes that contribute to adaptability and survival than are men. Women, on the whole, possess a greater number of biological advantages than men, yet it is not their number but their overall quality that is important. These many qualitative differences confer biological advantages upon females. Many of these differences have not even been acknowledged, and where they have, they have usually been slighted or totally ignored. The traditional mythology has made it possible to bypass the facts or to render one insensible to them.

Traditional myths concerning women have grown hoary with age and have been accepted as eternal truths. Custom and rationalization have served to keep them alive. The seventeenth-century French philosopher François Poulain de la Barre, writing on this subject, said, "Men persuade themselves of very many things, for which they can give no Reason; because their Assurance is founded upon slight Appearances, by which they suffer themselves to be hurried: and would have as strongly believed the contrary, if the Impressions of Sense or Custom had thereto determined them after the same manner." Quite so, but the fact is that men have always found it easy to provide reasons for their belief in feminine inferiority. For surely, went the "definitive" argument, was it now clear to anyone with common sense that women were inferior to men? This is the kind of "clarity" and "common sense" which informed the medieval inquisitor's handbook, the *Malleus Maleficarum*, produced in 1487 and sanctioned by Pope Innocent VIII, and for two centuries thereafter a widespread influence as the supreme authority on the methods of detecting, bringing to trial, and punishing the "witches" of the world.[6]

Unfortunately, common sense is not very common, and it is not quite enough to disprove an argument, based on false premises and reasons, that has assumed the form of a secular religion. The myths have recreated reality: We tend to fall back on the readiest of explanations. Belief in the myth of the inferiority of women is indeed part of the religious system of many faiths, not only those of the Western world. What seems clear or obvious to us is not necessarily true. Locked into perceiving reality in certain traditional ways we become the prisoners of our perceptions, and our beliefs in the unreal become more real than reality itself. Fortified by all sorts of rationalizations, not clearly known to ourselves, and devices for believing what we want to believe, we proceed to act upon our prejudices with ritual fidelity. The first of the great feminists understood this quite clearly: Mary Wollstonecraft, in her *A Vindication of the Rights of Women* (1792), wrote, "Men, in general, seem to employ their reason to justify prejudices, which they have imbibed, they cannot trace how, rather than root them out."

Most women will not like talk of "superiority" and "inferiority" any more than I do. We have had altogether too much of these terms in the recent past in connection with the so-called superior and inferior races. The unspeakable horrors that have been committed in the name of such pathogenic ideas constitute the most awful record in the history of humankind. I should not have written this book had I thought there was any danger that women would adopt superior airs and deal with men as men have dealt with women. Most women have better sense than that. The one thing of which we may be certain women will never do is to be overbearing toward men as men have for so long been toward women. The truly healthy minded person experiences not the slightest need to establish supremacy over anyone. It is only the individual of weak and insecure character who, like the bully, is impelled to such contemptible devices.

Men are both numerically and biologically a minority group, while women are both numerically and biologically the majority. One need not emphasize, therefore, the peculiar necessity of generosity toward the minority group. The greatest victory one can yield to one's traditional enemy is to become like him.

In this book I bring some of our rationalizations and the reasons for them into the light of day for everyone to see plainly and clearly, to make available the relevant facts—all too little known and all too seldom discussed—concerning both sexes. With the facts thus placed, and the conclusions soon to be drawn, it is to be hoped that men will rethink the foundations of their beliefs concerning feminine inferiority and not permit themselves to be deflected from the truth by prejudice and entrenched traditional beliefs. The truth will make men free as well as women, for until women are freed from the myths that still impede their progress, no man can be free or mentally adequately healthy. The liberation of women means the liberation of man. As Richard Garnett put it many years ago, "Man and Woman may only enter Paradise hand in hand. Together the myth tells us, they left it and together they must return."

2

THE SUBJECTION
OF WOMEN

Why is it that in many Western cultures as well as those of the Middle East, North Africa, the world of Islam, and elsewhere, women have been, and still are, considered to be lower beings, creatures not quite as human as the male: not as wise, nor as intelligent; deficient in the development of virtually all the capacities and abilities with which the male is believed to be so plentifully endowed? How has it come about that women have occupied a position of subordination to men in so many cultures?

Humankind is about three and a half million years old. Since practically nothing is directly known about the social life of our earliest ancestors, speculation and conjecture by scientists and others has for the most part substituted for direct investigation. From the late eighteenth century until relatively recently, those who devoted themselves to the study of anthropology were all European males, who saw and interpreted their "primitive" societies through the ethnocentric eyes of their own cultures. The very term *primitive* reflected their ethnocentric bias, just as the term *mankind* indicated their gender bias in favor of themselves and underlined their cultivated slighting of the *other* half of the human species. *"Humankind"* hardly occurred to *mankind*.

So-called primitive peoples are *culturally* different from peoples of technological societies in precisely the same sense that all ethnic groups differ from one another culturally. In their languages, kinship systems, religions, and social organization, so-called primitive peoples are as well developed or more so than so-called civilized peoples, and on the whole, *more* civilized, if one understands by *civilized* a community characterized by people who live in courtesy, thoughtfulness, cooperation, and peace with each other. The only things they are less advanced in compared with "civilized" peoples are written language and technology.

The truth, however, is that indigenous peoples with oral rather than written cultures have no need for writing or for anything more than the ingenious technology which is perfectly adapted to their requirements. Writing and complex technology develop when the need arises for them in urban societies. Hence, modern anthropologists abjure the term *primitive*, and prefer the term *indigenous*.[1]

Thanks to the work mainly of female anthropologists and archaeologists during the second half of the twentieth century, the male-created mythology concerning women in prehistoric and indigenous societies is being completely recast by a vastly more interesting and undoubtedly more accurate picture than the long-held view of women of these societies as nothing more than beasts of burden, slaves, chattels, economic assets, commodities, and sexual conveniences dominated and enforced by the "superior" males, a view that is wholly unsound.

In the class-bound hierarchical societies of the civilized world the classification of persons by status is the rule. In indigenous societies it is not. In the past, the male anthropologists and archaeologists were so blinded by their own prejudiced, male-oriented ethnocentrism that they simply failed to see women as they really were. Women in prehistoric and indigenous societies were viewed in the same discriminative manner as were women in their own societies. The result was a complete distortion and misinterpretation of the conditions prevailing in indigenous cultures the misconstruction of those prevalent in prehistoric societies.

John Pfeiffer has put the situation very well. "Human evolution," he writes, has been long regarded as a male achievement, a product of male aggressiveness and initiative. The ringing phrase *man the hunter* evokes an image of to-the-death combat at the human dawn: A mammoth at bay, trapped in a pitfall, trumpets its pain and rage while men hurl rocks and spears at it. The accent on such encounters as the major moments in the emergence of the genus *Homo* makes fine pedagogy, providing an exciting story line of men in groups learning to cooperate and conquer. The putdown of women is generally implicit. They were bit players in the human drama, concerned primarily and unadventurously with having babies and gathering plant foods, making only minor contributions to the cultural advancement of the species.[2]

Cartoonists completed the picture by displaying brutish looking men garbed in animal skins carrying knotted cudgels in one hand and with the other dragging women by their hair along the ground. The caricature still makes its appearance quite frequently, at best supposedly funny, but in fact significantly contributing to the prevailing misjudgments concerning pre-historic times, as well as those of indigenous women. This caricature greatly narrowed the definition of humanity.

From the eighteenth century, throughout the Victorian period, and well into the twentieth century, childbirth meant the "confinement" of the mother to her bed for at least two weeks, and she was often treated as a convalescent for a durable period thereafter. Add to this the prolonged period of breastfeeding, and the Victorian anthropologists could only think of women of nonliterate societies as of secondary consequence. Most of these armchair anthropologists had never in fact even seen a woman of an indigenous society. When some anthropologists eventually did encounter such women, the projection of their Victorian image of European childbirth practices upon these "savages" prevented them from paying more than the most perfunctory attention to the conditions of childbirth as they really were.

Certain biological facts are pertinent here, or rather it is not these facts so much as the *interpretations* that have been given them. It has long been held that because women bear children and nurse them, they are forced to be much more sedentary than men. Woman in the Victorian period was taken to be the cricket on the hearth; man, the eagle on the wing. Women stayed at home to nurse and care for their children, prepare meals, and perform virtually all other domestic duties. Men left the hearth for the hunt. That was how the traditional scenario was written, but is it sound?

It is necessary to understand that during a great part of the long history of humankind, its economy was at first characterized by foraging—eating foods as they were gathered, or by scavenging—eating foods that were killed by predators or died by accident. This was later followed by food gathering and hunting. Agriculture and herding of animals were unknown; habitations were of the most primitive kind, like windbreaks, probably similar, to those built by Australian aborigines. Tools were probably fashioned of wood or bone, the remains of which have long disappeared. Implements were simple and few. Most of these were probably developed after our ancestors had made the transition from foraging for food, which may have included scavenging, to food gathering. It is important to remember that food gathering came long before the invention of hunting. It is probable that women made the tools they needed in digging for tubers and other plant foods.

The belief has been that since women had babies to nurse and care for, they were sedentary. But the gathering of food is a shared activity in which children as well as several other women may participate, apart from men. Observation of the conditions among gatherer-hunter peoples tells us that women are seldom incapacitated by childbirth and are quite active shortly following it, carrying their infants in a sling. In some cultures women even hunt while carrying an infant with them in some sort of sling or carrier. There was almost certainly no significant division of labor between the sexes, though it is possible that men and childless women were free to range more widely over their habitat than were women with children to care for.[3]

Contrary to the usual picture painted by earlier anthropologists, it is probable that both sexes foraged for food, that both were food gatherers, and women later continued to hunt with men as well as with other women, and sometimes alone, as women still do in some indigenous cultures. For example, Drs. Agnes Estioko-Griffin and P. Bion Griffin have described the Agta, the Philippines Negrito peoples of Eastern Luzon, and characterized the women as "superb hunters" who eat animal protein every day and hunt frequently. Women make their own bows, though projectile points are a male craft. Men and women hunt together or alone. Women also fish. Girls start hunting shortly after puberty, and postmenopausal women hunt into old age. Among other things, women generally carry the carcasses of the animals they have killed, no mean feat, for the bodies of wild pigs and deer are quite heavy. Finally, Agta society is completely egalitarian.[4]

As the Griffins point out, the probabilities are high that women were hunters in prehistoric times, and that the custom continued into relatively recent times. The striking egalitarianism and cooperation between the sexes among the Agta is in keeping with modern anthropological findings that gatherer-hunting peoples are for the most part all egalitarian and that egalitarianism and cooperation was the rule among early humankind.

Professor Richard Borshay Lee, our greatest authority on the Bushman of the northwest corner of Botswana, has shown[5] that "the nature of early society can never be constructed with complete confidence, nevertheless, the hunter-gatherer data should make us view with suspicion any theory that seeks to *prove* that the male dominance in our present social order is a part of our evolutionary heritage."[6]

As among the Agta, men and women in early societies very probably had a partnership in marriage. There was no supremacy of one sex over the other. Women were characterized by several biological advantages which the male lacked; for example, women replenished the group by having babies; they breast-fed the babies for about four years or more and cared for them for years thereafter. Furthermore, a bond was created between mother and child, which constituted, as it still does, the basic family unit.

The general myth is that the male provides most of the food in gatherer-hunter societies, but the truth is that some 80 percent or more is provided in most societies by the female. For that reason such societies should be called gatherer-hunters rather than hunter-gatherers. (And, we may remark in passing, even in terminological matters women have been denied their well-earned rights!)

In some early societies there may have been some division of labor between the sexes based on such biological differences as greater male physical strength and women's ability to bear babies. Males may have been perceived as more active than females. At all ages males are on average taller than females, by about 2 percent of total body height until puberty, and between 5 and 8 percent taller in adult life. Males cross-culturally have a higher metabolic rate, some 5 to 7 percent greater than females, apparently correlated with their continuous greater expenditure of energy.[7] The suggestion is that males seem to be operating like an engine at higher levels of speed—both producing and requiring greater levels of energy. But even here we cannot be certain that such differences are not, at least to some extent, culturally influenced. However that may be, even if the higher energy levels of the male are biologically determined, that does not mean males are therefore designed to be hunters, any more than the fact that women bear babies has biologically caused them to be more sedentary. The truth is that, whatever the biological influences, we are dealing with the assignment of roles and statuses, which is a cultural practice and not a biological effect.[8]

Role and status are socially imposed, and in this way frequently serve to emphasize the character of social expectations as well as control the nature of the responses made to them. Activity differences between the sexes do exist, though they are secondary differences, *not* primary ones.

At this point, before continuing with a discussion of the biological facts, let us attempt to answer the question posed at the beginning of this chapter: How did it come about that women, with all the biological advantages we today know they possess, have for so long been subordinated to men?

Scientific studies during the last sixty years or more have increasingly yielded evidence that in prehistoric societies women not only played a much more important role than would have been possible for them in male-dominated societies, but that from very early times they represented a powerful political and social force. Furthermore, the pantheon of the gods was perceived as mainly feminine, the natural mothers of god and humankind as well as of animals. There were indications of such preexisting institutions, but they were not really understood for many years for what they were. It was not until women scholars began to look into these arcane matters that progress in accurately interpreting them began to be made.[9]

It would seem evident that, in virtually every society, pregnancy and childbirth would come to be regarded as something of a miracle, supernatural, and that woman, the giver of life, sustenance, warmth, and caring, should come to occupy a central position in symbolism and religion. Birth is an epiphany, a manifestation of woman's mystery and supernatural art, the most powerful and creative living presences. The long extended experience of the nurturing mother would have created a reverence for motherhood in which everyone shared. By extension it was the nurturing being who was most valued, and following that model, women would have chosen as their mates men of nurturing disposition, both for their children and for themselves.

As Ranier Maria Rilke, the great poet, put it, "The deepest experience of the creator is feminine—it is the experience of receiving and bearing." The miracle of pregnancy, childbirth, and motherhood inspired the birth of creation myths—religious beliefs—and constituted the most powerful influence upon the cultural development of the human mind and of society.[10]

With the progressive development of culture, from foraging and gathering to gathering and hunting, together with its associated development of elaborate tools, art, and sculpture, we for the first time had tangible evidence of woman as goddess. That evidence for the idolization of women emerges from a period late in the development of humankind, roughly about thirty thousand years ago, but that regard is surely much older than that.

Toward the end of the nineteenth century the first statuettes and figurines of remarkably stylized figures of generally big-breasted corpulent women were discovered in Paleolithic sites dating back some thirty thousand years. During the twentieth century many more such art works of females—of stone and wood, incised carvings and sculptures—have been discovered. The figurines are especially interesting, for in addition to large breasts, the abdomen of pregnancy is enlarged, as are the hips and buttocks. The abdomen shows the navel, and frequently a swelling extending to the mons, suggestion the imminence of birth, in some cases actually showing birth in process. The external genitalia were carefully modeled. These anatomical structures formed what the late Marija Gimbutas, archaeologist and professor of European archaeology at the University of

California, Los Angeles, called "the pubic triangle," elaborations of which are found on many artifacts. The usually faceless heads of each of these figurines are topped by stylized coiffures, while halfway below the knees the legs and feet are frequently truncated or fused and tapered to a point.

For many years these statuettes of mostly gravid females of somewhat exaggerated corpulence were held to be fertility figures. Most of them, if not all, undoubtedly were, but they were much more than that: They were goddesses.

Marija Gimbutas, in her magnificent book, *The Language of the Goddess* (1989), dealt fully with this subject. The period in which these artifacts occur is known as the Neolithic, or New Stone Age. It is a period associated with the beginning of early agriculture in Europe, beginning some nine thousand years ago. After more than twenty years of study of the statuettes and numerous other objects, Gimbutas has shown that these artifacts, the so-called fertility figures, were, in fact, representations of goddesses. This had been glimpsed and suggested by a number of earlier workers, but it was Gimbutas who led the field and established the facts.[11]

The evidence indicates that there existed a whole pantheon of goddesses, each presiding over some vital activity: Giver of Life, Wielder of self-generating (parthenogenetic) life, Regeneratrix, Earth Mother, and Fertility Goddess. "The goddess-centered art, with its striking absence of images of warfare and male domination, reflects a social order in which women as heads of clans or queen priestesses played a central role."[12] That Old Europe and Anatolia, as well as Minoan Crete, were gylanies,[13] that is, nonpatriarchal and nonmatriarchal balanced social systems that were egalitarian, is revealed by studies of religion, mythology, folklore, and the social structure of Old European and Minoan cultures. All of these reflect the continuity of a matrilineal system in which descent is reckoned through the female line, as in ancient Greece, Etruria, Rome, and among the Basque and other European societies.

What Gimbutas is saying is not that there ever was a society governed by women, a matriarchate, but there were many societies (if not all) that were gylanic, where women and men shared an equal partnership, and that the deities these societies celebrated were predominantly feminine.

The striking fewness of male figurines and the overwhelming number of female ones suggests the powerful role women played in prehistoric societies. Finally it seems clear that such societies were characterized by peace, cooperation, and freedom. An outstanding example of such a society is the Minoan culture of ancient Crete. In that land women played a central role in the functioning of society, and complete equality existed between the sexes. Descent appears to have been reckoned in the female line; in other words, Crete was an egalitarian matrilineal society. For fifteen hundred years, its people pursued the even tenor of their way, without war or conflict of any kind.

The distinguished archaeologist Sir Leonard Woolley described the Minoan way of life as "the most complete acceptance of the grace of life the world has ever known . . . like the enchantment of a fairy world." Another archaeologist, Nicholas Platon, said that it was a society in which "the fear of death was almost obliterated by the ubiquitous joy of living." Riane Eisler, much influenced by Gimbutas, has beautifully described all this in her memorable book, *The Chalice and the Blade* (1988).

How, then, did it come about that the gylanic cultures of Old Europe were destroyed and replaced by male-dominated, patriarchal, warlike peoples? The answer to that question is also the answer to the question: How, when, and where did the subjection of women occur? It is Gimbutas who offers the clear and unequivocal answer. She writes,

> While European cultures pursued a peaceful existence and reached a true florescence and sophistication of art and architecture in the fifth millennium B.C., a very different Neolithic culture with the domesticated horse and lethal weapons emerged in the Volga basin of South Russia, and after the middle of the fifth millennium even west of the Black Sea. This new force inevitably changed the course of European prehistory. I call it the *Kurgan* culture (*kurgan* meaning barrow in Russian) since the dead were buried in round barrows that covered the mortuary houses of important males.[14]

It was by these kurgan invasions that gylanic societies were overturned and replaced by patriarchal dominator cultures in which women were subjugated by men.

The culture of Crete lasted from about 3000 B.C. to 1500 B.C. During that period its influence, maintained mainly through the trade with the aid of a large fleet, extended widely through the Aegean, most notably to the Mycenean and the Greek cultures that succeeded Minos. Part of the legacy of the Minoans lived on in these cultures, as it does in ours, but much amended by a dominator attitude of men toward women, and an addiction to warfare and other male aberrations.

There is strong evidence that from the Near East came yet another powerful influence in replacing a gylany with an andro-cratic culture. The evidence for this with which we in the Western world are most familiar is found in the Old Testament. This has been ably discussed by Professor David Bakan as well as other scholars.[15] The traces of matricentrism, matrineality, and matri-locism are quite clear in the Bible. In every major archaeological excavation in Palestine numerous figurines of goddesses have been discovered, and again, as in the Mediterranean, with a striking paucity of those of males. The eloquent abundance of these female figurines testifies to their significance in the cultures in which they occurred. These figurines are found over a wide area in the Near East. In Israel and neighboring lands, such figurines date back to the fourth millennium B.C. and earlier. The great luxuriance of these figurines in Palestine indicates the probable widespread religious worship of the goddess.[16]

An interesting thing about the figurines and the various other representations of the goddess is that they were almost certainly made by men, for it can hardly be believed that women would glorify themselves in such a blatant manner, and it speaks to the wisdom of prehistoric men that they recognized the vital creativity of women. As the archaeologist Emmanuel Anati has said,

> These Upper Paleolithic men . . . created a feminine figurine apparently representing a goddess or a being of fertility, and probably involving a religious concept which *Homo sapiens* has retained ever since: a pregnant goddess or mother of man (or mother of god) in whom he exalted the mystery of his own creation.[17]

From the very beginnings of art it is likely that women and men participated equally. Out of these, in later stages of cultural development, such designs had magical and religious signi-ficance. And in still later stages of cultural development, such designs were elaborated and put into nonobjective, abstract forms, or into purely representational forms. Whatever the facts, it cannot be doubted that where pottery decorating, weaving, and, later, basketmaking are concerned, women made their own indispensable contributions to society.

We may conclude, then, that the evidence drawn from many different sources indicates that early societies were in most cases egalitarian, that this is also true of most indigenous societies that exist today, that the subjection of women has not always been the rule, but constitutes a late social phenomenon, and that it was roughshod invaders who conquered the egalitarian societies and imposed upon them government and rule by males, together with the subjugation of women.

It should be clear that it is not in our genes for one sex to establish supremacy over the other. Our biology does not decree that one sex shall rule over the other. What determines that sort of thing is, tradition, culture. The forms of behavior that characterize us as human beings are determined by the socialization process we undergo, the cultural conditioning in which we are molded, the customs by which we are all made. And there's the rub, for we are the most educable of all the creatures on this earth. And since we possess no instincts, everything we come to be, to know, and to do *as human beings* we have to learn from other human beings. Indeed, educability is our species' trait. And that is why to be human is to be in danger, for we can easily be taught many wrong and unsound things, or right and sound ones. And when the sound and the unsound are combined, the result is not intelligence but confusion. And that is the state in which the greater part of humanity has lived for a very long time. This has been particularly true of the traditional views relating to the status and roles of the sexes. And especially of the appeal to biology as the justification for the subjection of women. For that reason let us turn now to an examination of those views in light of the facts.

Males have a metabolic rate that is between 5 and 6 percent higher than that of females, and from the earliest ages males are more active than females. Red blood cells are more numerous in the male: The average red-cell count per cubic millimeter is 5,200,000 in the male and 4,900,000 in the female. The red blood cells carry oxygen on their surface membranes, the hemoglobin, which ranges from about 90 to 100 percent in the male and from 85 to 90 percent in the female. Since the oxygen carried by the hemoglobin to the tissues of the body is the main supplier of energy, it will be readily understood why the female requires fewer red blood cells than the male: She doesn't need as much fuel. Furthermore, because of her lower metabolic rate, the female doesn't have to eat as much as the male and is also able to adjust more efficiently to extremes and changes in temperature, and perspire less than males in hot weather.

Socially observed differences in activity between the sexes, it cannot be doubted, are to a large extent acquired rather than inherited. In short, activity differences do not represent first nature, though they may become second nature. First nature is the biological equipment of potentialities with which one is born; second nature is what one's culture and society make of one's first nature, the habits and ways of life one acquires. Culture, the human-made part of the environment, is the way of life of a people, its language, institutions, customs, its pots and pans. The division of labor between the sexes represents a cultural expression of what are believed to be biological differences. The variety of cultural forms that this expression may take in different societies is enormous; what may be considered women's work in one society may be deemed men's work in another. In some cultures men and women may engage in common activities that in other cultures are strictly separated along gender lines. The important point to grasp is that the prescribed roles assigned to the sexes are not determined biologically but virtually entirely by culture. As anthropologist Ralph Linton says,

> All societies prescribe different attitudes and activities to men and to women. Most of them try to rationalize these prescriptions in terms of the physiological differences between the sexes or their different roles in reproduction. However, a comparative study of the status ascribed to women and men in different cultures seems to show that while such factors may have served as a starting point for the development of a division, the actual ascriptions are almost entirely determined by culture.[18]

As I have already mentioned, role and status serve to emphasize the character of social expectations and thus control the nature of responses made to them. In societies in which such categorizations are the rule, the cultural perception of what are presumed to be biological sex differences, whether they are in fact so or not, provide the grounds upon which are based the different social status and roles. But the significance of the biological differences is usually interpreted to convey the impression of a natural connection between conditions that are, in fact, only artificially connected through misinterpretation. For example, in many cultures pregnancy, birth, and nursing are interpreted by both sexes as handicapping experiences; as a consequence women have been made to feel that by virtue of their biological functions they have been naturally placed in an inferior position to men. But as we today well know, these biological functions of women are only minimally, if at all, handicapping.

It is worth paying some attention to the fact that in the societies in which such discriminations are the rule, one would have thought it unequivocally clear that women were superior to men, namely, in their ability to bear and nurture children. Instead women have been made to feel that their life giving roles are a handicap. The evidence relating to the conditions of childbirth and child rearing in indigenous societies is scant enough, but the indications are that women in such societies seem to have an easier time than they do in more complex ones. Unquestionably, under many conditions childbirth and child rearing from a conscious male viewpoint appear to be handicapping conditions. The *unconscious* male viewpoint, there is much factual evidence to show, is of a very different nature. In almost all societies birth has been culturally converted into a much more complicated condition than it in fact is: In general, it would seem that the more complex a society becomes, the more it tends to complicate the process of birth. One result of this is seen in Western cultures where women have, until recently, been made to spend anything from ten days to three weeks in "confinement," as the subjugation to helplessness so appropriately used to be called. Since the advent of natural childbirth, women are finding childbirth far less unpleasant and scarcely handicapping. Childbirth is neither a disease, a disorder, nor a handicap.

Today following the birth of a baby, whether in a family birth center or hospital, if there has been no problem, a woman may rise within a few hours and within a few days resume a normal ambulatory existence. In some nonliterate societies some women take much less time than that to return to their normal domestic activities. In gatherer-hunter cultures, such as those of the Bushman of southern Africa and the Australian aborigines, the fact that a woman is pregnant or that an hour ago she gave birth does not interfere with daily routines, except for the additional task of nursing. It sometimes happens that on the march, in moving from one food area to another, a woman falls out, gives birth to her child, catches up with her companions, and behaves as if nothing requiring heroic measures had occurred. If, as rarely happens, another child is born to her a little too soon after the last one, it may be disposed of, for it may constitute a real disability, since under the conditions of the gatherer-hunter way of life it is difficult to take care of more than one infant at a time. There must be adequate spacing between children, not for this reason alone but also because the responsibility of fostering a child is considered virtually a fulltime commitment. Owing to intensive breastfeeding lasting four or more years conception rarely occurs at less than four-year intervals.

Childbirth and nursing do introduce additional activities into the life of the female, but such activities do not necessarily constitute disadvantages. In comparison with certain forms of masculine mobility, and under certain social conditions, such activities *may* be disadvantages, and it would be wrong to underestimate them. It would, however, be equally wrong to overestimate such disadvantages; yet this has been done, and I believe the evidence strongly suggests that it has been deliberately done by male "authorities," if to some extent unconsciously. Besides, do we not have Divine sanction for such practice? Does it not say in Genesis 3:16 that God said "unto the woman, I will greatly multiply thy sorrow and thy conception; in sorrow thou shalt bring forth children." So it is ordained that labor and childbirth shall be hazards and painful. Clearly, then, if one can turn childbirth into a handicapping function, then that makes women so much more inferior to the sex that suffers from no such handicap. Those who resort to such devices are usually concerned not so much with the inferiorities of others as with their own superiority. If one happens to be lacking in certain capacities with which the opposite sex is naturally endowed, and those capacities happen to be highly, if unacknowledgedly, valued, then one can compensate for one's own deficiency by devaluing the capacities of others. By turning such capacities into handicaps, one can cause those thus afflicted to feel inferior, while anyone not so "handicapped" can then feel superior.

Farfetched as the idea may appear to some, the fact is that men have long been jealous of women's ability to give birth to children and have in some societies even envied their ability to menstruate; but men have not been content with turning these capacities into disabilities, for they have surrounded the one with handicapping rituals and the other with taboos that in most cases amount to punishments. They have even gone so far as to assert that pregnancy occurs in the male first, and that it is entirely dependent upon him whether the female becomes pregnant or not. For example, among numerous Australian aboriginal peoples it was the common belief that intercourse had no causative relation to pregnancy, and that pregnancy is the result of the entry of a spirit child into the female.[19] In many of these tribes it is the spirit child that has entered the male first, or he dreamed it. Should he desire a child, he tells his wife what has happened and the spirit child is then transferred to her. Even then she is merely regarded as the incubator of the child planted in her by the male. The idea is clearly expressed by the Greek dramatist Aeschylus (525–456 B.C.) in his play, *Eumenides*, in which Athene, the daughter of Zeus who sprang from his head, is made to say, "The parent that which is called her child is not really the *mother* of it, she is but the nurse of the newly conceived fetus. It is the male who is the author of its being, while she, as a stranger (that is to say, no blood relation), preserves the young plant."[20]

The very terms we use when we speak of male and female roles in reproduction, like the terms *male* and *female* themselves, and also *man* and *wo-man*, make women subservient addenda to men and reflect the ignorance and prejudice that have characterized dominant male attitudes. The male *fertilizes, fecundates,* or *impregnates* the female. The truth, however, is quite otherwise. The process of reproduction is not one-sided: Its antecedent condition is the fusion of two cells, the female ovum and the male sperm. It is not that an ovum is rendered fertile by sperm, but that ovum and sperm contribute to the initiation of those further processes that result in an embryo's development.[21] Furthermore, all embryos up to the end of the sixth week are female. The ovum has a volume approximately eighty-five thousand times greater than that of the sperm, because it carries the nutriment necessary for the development of the early conceptus.

Menstruation has been regarded among many peoples as woman's natural method of getting rid of evil humors that are believed to accumulate in the body. Since men lack such a natural means of achieving this desired end, the Australian aborigines perform an operation called *subincision* on the adolescent youth, at his second initiation. This operation consists of slitting open the urinary tube, the urethra, on the underside of the penis, often from the scrotum to the external orifice of the glans penis. A stone is then inserted into the subincised penis to keep the urethra permanently open. The aborigines call a subincised penis by the same name as the female vulva.[22] There can be not the least doubt that, among other things, the purpose of this operation represents an attempt to imitate feminine genitals. Every so often, especially at ceremonies and initiations, the subincised penis will be incised to make it bleed in imitation of menstruation. Similar operations are performed by the natives of Wogeo, one of the Schouten Islands off the north coast of Irian Jaya, Indonesia. Periodic incision of the penis and the flow of blood thus induced is often referred to as men's menstruation; such men are subject to much the same prohibitions as menstruating women, but the flow of blood is considered to be a necessary cleansing process.

What the female is endowed with, the male must, at great pain and suffering to himself, periodically reproduce by art; this constitutes further ground for jealousy of, and resentment against, the female. A similar operation is therefore performed upon girls at puberty. During this operation the clitoris and labia are cut away, at which time, in some Australian groups, all the initiated men proceed to have intercourse with the girl. Such an operation is still performed today in the thousands in some territories of Egypt and far up along both sides of the Nile. Furthermore, in North African regions where this operation is performed, the vulva is sewn up in such a matter as to leave only a small orifice for the exudation of the menstrual and urinary fluids; this operation is known as *infibulation.* Here the jealousy of the male has gone so far as to limit completely the female's capacity for pregnancy and childbirth. When the girl reaches marriageable age, the orifice may be enlarged to admit her husband's penis, and it will be opened up, by incision, shortly before childbirth, and after childbirth sewn up again![23]

Should anyone be inclined to think that it is only indigenous peoples and benighted heathen who indulge in such practices at the expense of the female, it has only to be pointed out that not so many years ago some American surgeons were performing clitoridectomies by the dozen, while today surgeons sedulously castrate thousands of women yearly, for even though the ovaries are not removed, that is what the operation of hysterectomy actually achieves. How many of these operations are really necessary? In 1969 at the behest of the New York State Teamsters Union an investigation of the cost and quality of medical and hospital care was conducted by the Columbia University School of Public Health and Administrative Medicine on the Teamster families. The relevant part of the report reads as follows:

> There were 60 cases in the sample where a hysterectomy (removal of the uterus) had been performed. From a review of the records, including the operative report and the pathology findings, the surveyor felt that one-third were operated on unnecessarily and that questions could be raised about the advisability of the operation in another 10 percent. At the very least these women should have had a dilation and curettage (scraping of the uterus) followed by a period of observation prior to the hysterectomy. In many instances, the dilation and curettage alone would have alleviated symptoms.[24]

Dr. Sidney Wolfe, testifying early in August 1975 before a House of Representatives subcommittee investigating the incidence of unnecessary surgery in the United States, stated that by the age of seventy the average woman stands a 45.3 percent chance of undergoing a hysterectomy. By contrast, women who were members of health maintenance organizations, which are prepaid group plans rather than fee-for-service plans, have only a 16.8 percent probability of undergoing a hysterectomy. A study by Cornell University Medical College found that some 787,000 hysterectomies were performed in 1975, resulting in 1,700 deaths. It was estimated that surgery was unnecessary in 22 percent of cases, resulting in 374 avoidable deaths. Even today, more than thirty years later, more than 600,000 hysterectomies are performed in the United States each year. Various sources put the percentage of unnecessary hysterectomies anywhere between 24 and 88 percent. More than one-fourth of the female population will undergo this procedure by the time they are 60 years of age. Can it be that in some cases the unconscious motivations for such operations differ from those consciously alleged? For further information on unnecessary surgical interventions the reader should refer to Dr. Diana Scully's important book, *Men Who Control Women's Health: The Miseducation of Obstetrician-Gynecologists* (1980).

Man's jealousy of woman's capacity to bear children is nowhere better exhibited than in the Old Testament creation story in which man is caused to give birth (from one of his ribs) to woman: "And the rib, which the Lord God had taken from man, made he a woman, and brought her unto the man" (Genesis 2:22). A frequent subject of medieval art is the birth of Eve from Adam's side. Milton considered the creation of woman a mistake. In *Paradise Lost* he wrote,

> Why did god Creator wise, that peopl'd highest heav'n with Spirits Masculine, create at last This noveltie on Earth, this fair defect of Nature, and not fill the World at once with Men as Angels without Feminine, or find some other way to generate Mankind?

Possibly the answer lies in Dr. Samuel Johnson's reply to a lady who asked him to define the difference between man and woman: "I can't conceive, Madam," he replied. "Can you?"

We begin to see, then, how it may have come about that childbirth as well as menstruation were transformed from perfectly healthy natural phenomena into a handicap and a curse. Men project their unconscious wishes upon the screen of their society and create their institutions and gods in the image of their desires. It would seem as if their envy of woman's physiological prepotencies causes them to feel weak and inferior, fear being often added to jealousy. An effective way for men to protect themselves against women, as well as to punish them, is to depreciate their capacities by devaluing their status. One can deny the virtues of women's advantages by treating them as disadvantages and by investing them with mysterious or dangerous qualities, hence, the tracking down of witches. The attitudes and the practices to which they lead constitute the palpable evidence of man's morbid fear of existential irrelevance. By making women objects of fear and something to be avoided as unclean, one can reduce the cultural status of women by simple inversion. Their biological advantages are demoted to the status of cultural disadvantages, and as cultural disadvantages, they are then converted into biological disadvantages. Once this is achieved, there need be no end to the belief in the cultural and biological disadvantages of these traits, and hence of their bearers. It is not here being suggested that this sort of thinking occurs, except occasionally, on the conscious level, for which there is a great deal of evidence, is drawn mainly from anthropological and psychoanalytic sources, as well as the above mentioned.[25]

From an early age females have been conditioned to believe that menstruation is a curse and a handicap.[26] Pregnancy, females were taught, put them in a precarious condition, while childbirth was enveloped in so many myths, mysteries, and dangers that most women in the Western world have until recently rarely approached or experienced the event without foreboding and anxiety. This also held true for the sympathetic husband. The fact is that infant and maternal mortality rates were quite high in earlier days, so there was some reason for fear and anxiety.

Through our social heredity and our traditions, we have fallen heir to a battery of beliefs concerning the "biological disadvantages" associated with being female. Even today we have not yet fully emancipated ourselves from these errors. We have already seen what some of the origins of these beliefs may have been, and why, in part, they continue to be perpetuated. These beliefs are almost wholly unsound. We know today that menstruation is neither mysterious nor malignant but a perfectly healthy, normal function of women. Pregnancy need be neither precarious nor handicapping, nor need childbirth or childbearing. Women have been led to believe that these functions are handicapping, and that they must, therefore, at best, play a secondary role to men. Today, both women and men perhaps better understand how this belief came into being, and perhaps endeavor to make the necessary concession to the facts. This is a theme we shall take up in a later and more appropriate place. For the present, let us return to a consideration of the manner in which certain of the other alleged disabilities of women came into being.

Owing to the enlarging experiences that fall to the dominant male in the androcentric society and the restriction of women's opportunities, the male has everywhere acquired a broad experience and varied knowledge, which has been denied the female. The male develops certain highly valued traits and skills far more various and extensive than those which the female is privileged to command. It will readily be understood that such traits immediately give their owner an advantage. It will also be readily understood why it is that men, under such conditions, consider women their inferiors and themselves incomparably more important, for while it is woman's work to concern herself with the preservation of the individual—so goes the rationalization—men are concerned with no less than the perpetuation of the their manmade rules. Were it not for the basic support that men provide for the family (so they consider), the species would die out. Even though this has always been a highly questionable view, such, nevertheless, has consistently been the opinion of the "head of the family." It is an open question whether the real mainstay and support of the family in the psychological, if not entirely in the material, sense has not always been the wife and mother.

However that may be, whoever pays the piper calls the tune, and the head of the family has always insisted upon the respect due the superior person, naturally at the cost of making all other family members feel subordinate. And indeed, by comparison everyone else in the family was inferior, for the wife possessed no such skills as her husband, nor was she anywhere nearly as knowledgeable about so many things her husband had experienced; furthermore, he was bigger and stronger than she, that in itself testifying to the biologically determined differences. The children, of course, were even more inferior to their father than was their mother, and boys, of course, were superior to girls. To this day, most parents in the Western world hope that their firstborn will be a boy. In societies that practiced infanticide, girls were invariably the principal victims. Growing up in such male dominator societies it would be difficult to avoid the belief that males were superior to females. Everyone, including the mother, drew the erroneous conclusion from the cultural facts that these differences of superiority and inferiority were biologically determined; women, it was assumed, were naturally inferior to men, and that was that. There were always women who entertained grave doubts on the subject. One of the earliest, "Miss S. Hadfield," in her little-known brilliant book, *Letters on the Importance of the Female Sex: With Observations on Their Manners and Education*, published in 1803, called upon women everywhere to look beyond the traditional role expected of them by men. In her preface she wrote, "Men have, indeed, too long thought it an advantage to consign the Fair Sex to ignorance, that, by a monopoly of knowledge, their superiority might be supported. Women were not permitted to possess just sentiments of their own importance, and of their native dignity—but were encouraged, or controlled—were gained or lost—by the most childish, narrow, and degrading methods." Two centuries later, that truth still holds true.

In our own time, although much progress has been made, owing largely to the feminist movement, male dominator attitudes linger on almost everywhere in the civilized world. There clearly remains a great deal of work and reeducation to be done. The damage that has been done appears to have been the doing largely of male dominator conquerors and their continuing, though attenuated, influences. In short, the change from a matricentric to an androcentric culture is only about seven thousand years old. In male supremacist cultures women were never afforded equal opportunities with men—opportunities for the development of their intelligence—and were severely restricted by what was traditionally considered permissible to women. Women were prejudged rather than fairly judged; and they were condemned to a caste system of lower status from which they could never emerge unless, on a rare occasion, granted the opportunity to do so. In the 1840s a writer in *Godey's Lady's Book* put it very plainly, "As a general hint there was much wisdom in the advice given by an old mother to a young one: Stimulate the sensibilities of your boys and blunt those of your girls." Depressing advice, but well adapted to the realities of the time.

Charlotte Brontë's friend Mary Taylor wrote in 1854, "There are no means for a woman to live in England, but by teaching, sewing, or washing. The last is the best. The best paid, the least unhealthy, and the most free." In 1864 Walter Bagehot, the famous English economist, wrote to Emily Davies, the woman's rights leader,

> I assure you I am not an enemy of women, I am very favorable to their employment as laborers or in any other menial capacity. I have, however, doubts as to the likelihood of their succeeding in business as capitalists. I am sure the nerves of most women

would break down under the anxiety and that most of them are utterly destitute of the disciplined reticence and self-constraint necessary to every sort of cooperation. Two thousand years hence you may have changed it all, but the present woman will only flirt with men and quarrel with one another.

Indeed it is estimated that in the 1850's, among the 876,920 "surplus" gentlewomen of England, there were some twenty-five thousand governesses suffering pittance wages and a multitude of petty humiliations for the sin of not finding a husband. The truth is that until 1914 women lived in a world in which they were forced to be totally dependent on men, and were deprived of all legal autonomy as human beings. Bagehot was a highly intelligent and civilized man who was typically reflecting the cultural prejudices of his day, and this in spite of the fact that John Stuart Mill had published *The Subjection of Woman* five years earlier, in 1859.

Feelings of weakness and inferiority have their roots in other than purely cultural factors. It is a matter of fact that men are usually bigger and physically more powerful than women. Being bigger and more obviously physically powerful generally makes a person feel and act in a big and powerful manner. In the presence of such persons, the smaller and less powerful are likely to feel dwarfed. At any rate, where the sexes are concerned, the factors of size and power, added to other prerogatives and statuses, put the male decidedly in the position of dominance.

Most women have been so long conditioned in an environment of masculine dominance that they have come to expect the male to be dominant and the female subservient. The psychological subservience of the female has assumed innumerable ramifications in almost all human societies and constitutes yet another illustration of the effects of the cultural differentiation of the sexes. Among the many ways in which the downgrading of women traditionally proceeds, and one of the most blatant, is patronymy, in which names descend in the male line and women assume the surname of their husband. This is the rule in male dominator societies, and as Sharon Lebell says in her important book, *Naming Ourselves, Naming Our Children,*

> Whenever a woman automatically changes her name at marriage,
> or whenever a couple names a child by the patronymical code,

they are recreating and reinforcing the universal perception that males are more important and therefore superior to females, more deserving, better in every way. We accept, even warmly embrace, patronymy as if it were a natural law.[27]

Another of the many channels through which such ideas are transmitted is the formal processes of education. In a study of children's textbooks and personality development, Drs. I. L. Child, E. H. Potter, and E. M. Levine found that the third-grade-level primers they examined presented females in an unfavorable and indifferent light. Females were nurturing and gentle but seldom active, adventurous, constructive, achieving, or worthy of recognition. Girls and women are thus being shown as sociable, kind, and timid but inactive, unambitious, and uncreative. The characters in the stories who were nurtured and given support were generally female, suggesting that females are in a relatively helpless position. On the other hand, the knowledgeable people were males. Males, in short, are being portrayed as the bearers of knowledge and wisdom. In some instances females were portrayed as being morally inferior to the male. They were portrayed as acquiring things in socially disapproved ways much more often than were males, and less often by the socially approved means of effort and work. They were shown as lazy twice as often as males. In addition to females being slighted, males were predominantly the heroes of stories—73 percent of the time. The implication, write the authors of this study, is that being female is a pretty bad thing, and the only people in everyday life who are worth writing and reading about are boys and men.

If the content of these readers is typical of other social influences, small wonder that girls might develop for this reason alone an inferiority complex about their sex. The many schoolgirls who will at some future time have to make their own living are failing, if they identify with female characters, to receive the same training in the development of motives for work and achievement that boys are receiving. To the extent that this distinction is characteristic of many other aspects of the training the child receives from the environment, it should cause little wonder that women are sometimes less fitted for creative work and achievement than men of similar aptitude, for there is certainly much difference in the motivational training they receive for it.

It is the general rule throughout the animal kingdom that wherever one sex is larger or physically more powerful than the other, the larger or physically more powerful sex will occupy the position of dominance. Humans, we know, are something more than animal, but not all men have quite realized that fact. If, as Plato said, civilization is the victory of persuasion over force, it may be that men may yet be persuaded to consider some of the origins of their sexual dominance, and even to learn that the force of argument is eventually stronger and more beneficial in its effects than the argument of force.

It has already been pointed out that there is a remarkable parallel between the phenomenon of race prejudice and prejudice against women. This is nicely illustrated by an editorial comment on a woman's suffrage meeting held in Syracuse, New York. The editorial appeared in the *New York Herald*, in the September 1852 issue, and was probably written by the elder James Gordon Bennett, the *Herald's* founder and owner. Among other things, the editorial said,

> How did woman first become subject to man, as she now is all over the world? By her nature, her sex, just as the negro is and always will be to the end of time, inferior to the white race and, therefore, doomed to subjection; but she is happier than she would be in any other condition, just because it is the law of her nature!

Everything that has been said about almost any alleged "inferior race" has been said by men about women. We have already heard that their brains are smaller, that their intelligence is lower, that they are not very good at mathematics, that one can't trust them to govern their own affairs, that they are like children, emotional, unoriginal, uncreative, unintellectual, with a severely limited attention span, and so on, through the whole dreary calendar of fables. These are the familiar arguments of the racists, their stock in trade; and every one of them has been urged as a fact in racist contexts, as well as against women in general.

I hope that no reader of this book is naive enough to imagine that proof of the erroneousness of these beliefs would be sufficient to eliminate either race prejudice or the prejudice against women; for just as the "race" problem is in reality a problem in human relations, so the prejudice against women is therefore also a problem in human relations. Until we solve the human relations problem, we shall solve neither these nor any other difficulties of human beings. It is part of the purpose of this book to show how this problem may be solved.

Man is himself a problem in search of a solution, and the prejudices of some against minority groups and women in itself constitutes a social problem. That problem may, in a sense, be understood as groping expressions, at least in part, of confused attempts to solve the problem. When men understand that the best way to solve their own problem is to help women solve those that men have created for women, they will have taken one of the first significant steps toward its solution. And what is woman's greatest problem? Man. For man has created and perpetuated her principal difficulties, and until man solves his own difficulties there can be no wholly satisfactory solution of woman's. Once again it is like the black's problem, that is, the white man. Until the white man solves his personal hangups, blacks will continue to afford a convenient scapegoat. These difficulties in human relations are not simply problems in the communication of facts. One doesn't help anyone suffering from delusions by telling them that they are playing tricks with reality, or that the facts are other than they believe them to be. Deep and complex psychological conditions are involved; we must make the creators aware of them before we can hope for any possibility of relief. Prevention is so much better than cure, so painless, and so much less costly in the service of the greater health of our society, that it is worth hanging a big question mark on some of the things we take most for granted.

3

THE SOCIAL DETERMINANTS
OF BIOLOGICAL "FACTS"
AND SOCIAL CONSEQUENCES

In all societies women have played a much more important role than their menfolk have been generally inclined to admit. After all, if one is afflicted with feelings of inferiority, especially unadmitted ones, as the male is with respect to the female, strong overcompensatory tendencies develop. It is difficult to admit, even though the dark suspicion may have dawned on one, that women are one's equals—and perish the thought— they certainly are not one's superiors. After all, is not the evidence, the biological evidence, of male superiority unequivocally clear? The answer is that it is far from clear that man is biologically superior to women, and that, on the contrary as we shall see, the evidence indicates that woman is, on the whole, biologically superior to man.

Since we have already used the term *superior* without having defined it, and since it is a significant term for our discussion, we had better define it now. The term is used in its common sense meaning as being of higher nature or character. Of higher nature or character in respect to what? The question is a crucial one, and upon its correct answer turns the whole theme of the book. The answer is: Superiority in any trait, whether biological or social, is measured by the extent to which that trait confers survival benefits upon the person and the group. If you function in such a way as to live longer, be more resistant, healthier, and behave in a manner generally calculated to enable you and your progeny to survive more efficiently than others who do not function as efficiently, then by the measure of the definition of superiority you are superior to the others. The reference here is not simply to immediate survival but to the long-term survival of the group.[1] And by group, for the purposes of this discussion, I mean the immediate family, and then the social group of which the family is part, and finally, the whole of humanity.

Allowing for the usual variability, men, for example, are bigger and physically more powerful than women. Are these, then, traits in which men are superior to women? In other words, do greater size and muscular power increase the probability of survival? The comparison is between men and women, not between men and other men. There can be no doubt that culturally we value tall men and powerful ones, but we may legitimately entertain the suspicion that this, too, is a male-determined value. In fact, we place a negative value upon unusually tall and powerful women. Women almost always prefer a man who is taller than themselves. Why? Can it be that women have been taught to look up to men so that (to give the unexpressed corollary) men may look down upon them? May not the bruited advantages of larger size and muscular power constitute yet another of the male-made myths foisted upon an unsuspecting feminine world? Are larger size and greater muscular power biological advantages? The dinosaurs had a long run for their money, but eventually size and muscular power may have proved their undoing, and the creatures vanished from the face of the earth. Man, by means of the development of size and power, finds himself in a dangerous position, in a deadly parallel with the long-extinct dinosaurs.

My reference is not simply to misuse of size and power; it is intended to suggest that the very existence of size and power seems to constitute in itself an incentive and an irritant to man to make use of them. With the accumulation of armaments there is a strong tendency not to control them but to employ them. In terms of size and muscular power man has exercised a physical and psychological dominance over woman. However, that is a very different thing from saying that from the sociobiological point of view such supremacy endows man with a superiority over woman.

If, as a consequence of the possession of greater size and muscular power, one is better able to pull and move heavy loads, run faster, and better accomplish all those things that minister to the survival of the person and the group, then it should be plain that men are in these respects superior to women. But while men have, in part, used their size and greater muscular power in a manner calculated to confer survival benefits upon themselves and upon the group, they have also misused these qualities in such a manner as to confer negative survival benefits upon themselves and upon the group. The muscle man likes to feel his bumps and is, therefore, inclined to be bumptious, to fall back upon brawn, when brain is indicated. His size inclines him to throw his weight around, and not only to persuade his woman that he loves her most when he is showing his fellows in the pecking order that he is not to be trifled with. Since there are likely to be other men around who feel much the same way, trouble is inevitable. Such conflicts that arise within the group in this way make no contribution to its greater chances of survival. Many a good and valuable man has been unnecessarily lost to the group by relying upon his muscles rather than upon his mind, and the group has suffered. Vendettas and internecine conflicts are socialized masculine activities, and the most pathological form that such activities take, namely war, is exclusively a masculine invention and iniquity. Such activities do not contribute to the survival of the individual or of the group.

Since greater size and physical power are overt evidences of masculinity, boys are in most cultures of the Western world encouraged to demonstrate their superior masculinity by indulging in so-called games or sports. Sports such as football, baseball, ice hockey (otherwise known as "war on ice"), boxing, wrestling, rugby, and similar activities, are calculated to underscore the inferior power of girls. And this occurs at a time when girls may be, at the same chronologic ages, larger in size and physically more powerful than boys! Boys are encouraged to be tough and rough, to play with guns and other weapons of destruction and indulge in sports that are rugged. In addition, because boys are supposed to be able to endure more pain than girls, boys may be corporeally punished (and so unconsciously encouraged in the development of additional hostilities), whereas girls are usually punished by deprivation or by the assignment to uncongenial tasks.

It should be clear, then, that the greater size and power of the male may constitute biological advantages or sociobiological disadvantages, depending upon the response to them.

In a society in which the "strong" tend to be destructive even to the point of destroying themselves, it is obvious an advantage not be inclined to muscular aggressiveness. Here we are concerned with the relation of the male's greater size and physical power to the comparatively lesser size and physical potency of the female. Because muscles account for 42 percent of the total body weight in the male and only 36 percent in the female, the male is able to implement his commands and to enforce his will by the misguided exercise of his muscular powers. Obedience is commanded in this way when it can be in no other. The long training of men in securing obedience through the use of force is almost certainly related to the ease in which they fall back upon this means of compelling attention and securing obedience. As the distinguished zoologist Professor Jon Berrill of McGill University has said, "Men and boys are troublesome creatures, but being larger, stronger, and louder than the females, they have succeeded in putting over the biggest bluff the earth has ever seen." And perhaps not altogether with tongue in cheek Professor Berrill adds, "For when you come to the point, what use are males apart from keeping some sweet young things happy and keeping other males at bay?"[2]

I am not writing an unapologetic indictment of man. I am writing part of the story of the origins of masculine tyranny. Men have been perplexed and scared for a long time, and like most scared and confused creatures conscious of their physical superiority to the opposite sex or to members of their own sex, they are likely to take on something of the character of the bully. Men have browbeaten and physically and mentally abused women for ages, and one of the subtlest of the ways in which they have accomplished this has been through the development of elaborate codes of chivalry and etiquette. The forms of chivalry and etiquette, though they may have been and may continue to be valued by women, were originally not really intended as friendly acts. They really represent ritualized performances by Henry the Eighth (who cut off the heads of two of his wives), a patronizing superior who, in effect, is saying: "As your superior, I am called upon to give you my support and make things easier for you. You, as an inferior person, are in all respects less capable than I; and as long as you continue to recognize the facts and remain submissive and dependent, I will continue to show you the respect you believe you deserve." Chivalry was thus a kind of fictitious benevolence, the gloss put by good manners on selfishness, self-conceit, and contempt for the rights of women. In other words, a putdown.

Observe how chivalry and the ordinary rules of politeness break down as soon as women begin to compete with men on their own home ground. Men no longer offer their seats to women in conveyances, "Don't get up," I have heard men say, "they're just as strong as we are." In short, when one could keep women in their "proper" place, chivalry was a useful device, but when women begin to assert themselves as equals chivalry is no longer deemed to serve a useful purpose. This is not to deny, however, that the chivalry of many men has been a genuine unconscious or conscious recognition of the value and quality of women, and the debt of men to women.

Because by virtue of his greater physical power, man has been able to determine the fate and development of woman, men and women have come to assume that it was natural for men to do so, and both have come to mistake their prejudices for Nature's law. That men may bully women into a state of subservience is not a biological fact but a cultural sleight of hand, a cultural misuse of a physical dominance. This is a very different thing from saying that women are biologically designed to occupy a subservient relationship to men, and that the male is biologically determined to keep the female in such a subservient position. Female subservience is a culturally, not biologically, created condition. It is one of the consequences of the misuse of masculine power. As the insightful Thomas Jefferson wrote, "The stronger sex imposes on the weaker. It is civilization alone which replaces women in their enjoyment of their natural equality."[3]

At this juncture it may be useful to list some of the presumed social consequences of the biological differences between the sexes, thereby enabling us to perceive at a glance some of the biological pegs upon which men have hung the cultural disabilities of women. Looking at the table that follows, we see that there are quite a number of biological sex differences and their social consequences which we have not yet considered.

BIOLOGICAL SEX DIFFERENCES	FUNCTIONAL EXPRESSION	SOCIAL EXPRESSION
Men bigger, more powerful	Greater capacity for heavy labor	Dominance of males
Women bear children, nurse them	Movements impeded, kept closer to home	Different jobs, roles, assigned each sex; in anticipation, different training given to each
Greater muscular development	Urge to physical exertion, greater pride in it	Greater interest of male in sports, etc.
Male's larger size, higher metabolism, greater activity	Need for more food, more expenditure of energy	Greater drive in work, achievement
Lesser strength of female	Inability to cope with male physically	"Feminine" devices to achieve ends
Male's clumsiness	Tendency of men to treat women gently	Codes of chivalry, etiquette
Differences in genitalia and body	Garments adjusted differently for comfort, utility	Differences in dress, styles
Earlier puberty in girls	Ready for mating earlier	Girls permitted to marry; reach "age of consent" earlier
Menstruation	Effects on body, mind, consciousness of blood issue, other symptoms	Taboos on women, psychological and social restraint
Chronic sex drive	Women can have intercourse without desire; men cannot	Prostitution confined largely to women, rape to men
Pregnancy in women	Greater risk in sexual relationships, uncertainty of paternity	"Double standard" of conduct, stricter codes of behavior for unmarried girls and women
Menopause in women	Reproductive capacity ends much earlier than men's	Men's marriage chances continue beyond women's
Female more resistant to disease, bodily upsets	Her life span longer; surplus of women increasing	Threat to monogamous marriage system, problems of spinsterhood and widowhood

Based on a table in Amram Scheinfeld's *Women and Men*
(New York: Harcourt, Brace & Company, 1944).

It has been said that the larger size and higher metabolism of the male finds functional expression in his greater need for food and a greater expenditure of energy. One of the presumed social consequences of these differences is the male's greater drive in work and in achievement. As we have already noted, it is extremely doubtful whether the physiological differences in metabolism and their functional expression have any real connection with the male's alleged greater drive in work and achievement.

I am not the first to suggest, and I am sure I shall not be the last, that the male's drive in work and achievement may actually be the consequence of his recognition of his biological inferiority with respect to the female's creative capacity to conceive and create human beings. One of the ways in which the male may compensate for this biological inferiority is by work and achievement. By keeping the means of making a livelihood almost exclusively a masculine prerogative, men have unconsciously, as well as consciously, been able to satisfy themselves that they are by nature the "breadwinners," the pillars of society, the guarantors of the species. Hence, the great opposition to women when they begin to enter into competition with men in earning a living.

Married men, in particular, frequently object to their wives' working, considering it a reflection upon themselves. These men fear it will be said that they are unable to support their family. "My wife doesn't have to work. Why should she?" The arguments will be familiar to the reader, whether married or not. But the fact is that today the wife, faced with the high cost of living, must work in order to help support the family.

Many women enjoy being in the workaday world, even though in general they do not yet receive the same payment for the same work. Let men honestly ask themselves why they object to women working, particularly their wives, even though they may be largely free of those domestic duties that would otherwise keep them at home. Some quite illuminating answers might begin to break through the barrier of the unconscious. A wife, or almost any woman, working for a living, particularly in a field considered the special preserve of the male, is held by many males to constitute a challenge to their masculinity. When the question arises relating to the employment of a woman in some position that has hitherto been filled by a male, masculine reactions are often very revealing. The violence of the emotion and the irrational behavior that many males have exhibited, and many still continue to exhibit on such occasions, indicates how profoundly they are disturbed by the idea of a woman challenging their supremacy.

The male, in all societies, is at greater risk than the female. As Professor James Ritchie of the University of Wakaito, New Zealand, has pointed out, "The female, as she grows older and develops, has before her in more or less continuous relationship, the model of her mother. The man, as he grows through life, begins his life also in primary relationship to a maternal object but he has to give it up, he has to leave off identification with the mother, he has to take on the full male role. Males have to switch identification during development, and all sorts of things can go wrong in this."[4] And, unfortunately, they frequently do. The male has a much more difficult time than the female in growing up and separating himself from the loving mother and in identifying himself with a father with whom he is nowhere nearly as deeply involved as he remains with his mother. This often puts a strain upon him. The switch in identification he is called upon to make results in an enduring conflict. This he usually seeks to resolve by, in part, rejecting the mother and relegating her to a status inferior to that into which he has, so to speak, been thrust. Masculine antifeminism can be regarded as a reaction-formation designed to oppose the strong unconscious trend toward mother-worship. When the male's defenses are down, when he is *in extremis*, when he is dying, his last, like his first, word, is likely to be "mother," in a resurgence of his feeling for the mother he has never really repudiated, but from whom, at the overt level, he had been forced to disengage himself.

The trauma of rejection and separation from his mother, with whom he was most involved and whom he most trusted, constitutes an enduring frustration, and the reaction to frustration is usually aggressiveness toward the generalized representation of the frustrating object. This for the most part has to be repressed, but may later express itself in many ways toward women. A deep bitterness toward women, expressed in various misogynistic ways, such as contempt, sexual harassment, battering, rape, cruelty, and murder, may result. It is today well established that rape is not a *sexual* crime, but a crime of *violence* against women, suggesting that the cause of rape is in many cases due to the disordering maternal rejection. Mothers and educators need to be aware of this.

Rape, it has been said, is the only crime for which the victim is on trial. (It is also a frequent cause of family breakups, in which the husband leaves his wife for her crime of having been raped.) For this and other reasons rape is, as the FBI acknowledges, the most underreported of all serious crimes. Furthermore, the police generally throw out about 20 percent of reported rape cases as "unfounded" on the usually mythological ground that women are often vengefully likely to bring the charge against a man when no crime has actually been committed. The opposite is, of course, the truth. Knowing the obloquy and disgrace that will follow any publicity attaching to their plight, many women will nevertheless courageously report the crime.[5] Judges are, of course, mostly male, and are inclined to see that "justice" is done to the individual accused of rape. Was it not Eve who seduced Adam? The prejudiced treatment of the rape victim in a patriarchal society brings out in high relief the internalization of social attitudes toward women—even by many women toward their own sex.

Marriage, that "ghastly public confession of a strictly private intention," as a typically "ghastly" Victorian once put it, used to be the one institution by means of which the female could be securely kept in her place. Men used to be able to work and create without feeling challenged by their own wives. Wives stayed at home, had babies, and looked after them and the breadwinner too. God was in his Heaven and all was right with the world. As another Victorian male put it, "A man whose life is of any value should think of his wife as a nurse."

Most of the tens of millions of women age sixteen and over in the labor force in the United States at the present time have demonstrated that they can work as hard as men at all occupations and that they do a great deal better at some than men ever did, clerical work, for example, especially work demanding great precision and delicacy, as well as heavy labor. Men, therefore, cannot honestly object to women on the ground of lack of capacity or inefficiency. Women will be the major source of new entrants into the labor force into the next century. Men have resisted the "intrusion" of women into their workaday world to the last ditch, and many are still doing it. Why? May it not be that such men feel that the working woman constitutes a threat to their belief in themselves as the pillars of society, the creators of civilization? Or do they fear in the face of women's advances they may become merely flying buttresses? May it not be that men don't want their fears and insecurities about women disturbed? In the unconscious, these fears and insecurities are buried so deep beneath the surface of a myriad of repressions and rationalizations that they would seem to be beyond reach. However, when confronted with a serious challenge, such as a woman holding a male-dominated position, the male often loses his balance. Rocking the boat is what it is. The best way, therefore, to avoid such disturbances is to restrict women to the role of the helpless female who wouldn't know what to do with an oar or an engine if her life depended upon it. It's "*man the boats. Women and children first.*" And, of course, a certain number of men have to get into the boats; otherwise the women wouldn't be able to manage.

The origin of the English word *woman* indicates that the female's very right to social existence was determined in the light of her secondary relationship to the male, for the word was originally "wifman," that is, "wife-man," the wife of the man; in the fourteenth century the *f* was dropped and the word became "wiman," and later, "woman." Men unconsciously have desired to keep women in a secondary position, and all the rationalizations they have offered for keeping her there have avoided the statement of their actual motivation, because in most cases they have not consciously been aware of the nature of that motivation. Men must toil and women must spin, because if women stop spinning and start toiling, man's claim to creativity and indispensability as breadwinner is undermined and this he must resist.

Such motivations seem to be even clearer with respect to achievement or creativity proper. If men cannot conceive children, then they can conceive great ideas and great works, gestate them, and be delivered of them in the form of all the things that make up our complex civilization: art, science, philosophy, music, machinery, bridges, dams, automobiles, kitchen gadgetry, and the million and one things men create and women buy. How often have we heard men exclaim, "That's my baby," when referring to some product of their creation, whether it be an idea or an object? True enough, it is a way of speaking and may represent merely an analogy, or a metaphor. Perhaps, and perhaps not. "This is my brainchild," is another such expression. "I want to nurse this idea," is yet another. And there are many more. Why, it may be asked, should men use such expressions when in practically every other instance they use purely masculine phraseology and take great pains to avoid anything suggestive of the feminine? To be "pregnant" with ideas, to be "delivered" of a great idea, to "give birth" to a plan may not these and other obstetrical expressions possibly indicate, when used by males, an unconscious desire to imitate the biological creativity of the female? The conversion process takes the form: "Well, if I can't create and give birth to biological babies, I can, at least, create and give birth to their social equivalents."

Man's drive to achievement can, at least in part, be interpreted as an unconsciously motivated attempt to compensate for the lack of biological creativity. Witness how men have used their creativeness in the arts, sciences, and technologies as proof of their own superiority and the inferiority of women! The fact is that men have had far greater opportunities for cultural creativities than have women, and in this respect they have a far more profoundly motivated drive to achieve than women. The evidence strongly suggests that were women motivated by as strong drives to achieve as men, and afforded equal opportunities to do so, they would be at least every bit as successful as men. Because women are for some time yet likely to remain, on the whole, less strongly motivated than men, I think it probable that men will continue to show a higher frequency of achievement, not because they are naturally superior, but because their opportunities will for some time remain greater, and because among other things, they may be overcompensating for a natural incapacity to bear babies.

The female's inability to cope with the physically more powerful male obliges her, from an early age, to develop traits that will enable her to secure her ends by other means. Being forced to sharpen her wits upon the whetstone of the male's obduracy, the female develops a sharper intelligence. From their earliest years, girls find it necessary to pay attention to nuances and small signs of which the male rarely recognizes the existence. Such small signs and signals tell the girl what she wants to know, and she is usually ready with her plan for action before the male has begun to think.

The evidence proves that women naturally have better brains than men (see chap. 4). Women pick up the nuances in life, the different shades of meaning, in seeing and getting to the point quickly. Let men ask themselves the question, and frankly answer it: Which is the superior sex? Let it be remembered that I am not speaking about all women any more than I am speaking about all men; I am speaking about women and men in general. There are slow-witted members of both sexes just as there are quick-witted ones. My point is that women are, on the whole, more quick-witted than men, because they are born that way, but in addition to their natural endowment they are culturally forced to develop a sharpness of attention to small detail and hardly perceptible cues, of which the less sensitive male remains quite unaware. Thus "woman's intuition" is something more than merely man's transparency, constituting a comment on man's comparative opacity.

Woman's training in picking up such subliminal signs, which by comparison seldom impinge upon the consciousness of the male, is in part responsible for her greater thoughtfulness, tact, and discretion. There are, however, many other factors that contribute to form these qualities in women. When faced with the varying intractabilities of the average male, women early on developed a strategy of devices, tactics, and artful dodges for dealing with this problem. Swooning, weeping, hysteria, the vapors, and other emotional simulations of "feminine weakness" were, up to the beginning of the twentieth century, standard equipment. The utterly dependent, "clinging vine" syndrome or pose was, in many cases, an adaptive response to an otherwise impossible situation. The "little woman" attitude was anything put a pose. Such females had often been rendered so infantile that they were governed by a powerful need to feel dependent upon a strong person, usually but not necessarily always a male, who not infrequently referred to them as "baby." And, of course, a large number of females were brought up to believe that their natural state was to be dependent upon a male; in fact, many of them were taught to avoid all evidence in themselves of independence and to cultivate those traits that would appeal to the "protective instincts" of the male. Such females often acquired so high a competence in the use of the "appropriate" behavior that they themselves came to believe it to be natural. In many women these responses have become almost second nature, and it is often difficult to distinguish between what is primary and what is secondary or acquired in human nature.

How strong the clinging-vine syndrome was in some women was forcibly brought home to me years ago in the case of a very attractive young woman of about twenty-five who had already been married and divorced twice. She wished to marry again; she could see no purpose to her life other than marriage, an idea upon which she was thoroughly concentrated. I suggested to her that she had a good mind and that while she was waiting to marry again she might improve her interest in anthropology. Her answer was: "I'm the clinging-vine type. I couldn't be any good at studies." Striking a bargain with her, I sent her to take a course with a brilliant colleague at a neighboring university. The essence of our agreement was that if she could prove to herself that she really had brains, she was to continue her studies, take her degree, and possibly think of making a profession of the subject in which she declared some interest. At the end of the year she was very near the top of a class of sixty students! My colleague took special pains to discuss her abilities with me and thanked me for sending him so bright a student. The sequel to the story is that as soon as the results of the examinations were announced, she immediately disappeared, and neither my colleague nor I saw her again until many years later. The shock of discovering that she really had the necessary abilities and that she could, if she wanted to, rely upon her own merits was more than she could bear; it was a fact that she refused to face, for its consequences were unpleasant to her even in contemplation. She married a third time, and I lost touch with her. I hope she finally came to rest.

The varieties of techniques women have been forced to develop in response to the challenges presented by men have reflected more upon the male's deficiencies, than upon the female's responses. The result of this was unavoidable development. Women have to keep an eye on the main chance; they have to be constantly on their guard, with their antennae always unobtrusively extended, operating on the appropriate wavelength and picking up the proper signals without anyone noticing, as it were. All this makes for a certain artfulness. Elegantly decorated, such artificiality is not displeasing to men, even when they are able to distinguish it as such, any more than the artificially deformed feet of Chinese women were displeasing to the perpetrators of such deformities, for it was considered beautiful to have feet that peeped like mice from beneath the skirts or trousers of women. The artfulnesses of women of Western civilization possess an elegance of a different kind, for they represent a concocted admission of inferiority. It is a form of feminine wooing of the male. There he sits, this demigod, upon his throne, and all women who appear in his presence must genuflect before him, and they do, or at least most of them do. Men, of course, do everything in their power to constrain women to maintain these artificial obeisances.

The most effective feminine devices to which women resort in dealing with the male are sexual. This is a province that women have made their own. Even Sigmund Freud, that genius in the study of human nature, was badly deceived upon this point, for he mistook the overweening cultural emphasis placed on sex for a biologically motivated function. On the contrary, our preoccupation with sex is one of the unfortunate *social* consequences of the inferior position in which women have been placed by men. Under such conditions sex becomes one of the principal means by which men are able to promote themselves and secure their ends. Sex is, of course, a biological drive; what is not a biological drive, but a cultural development of a means by which the female may find her way about in the world, is the social expression of sex. This development has been constrained by the male. As a consequence, sex has been given an emphasis and value that magnify out of all proportion its real place and importance in the organic scheme of human needs. Socially, sex has become an almost pathologic metastatic growth. Its true beauty and meaning have largely become perverted and deformed to degrading ends and purposes. The true significance of love and sex has become beclouded to such an extent that few people in our culture really understand what it is. Sex is equated with intercourse as an end in itself, and love is confused with sex. Love, for far too many in our time, consists of sleeping with a seductive woman, one who is adequately endowed with the appropriate distribution of curvilinear properties, one upon whom a permanent lien may be acquired through the institution of marriage.

One of the most unfortunate consequences of the fixation on sex in our culture is that marriages are contracted by most males on the basis of physical attractiveness. It is a matter of prestige with men to acquire for a wife the most attractive female, that is to say, the most superficially attractive. It is not love but what may be called the "fakelore" of loving that reduces tenderness to a physiological exercise. Males in our culture tend to marry objects rather than persons. Marriages contracted upon such a basis are not likely to endure, for physical traits without genuine love have a way of waning with time, while character not only endures but enhances the wonder of marriage. Is it any wonder, then, that with the neglect of character and the emphasis on sex, more than one out of every two marriages in the United States ends in divorce? Think of the many more unhappy marriages there must be which, for one reason or another, never terminate in divorce. It was not merely the desire to be witty that caused George Bernard Shaw to describe contemporary marriage of his day as in many cases nothing more than licensed prostitution. It is a correct description of innumerable modern marriages. Such marriages are the product of a masculine attitude that looks upon the world of women as an open market in which one may trade old models for new.

The first and most fundamental basis for any marriage is character and friendship, and not so much marrying the right person as being the right person. Marriages between persons of character who can be friends tend to last and grow in reward and happiness. It was no less a person then Honoré Balzac who held that marriage was the best school for a man's character that was ever devised. Were people to marry for friendship rather than for that frenzy miscalled "love," but for friendship, for friendship, in a very real sense, is a form of love, and from it, in marriage or partnership, the full florescence of love will grow. Such are not the kinds of marriages or partnerships that man's present view of woman tends to encourage. Hence, men must be held responsible for the present unfortunate state of marital relationships existing between so many human beings who are tragically caught up in a web of punishments for offenses of which both are the innocent victims.

To listen to most men dilating authoritatively on the subject of women is to suffer a positive increase in one's ignorance. When men speak of women, they usually utter the most abject prejudices under the impression that they are truths, pure and simple. As Oscar Wilde remarked, few things are pure, and they are seldom simple, and of all the impure and unsimple things in this world which befog and bedevil the minds of men, their ideas about women take first place. When toward the end of the fifteenth century the Pontiff-appointed inquisitors drew up their infamous handbook of instructions for dealing with witches, the *Malleus Maleficarum* (1487), or *Hammer of Witches*, in answer to the question, Why were a greater number of witches found in "the fragile feminine sex" than among men? the answer was as simple as it was succinct. Said the authorities, "It is indeed a fact that it were idle to contradict, since it is accredited by actual experience, apart from the verbal testimony of credible witnesses" (Question 6, Part I). And that was all the evidence required. And that, alas, is the kind of evidence on which men have usually based their prejudgments of women. The myth of feminine evil has been illuminatingly examined by H. R. Hays in his book, *The Dangerous Sex*.[6] It is a sorry story of hysterical fear and hatred. The story of castration and impotence fantasies, the freezing touch of the witch, vaginas equipped with teeth and snapping like turtles, phallic women and succubae, the femme fatale, the virgin-prostitute alarum, the taboos against menstrual blood, the fear of losing male power, all testify to the deep anxiety underlying male attitudes toward women.

One of the most pervasive of myths which men have created concerning women is that women are possessed by sex. As a young Viennese writer, Otto Weininger, put it in 1903 in a famous book on sex and character, "Men possess sex, women are possessed by it." Never was the truth so madly inverted. The truth is that men are possessed by sex, while women possess it. Even among adolescents, as the Purdue study of the American teenager showed, for every girl who admitted "thinking about sex a good deal of the time," there were two boys who did so.[7] Telling evidence of the male's obsession with sex is provided by innumerable magazines and other pornographic materials that cater exclusively to the male's needs for sexual titillation. The equivalent erotica for women are minuscule in number. Biological evidence of the hormonally influenced greater aggressive sex drive of the male is curiously observed when a female suffers from a masculinizing disorder produced by excessive secretion of male hormones. When this occurs the female becomes as sexually preoccupied and as aggressive as the male. Removal of the cause of the disorder (usually a tumor of the adrenal glands) results in a decline in the circulating male hormones, and she returns to her former normal balanced state.

Men, in the cultures of the Western world, not only appear to be, but in fact are, in a chronic state of sex irritation, "erotosaurs," ready to indulge in intercourse with any presentable female at almost any available moment. This is not the case with the female, who has to be psychologically adequately prepared before she is willing to accept the advances of the male. It is a tragic but significant commentary upon our culture that there are vast numbers of men who are unaware of this simple fact. This is understandable because women seem to be so much more preoccupied with sex than are men. The cosmetics, the beauty treatments, the hairstyling, the concern with emphasizing the sexually attractive parts of the body by sexually stimulating kinds and arrangements of apparel, the décolletages, the miniskirts, the cleavages, and the thousand and one other devices calculated to produce similarly stimulating effects prove to the male the greater sexuality of the female. This is, of course, another significant misinterpretation of the facts, again calculated to establish the inferiority of the female, for what the male fails to realize is that the female's very real preoccupation with rendering herself sexually attractive, so that she looks like a movie star, represents nothing more nor less than an expression of the male's power in compelling her to conform to his reactionary requirements.[8]

In January 1995 the population of the United States was 264 million. Of this number, 49 percent were males and 51 percent females. Thus, there are always more women of marriageable age than men. While these are mostly at the older ages, if women are to find mates, they must make themselves attractive to males, and this by the standards that happen to codify feminine attractiveness at any particular time in any particular culture. In the Western world the criteria are concentrated upon sexual attractiveness, and the female, therefore, adaptively attempts to fit herself to those requirements. The behavior of women in Western culture has largely been conditioned by and represents a response to the behavior or males towards them. Studies carried out as late as 1990 found that the average American male thinks of sex every fifteen minutes. Men have placed a high premium upon sexual attractiveness; the promised dividends are high, and women, therefore, concentrate on making themselves sexually attractive. But, we repeat, it is the men who are possessed by sex, not the women. Yet there are so few men in our culture who have learned this that as a result, when women behave normally, according to their physiological state and psychological mood, men are inclined to consider them cold and frigid. And this, again, frequently leads to a disastrous dénouement to what might otherwise have been a successful marriage. Infidelity, broken homes, divorce, and suffering on the part of everyone involved, including the children, are a few of the consequences of the perfidious standards that men have set for women. Men frequently condemn women for employing artificial embellishments to make themselves more attractive. Oh, inconsistent male, be consistent in something, and as John Donne urged long ago, "love her who shows her great love to thee, in taking this pains to seem lovely to thee."

Even the diseases that men visit upon women, they saddle by implication upon them, "venereal disease" literally meaning the disease acquired from women. It would be silly, if it were not also offensive, to speak in terms of drawing up a bill of attainder against men for the crimes they have committed against women. These have been for the most part ritualized crimes, crimes that were no more regarded as crimes than a customary day's greeting. On the whole, the motivations of men have been socially ritualized inheritances like any other custom; in other words, the behavior of men toward women has been conditioned by the social heredity represented by their tradition. Men as well as women have been the victims of tradition, and as long as that tradition continues, injustice will continue to be done.

We have already considered some of the social consequences of the fact that the female is capable of being pregnant and a male is not. One of the peculiar consequences of this fact is that, while there can be no doubt that a woman is having a baby, there can be some doubt about the baby's paternity. While a man may be reasonably certain that a child is his, he cannot always be absolutely certain of it. This fact has given rise not only to strict codes of conduct for women but also to mistrust and fear of them. Men find the idea of "betrayal" intolerable, although when men choose to betray the betrayal is called by some more elegant name. In the eighteenth century Oliver Goldsmith had a revealing solution to this problem in a poignant poem:

> *When lovely woman stoops to folly*
> *And finds too late that men betray,*
> *What charm can soothe her melancholy,*
> *What art can wash her guilt away?*
> *The only art her guilt to cover,*
> *To hide her shame from every eye,*
> *To give repentance to her lover*
> *And wring his bosom, is—to die.*

Naturally, not the man, but the woman had to die. The double standard of sexual morality is immemorially old, as is the suspicion and fear of women. Such mistrust and fear actually revolve about the male's feeling of uncertainty about paternity, and therefore to compensate for his feelings of insecurity, men have created harsh punishments and practices within which to secure the chastity of their women. The operation of infibulation, referred to in the previous chapter, is an extreme example. The medieval chastity girdle represents another; although perhaps less brutal, it was calculated to secure the same end.

In a large proportion of societies adultery was and is punished by death or payment of a heavy penalty, that is, when the adultery is committed by the female. Adultery committed by the male has almost invariably gone unpunished. In some societies even more horrendous punishments than death were threatened or visited upon the adulterous female, death in such cases being but the final release. The stoning to death of women taken in adultery is but one of the more gentle methods with which such women were rewarded. We need not go any further into the inventory of horrors that have been visited upon women for this "crime"; it is sufficient to say that the penalties have been out of all proportion to its heinousness. In the civilized world of today we do somewhat better than our ancestors, though the emotional response of men to the unfaithfulness of their wives tends to be so excessive that one cannot help suspecting that the same ancient motives, at least in part, play a significant role in shaping their reactions. The emphatic paramountcy placed on premarital chastity largely has its origins in male insecurities rather than in concern for the welfare of the female.[9]

Emphasis on chastity has, in effect, produced in most persons brought up on the tradition of the Western world a calculated ignorance of the facts of human growth and development. As a result, there has been a conspicuous failure to prepare for the rights, duties, and privileges of becoming a spouse and parent. The amount of damage and tragic suffering this devastating ignorance has produced is incalculable. It is not being suggested that premarital intercourse as such is a desirable thing. It is being suggested that one of the byproducts of the early and continued emphasis on premarital chastity has been the production of a deplorably damaging ignorance of the so-called facts of life, of human creation, growth, and development. Such ignorance is harmful to the healthy development of the individual and therefore to the healthy development of society.[10]

4

WHO SAID,
"THE INFERIOR SEX"?

The myth of female inferiority is so old, and has been for so long a part of the ideas and institutions of civilized men, that it has been generalized for almost every aspect of the female being. Is there a trait in which women have not been considered inferior to men? It would be difficult to think of one. The idea seems to be that where women are different from men, they are inferior to men. In societies in which women have been allowed certain exclusive privileges, such privileges have not necessarily rendered them, in those or any other respects, superior to men, only different, with certain rights and privileges of their own. The myth of female inferiority has been extended not only to mental functions but also to physical traits. The lesser muscular power of the female has lent the strongest and most obvious kind of support to this belief. The female, it has been "clear," is weaker than the male. That is all men have known about the facts, which is all, they have felt, they needed to know. The facts, after all, speak for themselves. What countless errors and unspeakable crimes have been committed in the name of the authority carried by such words as, "The facts, after all, are obvious." But what is a fact? And what does "obvious" mean?

For most people a fact has always been something they could perceive, a thing they could grasp; but what most people have not understood is that a fact for them has been an experience they have endowed with a certain meaning. An experience is anything lived or undergone; a meaning is an interpretation, adding significance to the experience undergone. *Homo additus naturae.* And what men will add to each experience depends upon the kingdom that is within them.

The kingdom that is within us is socially constructed,[1] and what we perceive we preconceive in terms of that social construct, in the sense that every new experience is evaluated in terms of an already existing mass of perceptions within the mind; the psychologist calls this process "apperception." Men have lived upon the earth for several million years, and for a long period of this secular time they knew it to be a "fact" that the earth was flat. After all, it was "obvious." For quite as long a time it was obvious that the earth was a stationary body and that it was the sun that "rose" and "set." For untold thousands of years it was believed that decaying matter generated insects. Most of us today would accept the same mistakes as facts were it not that it has now become part of our tradition to think otherwise.[2] Most of us have no more proved for ourselves the facts about the solar system and the generation of insects than we have proved the facts we accept and to which we subscribe concerning female inferiority.

Men are roughly about 10 percent bigger than women. The female is generally shorter, slighter, and less muscular than the male; these facts are obvious to everyone. The male, it is asserted, is clearly superior in these respects to the female. Let us here recall our definition of superiority in terms of the conferral of survival benefits upon those possessing the particular traits under discussion. Do the greater size and muscular power of the male, from the biological standpoint, confer greater survival benefits upon him? We have already answered that question in the negative in the previous chapter, but let us for a moment continue with question and answer from another point of view: Do lesser size and muscular power of the female confer lesser survival benefits upon her? The answer, on the basis of the facts, is a resounding *no!* On the contrary, the facts prove that the biological advantages are with the female. Insofar as sheer muscular efficiency and endurance are concerned, the performance of the shorter, slighter, "weaker" female as a cross-Channel swimmer, for example, suggests that the best women can do as well as the best men, and often even better. Ever since Gertrude Ederle of the United States, on August 6, 1926, swam the English Channel in fourteen hours, thirty-one minutes—two hours faster than any man or woman had ever done before—there have been striking performances by women that testify to their remarkable physical skill and staying power. On October 12, 1955, Florence Chadwick of the United States crossed the Channel from England to France, the more difficult route, in thirteen hours, thirty-three minutes. Abla Adel Khairi of Egypt, aged thirteen years and ten months, on August 17, 1974, made the same crossing in twelve hours, twenty-two minutes. The race from France to England in August 1957, in which both men and women competed, was won by a woman swimmer, Greta Anderson of Denmark, in thirteen hours and fifty-three minutes. In September 1967, Linda McGill, a twenty-one-year-old Australian, broke the women's record by swimming the Channel in nine hours, thirty-nine minutes, missing the men's mark by only twenty-four minutes. In September 1971, Connie Ebbelaar, a twenty-two-year-old Dutch swimming instructor, swam the Channel from England to France in ten hours, forty minutes, which was just twenty minutes away from equaling the men's record for the twenty-one-mile swim. Wendy Brook of the United States, in September 1976, swam the Channel from France to England in eight hours and fifty-six minutes, the fastest time by anyone, male or female. Even more astonishing is the performance of Peggy Lee Dean of the United States who, in July 1978, set a record for the fastest Channel crossing from France to England in seven hours and forty minutes. Finally, without adding any of the other Channel records achieved by women, there stand the unique accomplishments of Diana Nyad of the United States who, in 1975, became the first person to swim nonstop the thirty-two miles across Lake Ontario; this she did in twenty hours. That same year she broke the 1927 record for a swim around Manhattan Island, completing the circuit in seven hours, fifty-seven minutes. A dedicated marathon swimmer Nyad has swum in shark cages on all the challenging waterways of the world, and in August 1979 was the first person to make the sixty-mile swim against sharks, jellyfish, and the cruel Gulf Stream current from the Bahamas to Florida. She was in the water for twenty-seven hours and thirty-eight minutes. Not only had she done "the impossible," but she followed this by completing a sixty-seven mile swim in the North Sea, followed by other long-distance swims, some of them setting world records.[3]

Among many of women's physical advantages is a greater distribution of body fat than men: 25 percent of body weight is fat in females compared with 14 percent in males. The overall subcutaneous fatty layer of women renders them more buoyant and better insulated against cold than men. Women's narrower shoulders offer less resistance through the water. Women are also capable of calling on extra reserves of energy unavailable to men. In long-distance running, for example, while they may tire, few women "hit the wall," as the expression has it for the sudden pain and debilitating weakness that sometimes hits long-distance runners or swimmers. This difference may be due to the fact that when the glycogen, the main source of carbo-hydrates that power the muscles, is exhausted in men, women are able to draw upon their fat reserves.

Women are able to deal with heat better than men. Their body temperatures can rise two or three degrees above men's before they begin to sweat, and then they do so more efficiently than men, because women's greater number of sweat glands are distributed more uniformly over their bodies. Also, blood supply to the skin is more efficient, so more blood is distributed to the surface to be cooled. The male sweats sooner, but the female sweats physiologically more efficiently.

Women are also better equipped to deal with cold. Another sporting event in which women have excelled, but few have thus far entered, is the Iditarod Trail Sled Dog Race. This race is run under the some of the world's worst weather conditions on the more than eleven-hundred-mile Alaska trail from Anchorage to Nome. The first women to win with her dog team was Libby Riddles in 1985. In March 1990, Susan Butcher won her fourth consecutive Iditarod in record time. The race presents a grueling challenge requiring great stamina and strength of character. In addition to driving the sled, and attending to their own needs, participants must prepare meals for their dogs and care for their injuries, often with little or no sleep.

In a society in which, in the last resort, its institutions are maintained by force, physical power becomes a valued social factor; but this is a very different thing from claiming that it is either a valuable biological or indispensable social trait. Civilized societies in particular have been characterized by a great deal of both covert and overt hostility. The quantity of violence that characterizes our contemporary civilized socially dysfunctional societies presents a picture of a world at war with itself. The most widely read books of our day deal with death, disaster, and crimes of violence; theater and the motion pictures carry on the tradition, and television proffers, as the most staple article of diet for our children, murder, muck, mystery, and every form of violence. War or the threat of war is almost continuously with us, and whole generations have been educated to believe that war and conflict are natural concomitants of human living. Thrilling and dangerous spectacles draw large and devoted audiences. Slugging matches, miscalled boxing, and no-holds-barred wrestling matches draw the largest followings—and now that television has brought these spectacles into the home, the education in violence proceeds apace. In a land as civilized as the United States, the most common known reason leading to a homicide was an argument, representing 28 percent of all homicides, only slightly smaller than the percentage resulting from robberies. Males, it was shown for 1995, have a firearm fatality rate six times that of females (24 per 100,000 vs. 4 per 100,000 for women). The average firearm fatality rate itself is alarmingly high, nearly 14 firearm fatalies per hundred thousand persons. In 1995 alone, 35,987 persons died as a result of firearm injuries—18,503 from suicide, 15,835 from homicide 1,225 were from unintentional shootings, and 394 from undetermined causes. The United States Department of Justice reports that men are more likely to be the killers and the victims, they are more then nine times more likely than women to commit murder. Even more alarmingly, firearm homicides by young people, mostly male, aged 18–24 increased from about 5,000 in 1980 to more than 7,500 in 1997.

Though in our time we have increased the facilities for the wider education of humankind in the varieties of violence, violence in one form or another has characterized most civilized societies for a very long time. Where violence has been traditionally resorted to as a means of settling disputes, familial, group, tribal, and intertribal physical force becomes not only a valued trait but also a sanctioned form of behavior. For example, it is permissible to beat one's wife and one's children in many societies without in any way being penalized for doing so. Boys traditionally fight; girls do not. It should be clear that in societies that sanction a certain amount of violent behavior, men, owing to their greater muscular power, consider themselves superior to women in this respect, and women readily grant them this superiority. But it must be understood that such superiority is a socially conferred superiority, not a biological one, because the male's greater muscular power enables him by force to obtain and maintain certain immediate social advantages. If the adequate functioning and survival of the male depended upon violent conflict with the female, then there would be no question concerning the biological superiority of the male's greater muscular power; but the efficient functioning and survival of the male does not depend upon violent conflict with anyone. The greater muscular power of the male has, to a large extent, been an economically valuable trait, especially during the long period of history when so much of the labor expended in human societies was in the form of muscle power. Today, when machines do more than 90 percent of the work formerly done by muscle, muscular power has become an outmoded redundancy borne by men at a price that exceeds any return it can yield either to them or to society.

Let us apply another test. What is the answer to the question: Which sex survives the rigors of life, whether normal or extreme, better than the other? The answer is: the female sex. Women endure all sorts of devitalizing conditions better than men: starvation, exposure, fatigue, shock, illness, and the like. This immediately raises the question of the alleged weakness of the female. Is not the female supposed to be the weaker vessel? Weakness is a misleading word that has, in this connection, confused people. Feminine weakness has generally meant that the female is more fragile and less strong than the male. But the fact is that the female is constitutionally stronger than the male and muscularly less powerful; she has greater stamina and lives longer. Women who reach 100 years or more in age are much more numerous than men who do. Muscular strength should not be confused with constitutional strength, for constitutionally, women are stronger than men, and men are constitutionally weaker than women, in part because of their burden of muscularity. Furthermore, the female possesses a more efficient and powerful immunological system than the male, thus affording her greater immunity against infection and endowing her with a faster recovery rate. The male pays heavily for his larger body build and muscular power. Because his expenditure of energy is greater than that of the female, he burns himself out more rapidly and hence dies at an earlier age. The metabolic rate of the male, as I have already stated, is some 6 to 7 percent higher than that of the female.

Where, now, are the much-vaunted advantages of the male's larger size and muscular power? Are males biologically fitter in *any* way? Are these physical traits socially advantageous any longer? The answer is that whatever benefits men may have derived from larger size and muscular power in the past, they have in our own time outlived them. Today the advantages are mostly with the smaller bodied, less muscularly powerful female.

During the last century and the early part of the twentieth, one of the great standbys of men in arguing the inferiority of women was the lesser absolute size and weight of the male brain. Among Europeans, the average weight of the male brain is about 1,385 grams and the female brain about 1,265 grams; that is to say, the male brain weighs, on the average, slightly over three pounds, and the female brain, on the average, about four ounces less. Yet on the basis of this small difference of less than four ounces an elaborate mythology has been erected. The actual amount—four ounces—has been forgotten, if it ever was widely known, and the difference in magnitude has been bruited as a substantial, but unstated, quantity. The smaller brain of woman has always been dealt as the trump card that effectively put an end to any doubt as to who had more "brains." And since more brain was believed to be the equivalent of greater intelligence, there could be no further argument that the male was more intelligent than the female. It mattered not how often this canard was demolished by scientists. Despite the evidence, repeated again and again in edition after edition of Havelock Ellis's widely circulated book *Man and Woman* and in Amram Scheinfeld's more recent *Women and Men*, the myth seems to be as strongly entrenched as ever.

Scientific investigations on the relation between brain size and intelligence have been fairly numerous, and the general conclusion drawn from them is that there is no relation whatever between brain size and intelligence. The biggest human brain on record was that of an idiot; one of the smallest was that of the gifted French writer Anatole France. The idiot's brain weighed over 2,850 grams or five and a quarter pounds; the brain of Anatole France weighed only 1,100 grams or two pounds, six ounces. Within the limits of the normal range of variation of human brain weight, human beings with big brains are not characterized by intelligence greater than those with "small" brains.

The widespread and erroneous belief that a larger or heavier brain constitutes a criterion of higher mental faculties is understandable enough, but it happens to be false. Many prehistoric humans had larger brains than contemporary humans, for example: The Neandertals had an average brain volume of 1,550 cubic centimeters, while prehistoric humans of modern type, the Boskop of south Africa, had an average brain volume of about 1,600 cubic centimeters, compared with the modern European average of about 1,400 cubic centimeters.[4] There is no reason to believe that the bigger brained prehistoric men were any more intelligent than contemporary humans. The elephant and the whale have larger and heavier brains than we do, but no one has yet suggested that they are more intelligent.

An important point to understand is that a heavier or larger brain does not in itself constitute evidence of more gray matter. As is well known, the surface area of the brain is increased by being thrown into a number of convolutions or folds, thus enabling it to occupy a smaller volume of space than would otherwise be possible. The amount of gray matter, therefore, depends upon the number and complexity of the half dozen or more cellular layers of which the convoluted gray matter is composed. There is no known relationship between size of brain and number and complexity of convolutions, or between size or brain and complexity of cellular organization.

Finally, in relation to total body size the female brain is at least as large as, and in general larger than, that of the male. The heavier, larger male would be expected to have a slightly heavier, larger brain because all organs of the body are influenced and controlled by a general size factor and because each of the sexes possesses a brain that is proportionate to body size. However, when allowance has been made for general size, the female emerges with a slight advantage in brain size. The complete facts have been available for more than a century, ever since Professor T. L. W. Bischoff, the great German anatomist, published his study on the brain weight of man, *Das Hirngewicht des Menschen,* Bonn, 1880. Since then many other scientists have independently confirmed the findings of Bischoff. As I have already mentioned, in 1894 the facts were set out in detail by Havelock Ellis in *Man and Woman,* a book that by 1934 had reached its eighth edition. But as far as many members of the reading public of the Western world are concerned (not to mention the nonreading public) it would seem as if these studies and books have never been published. I have never met anyone outside, and few in, scientific circles who did not believe that women had smaller brains and therefore less intelligence than men. I shall spare the reader the spectacle of nineteenth-century scientists making fools of themselves in this connection by refraining from showing how they permitted their prejudices to become involved in their scientific speculations. As Havelock Ellis wrote:

> The history of opinion regarding the cerebral sexual difference forms a painful page in scientific annals. It is full of prejudices, assumptions, fallacies, overhasty generalizations. The unscientific have had a predilection for this subject; and men of science seem to have lost the scientific spirit when they approached the study of its seat. Many a reputation has been lost in these soft sinuous convolutions.[5]

Lest anyone who reads these words jump to the rash conclusion that there have not been scientists within the relatively recent period to whom this comment could be applied, let me hasten to disabuse them of so generous a judgment, for there have been many. Literary men have, on the whole, not improved much, if we are to judge from what may perhaps represent an extreme case, that of the well-known German writer Max Funke, who, in his book *Are Women Human?*, stated that woman, with her small brain, must be considered a sort of "missing link," halfway between man and the anthropoid ape, and should be labeled "semihuman."

What are the facts? Bischoff, and later others, showed that the brain weight of the female in relation to the male's brain weight is as 90:100, whereas her body weight is to the male's only as 83:100. If we then were to raise the female's body weight to the equivalent proportion of the male, namely, 100 units, then one would have to add 17 units to the existing 90 for the female proportion of the brain to that of the male, yielding a figure of 107 for the female as compared with 100 for the male. That is the proportion that most investigators have found when allowance has been made for body size. When one eliminates body fat from the weight of both sexes, the difference in brain weight in favor of the female is further increased.

Let us illustrate these facts in a simpler manner. As stated previously, we find that among Europeans the average brain weight of men is 1,385 grams, or 3 pounds and 1 ounce, while that of women is 1,265 grams, or 2 pounds and 12 ounces. Now, if the weight of the brain is considered in relation to the weight of the body, it will be found that women possess the relatively heavier brain. The average body weight of man is about 143 pounds, while that of woman is about 121 pounds; thus the average body weight of the male is about 22 pounds greater than that of the average female. Upon calculation it will be found that while man has 1 ounce of brain weight for every 47 ounces of body weight, woman has 1 ounce of brain weight for every 43 ounces of body weight. Roughly speaking, then, the brain weight of woman constitutes about 2 percent of the weight of the body, while the brain weight of a man is only 1 percent of his body weight.

How the mighty have fallen! But only from the rickety structure men have rather disingenuously erected to create a case for their own superior brain weight. As far as intelligence is concerned, it must be reiterated, the facts about brain weight prove that if there were any relation (within the normal range of variation of brain weights) between these two factors, the advantage would be with women; but since there is no such relation, the case against women on the basis of brain weight is completely demolished, as could be the case that might be argued against the intelligence of the male on the same grounds. So much, then, for the myth of brain weight and intelligence. Should anyone, however, for a moment think that this disposes of the brain boosters, let them prepare themselves for a shock: The brain boosters have other arguments.

Granting that the female has a slight relative superiority of brain size or brain weight, what about the size, shape, and form of the supposed seat of intelligence, the frontal lobes? We can dispose of this question rapidly: The frontal lobes are larger and more globular in the female than they are in the male. The great nineteenth-century French neurosurgeon and physical anthropologist Paul Broca, who was by no means an ardent feminist, was the first to show that if one took the cerebral hemisphere to represent 1,000, then the proportion of the frontal lobe to the hemisphere in the male is 427, whereas in the female it is 431. These findings have since been confirmed by other investigators. So much, then, for brain size and brain forms.

The absurd lengths to which some alleged male scientists would go in the attempt to keep women in their proper place is exemplified by Austrian writer Dr. M. Benedikt. Since women tend to have higher foreheads than men, and since it was (erroneously) believed that a high forehead constituted evidence of high mental capacity, Dr. Benedikt maintained that in women it constituted an indication of "convulsive degeneration." It is for this reason, he argued, women "instinctively" attempt to conceal a high forehead by lowering their hair over it![6]

It has been known for years that in women the cerebellum is much larger than it is in males; hence nothing of this part of the brain has been heard of in discussions concerning the relative intelligence of male and female. In recent years it has been found that the *splenium*, the hind part of the great commisure (the *corpus callosum*) through which it has been calculated almost two hundred million fibers pass to and from the hemispheres of the gray matter of the brain (the *cortex*), is larger in females, and on the whole contains more neurons. This suggests a probable advantage. There remain other parts of the brain which have been more or less frequently cited. One is the intermediate region on the side of the brain known as the parietal area. Most investigators appear to agree that this occupies a larger area in the male than in the female. This should not be surprising, for this is the general area of sensorimotor representation, and one would expect the more muscularly active organism to have a larger parietal area. The occipital lobe (the back part of the brain), most investigators find, is of equal size in both sexes. As for the convolutions, no one has ever found any kind of significant sex-based difference either in their pattern or in their complexity; nor has anyone ever found any difference of a sexual nature in the microscopic structure of the brain. Chemical differences have been found by one group of investigators, but no one has the faintest idea what the significance of these differences may be. While it has been claimed that the female has a better blood supply to her brain, in that the combined diameters of her internal carotid and vertebral arteries in relation to total brain mass are greater than those of the male, it would seem unlikely that this fact, if it is a fact, has any bearing upon the matter of intelligence. In the words of Havelock Ellis, "To sum up, it may be said that investigation has shown that the ancient view which credited men with a significantly larger amount of nervous tissue than women has been altogether overthrown. There is much better ground for the latter view, according to which, relative to size, the nervous superiority belongs to women."[7]

Beginning in the early 1990s, new methods were developed for detecting what happens while thinking. For this purpose various powerful imaging technologies were developed, such as magnetic resonance imaging (MRI), and positron emission technology (PET). By means of such instruments it now is possible to observe something of what is going on in the brain as it reacts to thinking, feeling, emotions, remembering, problem solving, mathematical activity, reading faces, making judgments, idling, and the like. These images tell us where, and in which side of the brain, things are happening. The fundamental discovery thus far is that the two lobes, or hemispheres of the brain function very differently in women. In women as well as men, the left hemisphere is found to be normally dominant for language functions, while the right hemisphere is prominently involved with spatial and nonverbal relations. This does not mean that each hemisphere is either exclusive or independent from the other, for every function seems to be capable of representation on either side. Hence, though one now speaks of the left/right brain, men tend to rely more on one or other hemisphere when processing information, whereas women will use both hemispheres; in other words, the male brain is more *lateralized*. Since processing infor-mation is what the brain does for a living, it is evident that women use their brains more efficiently than men.

The structural system that makes possible communication between both hemispheres of the brain is the corpus callosum, the largest fiber tract of the brain and the main highway of communication between both hemispheres. The corpus callosum contains more than 300 million nerve fibers, which are largely distributed within the six layers of the gray matter, the cortex, of the brain. The cortex has been estimated to contain as high as a trillion neurons, not surprisingly since that is where most of the business of the mind is conducted. Cortical neurons with different thresholds and kinds of excitatory responses, serving the nervous system, are always modifiable by environmental factors contributing to the structure and quality of the widely different functions, and ultimately the conditioning of behavior.

Furthermore, in women the corpus callosum is larger than it is in men, also each of its fore and aft regions, known as *commisures*, are enriched by additional bundles of neurons, which contribute to the more efficient coordination of both hemispheres. In short, neuroscientific studies have revealed that the female brain is structurally and functionally more highly developed and capable of thinking more soundly and intuitively than the male brain.

Finally, it should be noted that from their late teens until their middle age, men lose brain tissue at almost three time the rate of women, and tend to be mentally less lively then women.

One of the earliest experiences that drew my attention, as a student, to the natural superiority of women was the observation that in the general character of the skull the female appeared to fulfill the promise, the evolutionary promise, of the child rather more significantly than did the male. This idea was by no means original with me. I can no longer recall the circumstances that led to my encountering it, though I know that in my capacity as a physical anthropologist the study of many thousands of skulls helped. I think it was in the pages of Ellis's *Man and Woman*, or perhaps in the pages of someone quoting Ellis, that I first grasped the full significance of the differences that struck me when comparing male and female crania.

Ellis pointed out that the infant of the great apes (gorilla, chimpanzee, and orangutan) resembles the human being much more closely than does the adult ape, for the features of the ape as it grows older become more and more animallike. To the extent that *Homo sapiens* is apelike, the resemblance is, on the whole, to the infant and not to the adult ape. While man and woman in the course of their individual development fall somewhat away from the bountiful cranial promise of their early years, the ape in the course of its development departs very much more from the promise of its infancy than human beings do. Humans as they grow remain more like the infant than does the ape. The skulls of an infant gorilla and of an infant human being closely resemble each other, and the skull of the infant gorilla in many respects more closely resembles that of an adult human than it does that of an adult gorilla. But as the ape grows, the skull departs more and more from its infant form, so that the adult ape skull turns out to look so unlike the infant ape skull that, comparing one with the other, one would hardly believe they belonged to the same species.

The adult human skull preserves the promise of the infant human skull very much more than does the adult gorilla the promise of the infant gorilla skull. In other words, the adult human being is an infantilized or pedomorphic type, a type which has evolved by preserving some ancestral youthful characteristics; the adult gorilla is an aged or gerontomorphic type, a type that has undergone evolutionary change as the result of the accentuated development of already adult traits.

The skull of the human infant has a rather globular brain box, which relatively overshadows the small face; the bones are smooth and delicately made; the teeth are small and efficient. The more an adult skull approaches in appearance the human infant or late fetal skull, the more human it looks. The human female skull more closely resembles that of an infant than does the male skull. The human female, therefore, maintains the evolutionary promise of the fetal or infant skull more than does the male. The female is in the vanguard of evolution in this respect; the male falls somewhat behind.

As far as human beings are concerned, most authorities today believe that *Homo sapiens* is not only a predomorphic type, but even more a fetalized type; that is, the adult human being preserves many of the physical traits characteristic of the fetus. The infant shows these traits even more markedly than the adult; for example, in the general lack of body hair, the big head, the flatness of the face, and the root of the nose, which is associated with the epicanthic fold, the fold of skin of the upper eyelid that tends to cover the inner corner of the eye, that so many infants for a time exhibit. There are also the traits of the general smoothness of the bones of the skeleton, the correlated

absence of eyebrow ridges and other bony ridges and tuberosi-
ties, the short legs and long trunk, and fewer hairs to the square
centimeter. In other words, humans are in many ways very
much like a big fetus. Actually, the ethnic type whose adult
members most closely preserve these fetal traits is the mongo-
loid, and these are, perhaps, best represented by the Chinese
peoples. To a lesser degree these traits are characteristic of all
human beings, but in non-mongoloid people they are not quite
so marked in the adult stage as they are in earlier years.

Most authorities are agreed upon the important point that the
infant type is the type toward which human development is
directed and that human evolution has actually come about as
a result of the slowing down and stretching out of our development, in the womb and especially after birth. This kind of
development is known as *neoteny*.[8] For a species having one infant
at a birth and not a litter, it becomes very important for the survival
of the species that the baby be well nourished and prepared before
it is exposed to the dangers of postnatal life. This is as true of the
anthropoid apes as of humans; but, as we have seen, the fetalization
process becomes arrested in the ape much earlier than it does in
the human.

The progress of the human species has been a progress in
youthfulness, in growing young rather than old. Woman exhibits
that progress to a more conspicuous degree than does man, not
only physically but also behaviorally. As Sir Arthur Keith has
stated, "In mankind there has been a tendency to carry the joy
of youth and the carefree spirit into adult life; the retention of a
youthful mentality is commoner among women than among
men."[9] The female, in most respects, is a more highly fetalized
type than man, and adheres more closely to the line of evolutionary development indicated by the child than does the male. As
Havelock Ellis wrote in *Man and Woman*,

> When we have realized the position of the child in relation to
> evolution we can take a clearer view as to the natural position of
> woman. She bears the special characteristic of humanity in a
> higher degree than man . . . and led evolution in the matter of
> hairiness, simply because she is nearer the child. Her conserva-
> tism is thus compensated and justified by the fact that she
> represents more nearly than man the human type to which man
> is approximating.[10]

In more senses than one, Jesus' words have a profound meaning: "Except ye . . . become as little children, ye shall not enter into the kingdom of heaven" (Matthew 18:3).

If human beings continue upon this earth, they will probably continue to evolve in the direction of a greater prolongation of infancy and childhood and a progressively increasing slowing down of maturity.[11] Just as modern humans have lost the heavily developed brow ridges and protruding jaws of their prehistoric ancestors, so it is likely that they will continue to lose many of their present distinguishing adult characteristics. As Schiller wrote long ago in *Dignity of Women*, "From the bewitching gracefulness of the features shines forth the fulfillment of humanity."

5

WHEN "X" DOESN'T EQUAL "Y"

We have already seen that there is good reason to believe that the female enjoys, on the whole, a substantial biological advantage compared with the male. Does there exist some biological differentiating factor that may serve to explain or possibly throw some light on the origin and meaning of these differences? The answer is, yes. I do not know that anyone has previously made anything of a key fact that lies at the base of practically all the differences between the sexes and the biological superiority of the female to the male. I refer to the chromosomal structure of the sexes, the chromosomes being the small cellular bodies that carry the heredity material, or genes, which so substantially influence the development and fate of the organism.

In the sex cells there are twenty-three chromosomes, but only one of these is a sex chromosome. There are two kinds of sex chromosomes, X and Y. Half of all sperm cells carry X and half carry Y chromosomes. All female ova in the female ovaries contain only X chromosomes. When an X-bearing sperm and an ovum unite, the offspring is always female, XX. When a Y-bearing sperm unites with an ovum, the offspring is always male, XY. It is the initial genetic, or constitutional, difference between the sexes. This is not to say that the sex chromosomes are eventually entirely responsible for the development of all the differences in sex characteristics; it *is* to say that the chromosomes are decisive in determining whether an organism shall develop as a male or a female. The sex chromosomes regulate the transformation of the zygote, or diploid cell, resulting from the union of the male and female gametes, or haploid cells, each carrying half the number of chromosomes. *Fertilization,* the word usually employed to describe this process, is not the best term, for the essence of the process is the fusion of two cells which will develop into an embryo, not the supremacy of one cell over another. During the first few weeks of development the embryo remains sexually undifferentiated, though oriented toward femaleness. Up to the end of the sixth week of embryonic development the appearance of the external genitalia is identical in the two sexes. If the embryo is a genetic male, masculinizing organizing substances will enlarge the phallus, extend the urethra along its length, and close the skin over the urogenital sinus to form the scrotum for the testes, which will later descend into it. In the absence of the masculinizing hormone testosterone (which is normally derived from the gonad, the sexually indifferent organ that may develop either as an ovary or testes), the infant will develop as a female, even though a female organizing substance does not exist. This, as the distinguished experimental endocrinologist Dr. Alfred Hoet and others have suggested, indicates that the basic surviving human form is female and that masculinity is something "additional."[1]

Under normal conditions the sex rudiments are differentially affected toward maleness or femaleness depending upon whether the chromosomal constitution (the genotype) is XY or XX. The genotype of chromosomal constitution therefore is decisive in initiating the direction of sexual development; thereafter it is a matter largely under the influence of the developing hormones secreted by the endocrine glands. The development of all bodily structures and their functions, in relation to the environment in which they develop, is set by the sex chromosomes at the time the sex rudiments and the gonads are sexually differentiated. As Professor N. J. Berrill has written,

> In any case, the status of the female is never in doubt. Whoever produces eggs is essential to the future, for eggs are reproductive cells, whatever else they may be. Sperm are not so in the primary sense of the word. They serve two decidedly

secondary ends—they serve to stimulate the otherwise comatose eggs to start developing, like the kiss that awakened the Sleeping Beauty, and they serve to introduce considerable variability derived from the male parent.[2]

Eggs, of course, also contribute their variability to the offspring, but eggs alone have the capacity, under certain conditions, to develop readily into grown organisms, whereas sperms lack such a capacity altogether. In all sexual species the mature organism is the developed egg, with the extra touches added, usually but not always, only when a sperm is involved.

What is the difference between an XX and an XY cell? When one looks at a body cell containing a full complement of forty-six chromosomes there is no difficulty in recognizing the XX sex chromosomes because they belong with the group of quite large chromosomes. But if one examines a body cell with the XY complement of the male, say at a magnification of two thousand diameters, it will be seen that the Y chromosome is the smallest of the forty-six chromosomes. It is in that difference, and what it signifies, that there lies part of the answer to the question, How do the sexes get that way?

The chromosomes which are neither X nor Y (twenty-two in the haploid and forty-four in the diploid state) are called *autosomes*. There are twenty-two pairs of them in the body cells, but only twenty-two *single* ones in the sex cells. Each of the autosomes contains factors that tend toward the production of femaleness. Each of the X chromosome contains genes that tend toward the production of femaleness. The Y chromosome carries factors that are male-determining. (Among the genes contained in the Y chromosome is one responsible for the secretion of the masculinizing hormone, testosterone, from the gonads.) Hence, when a Y-carrying sperm fuses with an ovum, the XY chromosomes, in the presence of the twenty-two pairs of autosomes carrying genes directed toward femaleness, are insufficiently powerful to reduce the influence of those genes, and the result is the development of a male. On the other hand, the combination of two X chromosomes, one from the mother and the other from the father, is sufficient to overcome the influence of any possibly male factors in the autosomes, and the result is a female. The X chromosomes together have quite a pull to them; and the explanation of the biological superiority of the female lies in the female having two X chromosomes while the male has only one.[3] It is largely to the original X chromosome deficiency of the male that almost all the troubles to which he falls heir may be traced, and to the presence of two well-appointed, well-furnished X chromosomes that the female owes her biological superiority. As a consequence of the larger size of the X chromosome, the female's cells are about 4 percent greater in chromosome volume than those of the male. As Drs. J. H. Tjio and T. T. Puck, who originally determined the difference in sex-chromosome size in 1958, have remarked, "The female has a substantially richer genetic capacity than the male."[4]

The vital importance of the X chromosome as compared with the Y chromosome is unequivocally clear because no cell can survive long unless it contains an X chromosome. No matter how many Y chromosomes a cell may contain, if it does not also contain an X chromosome it dies. Males, therefore, survive only by grace of their having been endowed by their mothers with an X chromosome. In birds and some insects two X chromosomes produce a male and an XY combination produces a female, but otherwise the conditions are precisely the same as in humans, except that the autosomes contain the sex genes that are strongly organized toward femaleness, whereas the X chromosomes are strongly, and in double dose, more powerfully organized toward maleness. That it is the X chromosome that counts is borne out of by the incidence of embryo deaths, which is much greater among the female birds than among the males.

What the origin of the X and Y chromosomes may have been no one knows. It may be that the Y chromosome represents a remnant of an X chromosome. While the Y chromosome is the masculinizing agent, feminization will occur only when it is absent, while survival is impossible in the presence of a Y chromosome alone. On the other hand, development will occur in the presence of only one X chromosome, giving rise to a female with a condition known as Turner's syndrome, usually sterile and exhibiting a sort of webbing of the neck.

Thus far some twenty conditions have been traced to genes which sometimes occur only by fathers to their sons. Among these are barklike skin (*ichthyosis hystrix gravior*), dense hairy growth on the ears (*auricular hypertrichosis*), nonpainful hard lesions of the hands and feet (*keratoma dissipatum*), and a form of webbing of the toes in which there is fusion of the skin between the second and third toes.

It is probable that the biological disadvantages accruing to the male are not so much due to what is in the Y chromosome as to what is not in it. This is well exemplified by the manner in which the male inherits a serious disorder such as hemophilia (spontaneous or traumatic subcutaneous and intramuscular bleeding). This is due to a mutant gene carried on the X chromosome. A mutant gene is one in which a physicochemical change of a heritable kind occurs. It has been calculated that the normal gene for blood clotting mutates to the defective hemophilia gene in one out of every hundred thousand persons of European origin in each generation. Since most hemophiliacs die before they can leave any offspring, the number of such unfortunate persons alive at any time is relatively small. Hemophilia is inherited as a single, sex-linked recessive gene, that is, a gene that is linked to the X chromosome and that will not express itself in the presence of a normal gene on the opposite X chromosome. When, then, an X chromosome that carries the hemophilia gene is transmitted to a female, it is highly improbable that it will encounter another X chromosome carrying a similar defective gene; it is for this reason that hemophilia is of very great rarity in females. Since the survival rate of hemophiliacs to reproductive age is very low, it is obvious why females are the most unusual transmitters of the hemophilia gene, and it should also be clear why females practically never exhibit the condition. The males are affected because they lack the blood clotting factor on their Y chromosome which, were it present, would compensate for the deficiency in the X chromosome inherited from the mother. Women exhibit the condition only if they inherit one hemophilia gene from their mother and another from their father, but this is extremely unlikely to occur. If she derived a single defective X chromosome from either her father or her mother, the female would not suffer from hemophilia because her normal X chromosome would either compensate for, inhibit, or suppress the action of the hemophilia gene on the other X chromosome; if she then married a normal man and bore a number of children she would pass on the hemophilia-bearing chromosome to about half her sons and half her daughters. The girls who inherit the defective gene will show no ill effects, but the males who have received the gene may show the effects even before they are born and die of hemophilia *in utero,* or fall victim to the disorder at any time from birth to adult life, but exhibit the condition they will, and in the greater number of instances they will die of its effects.

There are actually two kinds of hemophilia genes; an A, or classical, occurring in one out of every ten thousand males; and B, or Christmas disease, occurring in one out of every forty-five thousand males.

The mechanism of color blindness (red-green, mostly) and its explanation are precisely the same as for hemophilia. About 4 percent of American men are completely red-green color blind, while another 4 percent are color blind in varying degrees to red-green or other colors. Only 0.5 percent of American women are so affected.

More than seventy serious disorders occurring in males are known to be due to genes present on the X chromosomes. These conditions occur in a woman only if her father is affected and her mother carries the gene. In the table below are listed some of the conditions occurring more frequently in males because of sex-linked genes.

Conditions Due Largely to Sex-Linked Genes Found Mostly in Males

---

Absence of central incisor teeth
Albinism of eyes (depigmentation of eyes)
Aldrich syndrome (chronic eczema, middle-ear disease, etc.)
Agammaglobulinemia (gamma globulin deficiency in blood)
Amelogenesis imperfecta (absence of enamel of teeth)
Angiokeratoma diffusum (lesions affecting many systems of body)
Anhidrotic ectodermal dysplasia (maldevelopment of sweat glands)
Borjeson syndrome (mental deficiency, epilepsy, endocrine disorders)
Cataract, total congenital
Cataract, congenital with microcornea
Cerebellar ataxia
Cerebral sclerosis
Choroidermia
Coloboma iridis (congenital cleft of iris)
Color blindness of the red-green type
Day blindness
Deafness, congenital
Defective hair follicles
Distichiasis (double eyelashes)
Dyskeratosis congenita (malformation of nails, pigmentation, etc.)

Conditions Due Largely to Sex-Linked Genes Found Mostly in Males (cont.)

Dystrophia bullosa (formation of swellings, absence of all hair, etc.)
Epidermal cysts (skin cysts)
Glaucoma of juvenile type (increase in fluids of eyeball)
Glucose 6-phosphate dehydrogenate deficiency
Hemophilia
Hurler syndrome (dwarf stature, generalized disease of bone, etc.)
Hydrocephalus
Hypochromic anemia
Hypoparathyroidism
Hypophosphatemia
Hypoplasia of iris with glaucoma
Ichthyosis (scalelike skin)
Keratosis follicularis (thickening of skin, loss of hair, etc.)
Macular dystrophy
Megalocornea (enlargement of cornea of eyeball)
Menkes syndrome (retarded growth and brain degeneration)
Mental deficiency
Microcornea (diminution of cornea of eyeball)
Microphthalmia
Mitral stenosis (stricture of bicuspid valve of heart)
Myopia (near-sightedness)
Nephrogenic diabetes insipidus
Neurohypophyseal diabetes insipidus
Night blindness
Nomadism
Nystagmus (rhythmical oscillation of eyeballs)
Oculo-cerebral-renal syndrome of Lowe (cataract, mental retardation, etc.)
Ophthalmoplegia and myopia (drooping of eyelids, absent patellar reflexes, etc.)
Optic atrophy (wasting of eye)
Parkinsonism
Peroneal atrophy (wasting of muscles of legs)
Progressive bulbar paralysis
Progressive deafness
Pseudoglioma (membrane formation back of lens)
Pseudohypertrophic muscular dystrophy (weakening of muscles with growth of
connective tissue in them)
Retinal detachment
Retinitis pigmentosa
Spinal ataxia
Spondylo-epiphyseal dysplasia (short stature, severe hip disease, etc.)
Thromboasthenia (defect in the thrombin, fibrin, and blood platelet formation)
Van den Bosch syndrome (mental deficiency, skeletal deformity, lack of sweat glands, etc.)
White occipital lock of hair

So much, then, for the conditions directly traceable to genetic factors. It should by this time be quite clear that to commence life as a male is to start off with somewhat of a handicap compared with the female—a handicap that operates at every stage of life, from conception on.

Even though male-determining sperm are produced in the same numbers as female-determining sperm, in the average ejaculation there are slightly fewer male-determining sperm, yet there are between 120 and 150 males conceived for every 100 females. Why this should be so we do not know, but it is a fact. The ratio at birth for American whites is 106 males to 100 females. In India the ratio is 98 boys to 100 girls. The ratios vary for different human groups, depending largely upon their socio-economic or nutritional status: the poorer the nutritional conditions, the greater the lethality of the males. Even fetal females are stronger than fetal males. The records uniformly show that from conception on, mortality rates before birth are higher for the male than for the female fetus and that males after birth continue to have a higher mortality rate than females for every year of age. Within every age range, more males die than females. For example, in 1987–88 three boy babies died in the first year of life for every two girl babies. At about the age of twenty-one, for every female who dies almost two males die; at age thirty-five, fourteen hundred men die for every thousand women; at fifty-five, eighteen hundred men die for every thousand women. After that the difference in death rate diminishes, though it remains in favor of the female.

In 1987, under the auspices of the National Institute of Aging, it became increasingly clear at the conference on biological and psychological differences between the sexes concludes that, as Professor James Neel of the University of Michigan put it, "we really are the weaker sex, biologically less fit than females every step of the way." The advantage in both psychological and biological robustness that females enjoy, appears to be due to the fact that females possess quantitatively and efficiently more innate immune responses than males. This probably explains why females recover more frequently from illnesses, and live longer than males.

Life expectancy at birth is higher for women than for men all over the world (except in certain impoverished parts of India), and

and this fact holds true for females as compared with males for the greater part of the animal kingdom. In the United States in 1996, the average life expectancy at birth females was 79.0 years and for males 73.0 years. At age 65, the average female could expect to live another 18.9 years, males at the same age could expect only 15.7 years. These facts constitute further evidence that the female is constitutionally stronger than the male. There have been some who have argued that women live longer than men because they don't usually work as hard. Most men, it is urged, work harder, work longer hours, and usually under greater strain and tension than most women. These statements are open to question. The exact opposite is, of course, the truth, as common experience and more than one study has shown. "Women's work is never done," as the old adage recognized. When forced to take over their wives' duties, at the end of a week or less most men are ready for a hospital bed. Furthermore, the stresses with which the average housewife with children has to deal are far greater than those which normally face her husband.

Male fetuses do not work harder than female fetuses in the womb, yet they die more frequently before birth than do female fetuses. Newborn males do not work harder than newborn females, yet they die more frequently than newborn girls. One-year-old boys die more frequently than the girls. And so one can go on for every age, with the difference in mortality in favor of the female.

In 1957 Francis C. Madigan, working at the University of North Carolina, published a study on the longevity of Catholic religious sisters and brothers who for many years maintained identical lifestyles. The same disparity in their mortality rates was found as among the rest of the general population. The data were obtained on nearly thirty thousand sisters and more than ten thousand brothers. The expectation of life at the age of fifty-four was found to be an additional thirty-four years for the sisters, but only twenty-eight years more for the brothers, a difference in favor of the sisters of five and a half years.

When we compare the longevity rates of unmarried men having jobs with those of unmarried women having jobs, we find that the advantage is again with the females. Unmarried women with jobs live longer than their unmarried male counterparts. In 1987 the age-adjusted death rate for single men was one and a half times that for married men, whereas among single women the death rate was only 10 percent higher than that for the married. It is an interesting fact that among both men and women, the married have lower death rates than the single, widowed, or divorced.

A fourteen-nation study of working mothers conducted under the auspices of UNESCO and published in 1967 showed that women in general work longer hours and have less leisure time than men. As Professor Alexander Szalai, the project director, put it, "To summarize our finding, let's say that the last state of human bondage still persists, even if its burdens have been considerably lightened. More precisely, both categories of women—the working and the nonworking—are at a disadvantage compared with men. The working women because they are overburdened with work; the nonworking women because their labors are underestimated and their existence is much more drab than that of the men."

Women are healthier than men—if by health one means the capacity to deal with microorganisms and illness. Statistics from the public health services of various countries, and especially the United States, show that, while after the age of fifteen the sickness rate is higher among females than among males, females recover from illnesses much more frequently than males do. Death from almost all causes are more frequent in males at all ages. Under the awful conditions in which men, women, and children were sadistically incarcerated by the Nazis during World War II, the morbidity and mortality rates for females were much lower than for men. Almost the only disorders from which women die more frequently than men are those subserving the functional systems of reproduction, namely, the reproductive system and endocrine glandular system. The female owes her superior constitutional strength to, among other important factors, the fact that she is equipped with immunoregulatory genes on each X chromosome. The double dose of such genes results in a higher serum concentration of immunoglobulins which function as antibodies to give the female superior ability to combat infectious agents. Hence, the female's superior immunological system affords her a higher resistance to bacterial and viral infections.

The facts are set out succinctly by Drs. David D. Portilo and John Sullivan in their classic study of the "Immunological Bases for Superior Survival of Females," in which they conclude,

In summary, males experience more frequent and severe illness and higher mortality from many common disorders than do females. We present evidence supporting the notion that evolutionary selection has equipped females with X-linked immunoregulatory genes for coping with many life-threatening illnesses. The superior immunocompetence of females probably compensates for the immunosuppression accompanying pregnancy. Thus the pregnant woman and the species survive.[5]

Epilepsy has about the same incidence in both sexes, but according to the statistics of the Bureau of the Census the death rate from epilepsy is about 30 percent higher for men than for women. For every female stutterer there are five male stutterers. The stutter-type personality, characterized by a certain jerkiness or "stutter" of movements as well as of speech, occurs in the ratio of eight males to one female. Word deafness, the inherited inability to understand the meaning of sounds, occurs very much more frequently in the male than in the female, and so do baldness, gout, and ulcers of the stomach. Need one go on?

The evidence is clear: From the constitutional standpoint woman is the stronger sex. The explanation of the greater constitutional strength of the female lies largely, if not entirely, in her possession of two complete X chromosomes and the male's possession of only one. The fact beyond question is that the natural, the biological, superiority of women is due to her having derived one chromosome from her mother and a second from her father, each chromosome differing from the other in the variety of genes it contains. This produces what is technically known as hybrid vigor, or heterosis, in the female, clearly contributing to her greater survival.[6] This may not be the whole explanation of the physical constitutional superiority of the female, but it is certainly scientifically the most acceptable explanation and the one least open to question.

To the unbiased student of the facts there can no longer remain any doubt of the constitutional superiority of the female. At the present time many insurance companies still charge the same insurance rates for women as for men. This hardly seems fair to women. But then when has anyone ever been fair to women? The occasions have been the exceptions. Man has projected his own weaknesses upon her, and as the muscle man

Some Sexual Differences in Susceptibility to Disorder & Disease

MALES		FEMALES	
Disorder/Disease	Preponderance M-F	Disorder/Disease	Preponderance F-M
Acoustic trauma	Almost exclusively	Acomegaly	More often
		Alzheimers	More often
Acute pancreatitis	Large majority	Anorexia nervosa	98%
Addison's disease	More often	Arthritis deformans	4.4-1
Alcoholism	6-1	Bunions	More often
Amoebic dysentry	15-1	Carcinoma of	
Angina pectoris	5-1	gall bladder	3-1
Aortic disease	More often	Carcinoma of genitalia	10-1
Appendicitis	More often	Cataract	More often
Arteriosclerosis	2.5-1	Chlorosis (anemia)	100%
Asthma	More often	Chorea	3-1
Atherosclerosis	More often	Chronic constipation	More often
Autism	4-1	Chronic mitral	
Bacterial infection	More often	endocarditis	2-1
Bright's disease	2-1	Cleft palate	3-1
Bronchial asthma	More often	Colitis	More often
Brucellosis	More often	Combined sclerosis	More often
C.S. meningitis	25-1	Depression	3-1
Cancer, buccal cavity	2-1	Diphtheria	Slight
Cancer, G.U. tract	3-1	Emotional Stress	More often
Cancer, head of pancreas	4.5-1	Gall Stones	4-1
Cancer, respiratory tract	8-1	Goiter, exophthalmic	6 or 8-1
Cancer, skin	3-1	Hemorrhoids	Considerably greater
Carsiovascular disease	More often		
Cerebral hemorrhage	Greatly	Hyperthyroidism	10-1
Cerebrovascular disease	More often	Influenza	2-1
Childhood		Lupus, systemic	9-1
schizophrenia	Slight		
Chronic glomerular			
nephritis	3-1		
Cirrhosis of liver	2-1		
Coronary insufficiency	3-1		
Coronary sclerosis	30-1		
Diabetes	More often		
Duodenal ulcer	7-1		
Dupuytren's disease	3-1		
Dyslexia	6-1		
Echovirus	More often		
Emphysema	More often		
Erb's dystrophy	More often		
Fragile X chromosome	3-1		
Gastric ulcer	6-1		
Gout	49-1		
Harelip & cleft palate	More often		

continued on next page

continued on next page

Some Sexual Differences in Susceptibility to Disorder & Disease (cont.)

MALES		FEMALES	
Disorder/Disease	Preponderance M-F	Disorder/Disease	Preponderance F-M
Harelip	2-1	Migraine	6-1
Heart disease	10-1	Mitral stenosis	3-1
Heart Disease	2-1	Multiple sclerosis	More often
Hemophilia	100%	Myasthenia gravis	10-1
Hepatitis	More often	Myxedema	6-1
Hernia	4-1	Obesity	Considerably greater
Hodgkin's disease	2-1		
Hysteria	2-1	Osteomalacia	9-1
Korsakoff's psychosis	2-1	Osteoporosis	More often
Legionnaire's disease	3-1	Pellagra	Slight
Leukemia	2-1	Purpura haemorrhagcia	4 or 5-1
Loneliness effects	3-1	Raynaud's disease	1.5-1
Lung Cancer	4-1	Rheumatic fever	3-1
Malnutritional effects	Considerably greater	Rheumatoid arthritis	Considerably greater
Meningitis	More often	Scleroderma	3-1
Mental deficiencies	3-1	Sinusitis	More often
Muscular dystrophy,	Almost exclusively	Stroke	Slightly more
		Tonsillitis	Slight
Myocardial degeneration	2-1	Varicose veins	Considerably greater
Paralysis agitans	Greatly		
Pericarditis	2-1	Whooping cough	2-1
Pigmentary cirrhosis	20-1		
Pineal tumors	3-1		
Pleurisy	3-1		
Pneumonia	3-1		
poliomyelitis	Slight		
Preclinical cardiomyopathy	More often		
Progressive muscular paralysis	More often		
Pseudohermaphroditism	10-1		
Pulmonary disease	4-1		
Pyloric stenosis, congenital	5-1		
Q fever	More often		
Respiratory infections	More often		
Sciatica	Greatly		
Scurvy	Greatly		
Syringomyelia	2.3-1		
Tabes	10-1		
Thromboangiitis obliterans	96-1		
Tuberculosis	2-1		
Tularemia	More often		

has maintained the myth of feminine weakness until the present day. But it is not woman who is weak; it is man, and in more senses than one. But the last thing on earth we want to do is give the male a feeling of inferiority. On the contrary, we consider it a wise thing for man to be aware of his limitations and his weaknesses, for being aware of them, he may learn how to make himself strong. The truth concerning the sexes will not only serve to set women free, it will also serve to set men free; for if women have been the slaves of men, men have been the slaves of their own prejudices against women, and this has worked to the disadvantage of both.

6

THE SEXUAL SUPERIORITY
OF THE FEMALE

There exists an old and widespread belief in Western societies that women are preoccupied with sex. This idea was somewhat stridently expressed in a book published in the summer of 1903 entitled *Geschlecht und Charakter*, in English translation *Sex and Character*, written by Otto Weininger, a brilliant Viennese young man who was in his early twenties when the book was published. He was "therefore," like other men, an "expert" on the subject of women and sex. The book created something of a sensation, and was widely read throughout Europe. In it Weininger proclaimed that "man possess sex, woman is possessed by it."

Every man is, of course, an authority on sex, and every man, of course, knows that beauty parlors, permanent waves, cosmetics, women's clothes, miniskirts, women's arts, and practically everything about women constitute abundant testimony to their greater preoccupation with sex. Men shave, comb their hair, and wear comparatively drab clothes. They are interested in sex, of course, but their interest is as nothing compared with the interest of women in sex, and by *interest* men usually mean *preoccupation*. So goes the myth, a myth which Kinsey and his co-workers were the first to demolish in *Sexual Behavior in the Human Female*;[1] the myth was finally scuttled with a much smaller sample of subjects by Masters and Johnson in their book, *Human Sexual Response*.[2] The Kinsey workers found their women subjects to be sexually superior in every way, except in the sexual athleticism of a multiplicity of partners upon which the male so overcompensatingly prides himself.

Since definitions are so much more meaningful at the end of an inquiry than they can possibly be at the beginning of one, let us postpone our account and definition of what we mean by sexual superiority until it has become so obvious to the reader in evaluating the facts that the formal definition becomes doubly meaningful.

Under the heading, "Psychologic Factors in Sexual Response," the Kinsey workers reported the following:

> In general, males are more often conditioned by their sexual experience, and by a greater variety of associated factors, than females. While there is great individual variation in this respect among both females and males, there is considerable evidence that the sexual responses and behavior of the average male are, on the whole, more often determined by the male's previous experience, by his association with objects that were connected with his previous sexual experience, by his vicarious sharing of another individual's sexual experience, and by his sympathetic reactions to the sexual responses of other individuals. The average female is less often affected by such psychologic factors. It is highly significant to find that there are evidences of such differences between the females and males of infra-human mammalian species, as well as between human females and males.[3]

Kinsey might have said not only infra-human mammalian species but for almost the whole of the animal kingdom. It has long been known that in almost all sexual species of animals the female is likely to be the more quiescent and the male the more active creature. This idea was explicitly stated by Geddes and Thomson in their famous book, *The Evolution of Sex*: "It is generally true that the males are more active, energetic, eager, passionate, and variable; the females more passive, conservative, sluggish, and stable."[4] Undoubtedly there is a profound phylogenetic basis for this difference between the sexes. Geddes and Thomson were the first to offer the hypothesis that the female organism is characterized by a predominance of constructive utilization of energy, by *anabolism,* the process of synthesizing simple substances into complex materials, as compared with *catabolism*, or the metabolic change of complex into simple molecules. This hypothesis has been widely adopted. It is a useful and an interesting hypothesis, but actually it doesn't go far enough in explaining the differences between the sexes with reference to the differences in the ends which they function to serve.

The ends which both sexes serve is reproduction of the species. But reproduction of the species is not enough; the species must be maintained. And this is where the difference between the sexes expresses itself, for while it is the function of the male to initiate conception, it is the function of the female to maintain the conceptus, and see it through not only to successful birth but through infancy and childhood. With comparatively few exceptions this is true of the whole animal kingdom. One may readily see, then, why the female is likely to be anabolic and the male catabolic. From the standpoint of survival the female is vastly more important biologically than the male, and it is therefore important that she be the creator of energy rather than the reducer of energy. As Tinbergen has pointed out:

> Since the female carries the eggs for some time, often even after fertilization, and since in so many species the female takes a larger share than the male in feeding and protecting the young, she is the more valuable part of the species' capital. Also, one male can often fertilize more than one female, an additional reason why individual males are biologically less valuable than females. It is therefore not surprising that the female needs persuasion more than the male, and this may be the main reason why courtship is so often the concern of the male.[5]

The overall biological superiority of the female lies, then, in the fact that she is "the more valuable part," as Tinbergen puts it, "of the species' capital" because she is the principal preserver and protector of the species during children's most tender periods of development. In this fact is also to be found the explanation of the difference in sexual interest between female and male. When, then, Kinsey records these differences in psychosexual response in as great detail as he does, he is probably quite right in seeing some significant connection between such differences in human beings and similar differences in infra-human mammalian species.

What are these psychologic factors in sexual response which Kinsey investigated? They are such factors as observing the opposite sex, nude figures, one's own sex, erotic art, genitalia, exhibitionism, movies, burlesque strippers and floor shows, sexual activities, portrayals of sexual activities, animals in coitus, peeping and voyeurism, preferences for light or dark, fantasies concerning sex, sex dreams, diversion during coitus, stimulation by literary materials, erotic stories, writing and drawing, wall inscriptions, graffiti, discussions of sex, and the like. Altogether there were thirty-three such factors investigated, and it was only in respect of three items—movies, reading romantic literature, and being bitten—that as many females or more females than males seem to have been affected. In respect of twenty-nine of the thirty-three items, fewer females than males were affected.

While there can be little doubt that social conditioning plays a considerable role in influencing patterns of sexual response, and that the male in this respect seems to be much more conditionable than the female in our culture, there can be equally little doubt that there is a profound biological difference between the sexes in this respect. The male seems to be in a chronic state of sexual irritation. The woman who in a letter to Kinsey described the race of males as "a herd of prancing leering goats" was not far from the truth. It is the male who is preoccupied with sex, and his preoccupation with sex, in our culture at any rate, is at a very superficial level of sensitivity. The male of the Western world is the gadfly of sex; he'll mate with virtually any woman he encounters. The female, on the other hand, is much less occupied with sex than the male. She is not in a chronic state of sexual irritation; she is not like the male in a state of continuous rut. Sexual response in the female has to be aroused, and it cannot be aroused by superficial stimulation. Sex means a great deal more to the female that it does to the male, and except for the highly abnormal instance of prostitution, she will not mate with just any male she encounters.

These differences seem to be biologically based, and from every point of view they confer superiority upon the female—biological, moral, social, and aesthetic. The fact that these differences are biologically based does not, however, mean that the male's behavior is either excusable or unalterable. It makes it, perhaps, a little more understandable. Certainly there have been highly sexed men who have managed not to be sexual gadflies or erotosauri, but who have exercised their claim to being called human by respecting themselves as much as they have other people, including women.

The promiscuous male is not destined by biology to be so, but is largely the result of an inadequate education in the meaning of human relations and a puritanical conception of sex. The biological drives require satisfaction, and they appear to have a much greater pressor effect and a lower excitation threshold in the male than in the female. We must learn to understand this and enable the male to order his drives in a more satisfactory manner than he has, for the most part, succeeded in doing in Western culture.

For the male in our culture, the satisfaction of the sexual drive is too often identified and confused with the conventional spurious conception of love. The female rarely falls into such error. Yet the tragedy of our culture's sex relationships, in the broad sense, is that the male fails to understand what sex means to the female, and assumes that it means little more to her than it does to him. Women marry, as Kinsey points out, to establish a home and a long-term relationship with a spouse and to have children. Men only too often marry in order to assure themselves an easy source for the satisfaction of their sexual needs. Though they may rationalize their needs in terms more acceptable to themselves, their wives, and their societies, it is probable, as Kinsey states, "that few males would marry if they did not anticipate that they would have an opportunity to have coitus regularly with their wives. This is the one aspect of marriage which few males would forgo."[6]

From an anthropological study published a few weeks after the appearance of the Kinsey report we learn that "throughout Brazil the idea is commonly held that men do not wish to marry. Several people explained that a young man does not willingly take on the heavy responsibilities of a permanent union and renounce the pleasures of sexual adventure."[7] We are not surprised—with sufficient encouragement men would everywhere take the same view. The fact is, however, that from the point of view of the biological and social health of a society such encouragement would have unfavorable results. Premarital sexual license is one thing, but the unwillingness to marry and become responsible for one's own family is quite another. It is here, too, that the pull of women to legalize illicit unions, to drag the unwilling male to the altar, has from the earliest times exercised a beneficial effect upon human society.

Women have been aware of the waywardness of the errant male, doubtless from the earliest times, and they have been caused thus to resort to every possible device in order to make themselves attractive to the male and to maintain their attractiveness in order to preserve the interest of this roving creature. Hence, the powders and the pomade, the paint and the pulchritude, and the equation in the male's mind (and in the minds of some women) of sex with love. The female's much higher threshold of sexual excitability, the ease with which she is distracted, even during intercourse, from what is for the male the focus of all his attention, led some readers of the Kinsey report to conclude that women are not very interested in sex. This is but one example of the dangerous kind of conclusions, and utterly erroneous ones, which could be drawn from Kinsey's data. By comparison with women, men are more superficially interested in sex and make up in quantitative activity what they fail to experience qualitatively. On the contrary, the female is more profoundly interested in sex, and the quality of her interest is very much more sensitively and passionately developed than that of the average male. Hence, the male's crass sexual approaches to the female are unlikely to elicit her happiest responses.

It is, however, doubtful that with the most continuous of perfect approaches the female would, on the average, ever respond as continuously as the male does to superficial psychosexual stimulation. The male can, as it were, turn the faucet of sex on at a moment's notice; it takes somewhat more than a moment in the average female.

For the female, sex is a human relationship; for the male, relationships with women tend to be largely sexual. Sex, without love is empty for most women, and it is the satisfaction of a chronic irritation for most men. Even the professional prostitute has one kind of sex for her customers and another kind for her lover. Most men, however, in their approach to sex, think of doing something to a woman that affords them relief and pleasure. These are not the words usually used; other less printable words are, and they convey the thought that the male satisfied himself on his quarry. Few women ever describe a sexual relationship with a man in such terms. Her relationship is with the man, and not with an adversary or victim. Today one has "relationships" without commitment.

In the sex relationship, as in other connections, women tend to humanize men. In the sex relationship what above all else they require from the male is tenderness, the tenderness which they so seldom receive. In this, too, the female, generally surpasses the male. The extraordinary thing is that in our culture there is a tabu on tenderness, a tabu which is customarily taught boys as a discipline, the emphasis being on masculinity. Tenderness and gentleness are looked upon as behavior fit only for a "sissy." Men have a great deal to learn about the nature of being human, and women have a great deal to teach them. Will they succeed? It is a consummation that will have to be more than devoutly wished. It would be greatly helpful if men began to understand the problem and commenced to cooperate with women.

By virtue of her gentle reticences woman is on the side of morality and the proprieties; in these respects, also, she is therefore very much more advanced than the male. The female seems to come by these qualities naturally, although there can be small doubt that social influences play a considerable role in determining what she will consider moral and proper. The male will always, obviously, have a harder time behaving himself, but that he can learn to keep himself happily in check has fortunately been many times demonstrated. The proper education in human relations will enable the healthy minded male to adjust himself to himself and to other human beings as he ought. It is time that we realized that the improvement he must make in the conduct of his sexual life will not be brought about through better sex education but through better education in human relations, for sex behavior is merely an aspect of human relations, of one's personal attitudes toward other human beings. It is possible that when the male of the future comes to look back upon the history of his sex he will perceive that its failure was in the realm of human relations.

Kinsey interestingly and conclusively demonstrated that while the male's sexual drives are at their peak in his early teens and shortly thereafter begin to decline, the female, on the other hand, develops her sexual urges much more slowly, and it is not until the late teens or early twenties that she really begins to mature sexually. Furthermore, Kinsey showed that the female never reaches an abrupt peak of sexuality, as does the male, but that she develops more slowly and steadily, and that while the male's sexual powers are waning hers are maintaining their steady level well into her fifties or sixties and even beyond.

Men have prided themselves on their sexual athleticism, but this is as nothing compared with what women are capable. Men may be able to muster a few orgasms at most in one session, but women can literally enjoy scores! The clitoris is a vastly more sensitive organ than the penis. Indeed, the penis has a very poor nerve supply, and compared to the clitoris it is much less sensitive. Men have tended to claim that with the menopause woman's interest in sex declines. Nothing could be further from the truth. It is at this time that most women experience a strong resurgence of sexual interest. That this is not merely mental is borne out by the fact that there is often an increase in estrogen, the female sex hormone. Hence, the menopause has been described as "the pause that refreshes." While the female's ability to experience multiple orgasms continues unfailingly into old age, the male's ability to manage more than one or two declines very markedly. In brief, the duration of the female's reproductive capacities is shorter than that of the male, but her sexual abilities are much greater and considerably outlast those of the male. It is the male sex, it should be noted, that is the impotent sex. Woman's frigidity is more often than not the product of an incompetent male.

Whatever may eventually be held accountable for these differences, the conclusion is obvious: In the duration of their sexual ardor women outlast men by a considerable margin. "There is little evidence," writes Kinsey, "of any aging in the sexual capacities of the female until late in her life."[8]

It may now be apparent to the reader what we have meant by sexual superiority throughout this chapter. Perhaps a definition may be acceptable on the basis of our findings. By sexual superiority we mean sexual behavior of a kind that confers survival benefits upon all who participate in it, as well as creative benefits upon all who come within the orbit of its influence. The female enjoys this sexual superiority by fiat, as it were, of nature, but there is absolutely no reason why the male cannot learn to adjust himself harmoniously to the differences which exist between female and male and acquire by second nature those controls with which the female has for the most part been endowed by nature.

Many avoidable tragedies of marriage are directly traceable to the ignorance which prevails concerning the fundamental differences that exist in the development of the sexual drives of female and male. In early marriage the male desires more coitus than his wife. In later life she wants more than he is able to provide, but she isn't anywhere nearly as concerned as the male is in the early years of marriage, when he finds that his wife isn't as frequently accessible as he thinks she ought to be. With deeper understanding of the facts of life it will be possible for both women and men to adjust these differences in a mutually satisfactory manner. In marriage, as in all human relations, happiness is necessarily reciprocal and is found only in being given. Success in marriage does not depend so much on finding the right person, as on *being* the right person.

The biologically based differences between the sexes insofar as behavior is concerned do not need to be changed; what needs to be changed is our traditional way of dealing with those differences. In short, it is not human nature that needs to be changed, but human nurture. Here the sexes can cooperatively work together to find a better *modus vivendi* than most of us have thus far been able to work out. It may be suggested that the best prescription for bringing about happier sex relations between the sexes is to begin with oneself, to set oneself in order as a basis for practicing good human relations, for if we are to live in an ordered world we must first put order in ourselves.

7

ARE WOMEN MORE EMOTIONAL THAN MEN?

Are women more emotional than men? Of course they are! And in this, too, they show their superiority. Women, unlike men, are not afraid to exhibit their feelings; they have not been trained to believe that it is unwomanly to display their emotions as men have been conditioned to believe that it is unmanly to reveal theirs. Women are not crippled as men are by an inability to express their feelings. As a consequence women are far greater realists than men. Men are the specialists in repression of feelings and what is unpleasant to them and call it "control." Women tend to permit their emotions to perform the functions they are designed to serve, the expression of feeling. Women know that without emotion nothing matters.

The function of the myth that women are emotionally weaker than men has been to maintain the prejudice that while man is the supremely rational and intelligent creature, woman is the creature of her emotions. When a family tragedy strikes, the strong silent man stands by with stiff upper lip and a face rendered immobile by a trained incapacity for emotional expression, and thus marmoreally ministers to the deep need for sympathy and support of his wife.

The interesting thing is that prior to 1945 the rates for virtually every emotional disturbance were greater among men than among women, but after that date these rates began to rise for women, until the present time, when they are appreciably higher among women. In spite of the fact that there were well over a million more women in the United States in 1951, there were ninety-five thousand first admissions to mental hospitals for males, as compared with seventy-six thousand for females. An exhaustive study of the subject by Drs. Thomas F. Pugh and Brian MacMahon, covering the years from 1922 to 1945 for first admissions in the United States, showed males far exceeded females. This is clearly seen in the table below. Forty-five years later these figures were almost exactly reversed. What can be the explanation for this change? The answer to that question is revealing, and has been dealt with by many investigators, including Phyllis Chesler (*Women & Madness*, 1972) and Maggie Scarf (*Unfinished Business: Pressure Points in Women*, 1980), as well as by others who have contributed much valuable additional research information and evaluation on the causes of mental illness in the sexes. The result is that today we better understand the many causative conditions of the hydraheaded forms such disorders may take.

First Admissions for Mental Illness per 100,000 per Year. Totals for All Ages.

	1922	1939	1941	1942	1943	1944	1945
Male	113.8	130.6	129.3	127.9	129.3	137.1	146.5
Female	86.5	93.6	98.7	97.2	96.1	100.2	105.6

Source: Thomas F. Pugh and Brian MacMahon, *Epidemiologic Findings in United States Mental Hospital Data* (Boston: Little, Brown & Co., 1962), Table 5, p. 17.

The more I have studied the research findings the more convinced I have become that the sex difference for the functional mental disorders, that is to say, those that do not have an organic basis, are due to the pressures of social experiences of various kinds, often beginning in childhood and lasting throughout life. Let us take as an example one of the most common disorders among us, namely depression. Depression is a state of conscious mental suffering and guilt, accompanied by a marked reduction in the sense of personal value, and a diminution of mental psychomotor and, not infrequently, organic functions. The causes of Vallombrosa, however as a broad survey suggests, it is a reactive condition often related to a loss of some sort, imagined or real. The outstanding cause is the failure of expected satisfaction, the loss of love, or its decline. For women such causes seem to be more effective in resulting the depression than is the case in men. Other pathways to depression include sexual and physical abuse, poverty, and reproductive issues such as miscarriage and surgical menopause.

Statistics indicate that from two to six times as many women suffer from depression as men. What the varying statistics indicate is that bias in diagnosis and reporting, absurdities in counting, neglect of significant grouping, and many other inadequacies account for the disparities. The more dependable statistical indications are that some 12 percent of the population of the United States will suffer from some form of depression during their lifetime; 10 to 20 percent of the female population will be diagnosed as depressive, while only 5 to 10 percent of males will be so diagnosed.[1] The ratio, then, of females to males being diagnosed as depressive appears to be two to one.

The conditions of life for women in our male-dominated society being what they are, it is hardly surprising that women should suffer more often from depression than males, even though women, by virtue of their greater resiliency, are better adapted to meet the challenges of the social and physical stresses to which they are exposed. The major factor for these differences is undoubtedly the fact that females from birth onwards are conditioned in dependency, while males are conditioned in independency. To summarize in a sentence a long story, being female means hardly ever being encouraged to become a self-sufficient person. The truth is that one can never become a self-sufficient person with an independent sense of self unless one has been in the habit of taking responsibility for dealing with life's experiences without completely depending upon one's original sources of love and support.

I know of no better description of the course of events that lead to depression than that given by Maggie Scarf, based on years of research and reflection on the subject. Women, she points out, are trained in a direction that leads away from thinking, "What do I want?" toward, "What do they want from me?" They then think of being successful in meeting the expectations of others. Since pleasure is related to the act of pleasing, this readily leads to a situation in which good feelings about the self—that is, self-esteem—become dependent upon the esteem of those around one. Feelings of emotional well-being, a sense of one's worthfulness as a person, are hostage to the moods, attitudes, and approval of others (or maybe to one critically important other person). One is likable/lovable/significant only to the extent that one is liked/loved/significant to someone else. It follows, then, that in times of interpersonal drought—when sources of emotional supply are unusually low, or not there— the "normally feminine, normally dependent" woman may experience her inner world as emptied of what is good and meaningful to her. The props of her self-regard, if they've been held in place primarily by feedback from the environment, may simply begin to crumble and fall down. Under the circumstances, a woman may become far too harsh in her assessment of herself and of her worth and usefulness as a human being. She may feel helpless about her life circumstances, and hopelessly ineffectual in terms of her capacity for mastering or changing them. She may, in a word, become depressed. "The depressed woman is someone who has lost. She has lost 'something' upon which she vitally depended. The tone is of something profoundly significant having been taken away, of some crucial life's territory having been surrendered." And what, "with amazing regularity," most frequently triggered a depressive episode in the women interviewed by Scarf, was the loss of a love bond.[2] The independent male tends to react very differently, frequently with disappointment, frustration, or hostility, or if he is depressed, it is not as long enduring.

Some of the factors that may have contributed to the biases in producing statistical distortions in rates of mental illness, were reported in the 1975 *Report of the Task Force on Sex Biases and Sex-Role Stereotyping in Psychotherapeutic Practices*. This study identified four major themes affecting female clients in therapy: (1) Therapists were often assuming that self-actualization and resolution of problems for women comes from marriage and family, and they did not encourage gratifications from work and careers; (2) therapists commonly demonstrated a lack of respect for women through demeaning comments and labels; (3) therapists often made use of use sexist psychological concepts such as penis envy and vaginal orgasm; (4) therapists held a double standard for male and female sexual activities and sometimes treated women as sex objects. In the twenty-odd years since this report, many changes have been made in the way therapists and physicians approach depression, though there is still much work to be done in this area.

Clearly, differences in the social experiences of the sexes are responsible for the differences in their rates of depression. There are, of course, many other factors that contribute to the greater vulnerability of women to depression. Some years ago Dr. J. L. Evans of the Institute of Living in Hartford, Connecticut, studied the records of fifty wives of physicians admitted to a private psychiatric hospital. Despite a high level of adaptation in the early years of marriage, these women later developed severe psychiatric symptoms requiring repeated hospitalizations. A precipitating factor in many of these cases appeared to be a feeling of increasing exclusion from the husband's life as he became more and more involved in his profession. Symptoms of depression, organic disorders, and addiction were prevalent and were clearly related dynamically and empirically to the profession of the husband.[3]

The feeling of exclusion after some years of marriage that many women experience, whether their husbands are professionals or not, is a major factor in contributing to the depressive illnesses from which so many suffer. It is yet another form of the widespread failure of communication, which is probably the married woman's most frequent complaint.

There is another factor in the causation of mental illness in women that must be mentioned here. It is the terrible wounds which many men inflict upon their wives, even when they do not physically abuse them. Sticks and stones may not break bones, but mutilating or denigrating words frequently do. As Kathryn Lasky Knight put it,

> The biggies like Hitler, Mussolini, Nero have been enshrined in the darker pages of history. But the petty tyrant too must be reckoned with. Although he . . . does not plan the extermination of a race, it is the petty tyrant that day in and day out causes the small deaths of the people closest to him. . . . And it is these small deaths that wear one down until a person is a mere shell, a husk of a former self through which the wind can moan."[4]

The frequency of this kind of abuse has, as far as I know, never been recorded, but it must be considerable.

Though women are more emotional than men, men are emotionally weaker than women; that is, men break more easily under emotional stress than women. Women are emotionally stronger than men because they bend more easily and are more resilient. If that is true, how then does it come about that women fall more frequently victim to depression than men? The answer to that question seems to be plain: In matters of interpersonal relations, especially where there is a loss of love, research has shown that women, more often than men, are the losers. In spite of very real progress women have made in recent years, their lives have in many ways become more stressful than they were in earlier days.

May Ann Mason has devoted a groundbreaking book to this subject, appropriately titled *The Equality Trap*.[5] The author, a professor of law and social welfare at the University of California, Berkeley, makes it abundantly and sorrowfully clear that we live in a time when even in marriage men and women have lost the touch for long-term commitment. Women are working more hours per week in the home and outside and are bedeviled by more problems than ever, often in low-paying jobs. In this brave new world men and women alike find it increasingly difficult to support themselves. The problems that married women face, especially those with children, in the double bind of home cares and the workaday world, add up to serious stresses that produce real damage to all concerned. The social changes necessary to accommodate the revolutionary changes that have occurred as greater numbers of women have entered the work force are complex and bewildering. This has put a severe burden upon women that far exceeds anything any human being should be expected to suffer. Women have come to stay in the workaday world, and it will be to the benefit of all were the appropriate arrangements made by our society to make that world a more comfortable place to live in and the family treasured. This is something I considered and made recommendations to follow in the first edition of this book in 1953, and in the third edition in 1974. I am not aware that anyone has paid much attention to them. Perhaps we shall have better luck this time. Meanwhile, Mason makes some additional valuable suggestions in *The Equality Trap* that deserve to be widely discussed and implemented.

Let us now resume the discussion of the evidence for the greater emotional strength and resiliency of the female. In the first place it should be clearly understood that women are quicker to respond to stimuli, both physical and mental, than men are. In tasks involving the rapid perception of details and frequent shifts of attention, women generally excel. Such aptitude tests as the Minnesota Clerical Test reveal that only about 16 percent of male workers in the general population achieve or exceed the average of female workers in checking similarities or differences in lists of names or numbers. Other investigations show a significant feminine superiority on the same test from the fifth grade through the senior year of high school. It has long been established that women possess a greater sensory acuity for color discrimination than men.

On tests measuring reaction time to a single expected stimulus, males generally do better than females, but this is not the kind of quickness of response to which I referred above. I meant quickness of response to a total complex situation, and tests reveal the superiority of the female in such situations. It is this kind of quickness of response that is often made a peg upon which to hang the myth of greater feminine emotional weakness. Quickness is equated with nervousness or jitteriness or excitability. The fact is that in a psychophysical sense woman is more excitable, and in the physiological sense more irritable or, as Havelock Ellis put it, more affectable. Irritability (perhaps the better word is "affectability"), that is, the ability to respond to a stimulus, is one of the criteria by which living things are distin-guished from nonliving things, and in a very genuine sense it requires to be said that by virtue of her greater affectability, her greater sensitivity, the female of the human species is more alive than the male is. Taken out of context, that might be an amusing sentence for a corner of a page in *The New Yorker*, but what it is intended to convey is that women in our culture are, on the whole, more sensitive to their environments than are men. This may in part be a matter of cultural conditioning, but the recent findings of neuroscientists suggest some biological basis, or perhaps a combination of both. In any event, women do, in general, seem to be "quicker on the uptake" than men.

I do not need to cite the results of the many studies that suggest that women are more emotional than men. It is an incontestable fact; but again, whether it is a matter of cultural conditioning or biological conditioning is not easy to decide. Certainly we know that cultural factors play an enormously important role in producing differences in personality with respect to the expression of emotion as well as other traits, but a biological factor cannot be altogether dismissed. In any event, by the measure of our biological test of superiority, how do the sexes stand concerning the expression, efficient use, and effects of emotionality?

The notion that women are emotionally weak and men are emotionally strong is based on the same kind of reasoning as that which maintains the female is physically inferior to the male because of the latter's greater muscular power. Trained in repression, or in the art of "schooling" his emotions, as it is sometimes called, the male looks with disdain upon the female who expresses her feelings in tears and lamentations. Such behavior is in the male's estimation yet another proof of the female's general weakness; her greater emotionality is proof of her lack of control. His own ability to "control" his emotions the male takes to be a natural endowment which the female lacks. This is gravely to be doubted. In the first place it is more than questionable that women are less able to control their emotions than are men.

What most men and, I fear, women, too, have overlooked is that men and women are taught to control and express different kinds of emotions. Thus, girls are taught that it is perfectly natural for them to cry but that they must never lose their tempers, and if they do, they must on no account swear: "It isn't ladylike." Boys, on the contrary, are taught that it is unmanly to cry, and that while it is not desirable to "fly off the handle" or to "cuss," well, men have always done so. Girls may not express their emotions in violent ways; girls may not fight. Boys may and do. Nineteenth-century ladies permitted themselves to swoon or call for the smelling salts; their twentieth-century scions are obviously not ladies. Twentieth-century ladies still do not curse, but many modern women do, and if they drink, though they are today at perfect liberty to drink what they wish, they still do not drink as men do. Though it is considered manly for men to drink, it is not considered womanly for a woman to do so. Women, in fact, don't drink nearly as much as men do, and, by comparison with the rates for men, they are seldom drunk. Alcoholism and deaths from alcoholism are considerably more frequent in men than in women. Here, indeed, is a very significant difference in emotional expression, for men drink, whatever they may claim to the contrary, largely for emotional reasons, much of the time because they are unhappy, or in order to reduce stress; and an enormous number of them are unable to control their drinking. Whatever the reasons may be, women are able to, and do, control their drinking incomparably more successfully than men. It is interesting to observe that about the only time many men are able to weep is when they are drunk, and it may be that some of them get drunk in order to be able to do so. Weeping is an effective way of reducing tension; with their inhibitions down men are no longer constrained to abide by macho rules, as they must when they are sober.

Women don't fight, don't curse, don't lose their tempers as often as men do; they don't get drunk as frequently, and exceedingly rarely commit acts of violence against other persons. Though quicker on the uptake, they do not jump to conclusions as hastily and inconsiderately as men. Women tend to avoid the trigger responses of the male; as a result, they do not go off half-cocked as frequently as the male does. Women tend to keep their emotional balance better than men do. In short, women use their emotions a great deal more efficiently than men, and not in the emotional manner that men imply when they use the word disparagingly in connection with women. In this sense women are positively less emotional than men; but in the accurate sense of the word, women are more emotional and have their emotions more effectively under control than do men. I am speaking, of course, in terms of the generality of women and men. There are exceptions to most rules in both sexes. As we shall see, from the biological and social standpoints the female orders her emotions in a manner far superior to that in which the male orders his.

Among the myths perpetuated by men is the canard that women are much more liable to fits of temperament, that they "blow their top" much more easily, and are much less self-possessed. Controlled studies calculated to throw some light on this have been conducted at Oregon State University and at

Columbia University. Under the same given periods of time and under the same conditions, it was found that the average man lost his temper six times to the average woman's three. Studies conducted at Colgate University showed that women have more aplomb than men, that they are less easily flustered and embarrassed, and that they retain this self-possession longer under adverse conditions.[6]

In the nineteenth century, women very frequently responded to psychological shocks by swooning. The swoon served many functions: It drew attention to a lady much in need of attention; it elicited concern for her which she otherwise frequently failed to receive; and while recovering she might often secure concessions from her "superior" mate which might not, under other circumstance, be forthcoming. In other words, a capacity for swooning in the nineteenth-century female was a positive accomplishment of considerable value, a constructive use of emotion or simulated emotion that the bewildered male never really quite fathomed, for he always considered it a mark of inferiority in women. Weeping often served a similar purpose; as a contemporary wit remarked, a woman's idea of a good cry was one that secured the desired results.

Under conditions of shock men kept a stiff upper lip, and that was supposed to be the long and the short of it. After all, women were the emotional creatures. Though nineteenth-century statistics are not always reliable, they indicate that there were many mental homes, and most of them seem to have been populated largely by males. For the twentieth century, the statistics are far more accurate.

Boys as behavior problems far outnumber girls. In one study covering ten cities, the ratio of boys to girls in the problem group was four to one.[7] Some of the types of undesirable behavior reported as occurring much more frequently in boys than in girls were truancy, destruction of property, stealing, profanity, disobedience, defiance, cruelty, bullying, and rudeness. And what is even more significant, a larger number of undesirable behavior manifestations per child were reported for boys than for girls. Boys are much less in control than girls.

An investigation of 579 nursery school children revealed that, among those from two to four years of age, boys more often grab toys, attack others, rush into danger, refuse to comply, ignore requests, laugh, squeal, and jump around excessively. Girls are quieter, more frequently exhibit introverted and withdrawing behavior, such as avoiding play, staying near an adult from whom they seek praise, and "giving in too easily." All investigators agree that boys at all school ages are more quarrelsome and aggressive than girls.

In the present state of our knowledge, it is quite impossible to settle the question: Is the greater aggressiveness of the male largely or in part due to an inborn factor, or it is it a result of the conditioning the boy receives from the earliest age? It is quite possible that a boy, in our culture, becomes much more frustrated during the process of socialization than a girl does and that this difference already expresses itself at nursery school age. The evidence, so far as I have been able to study it, suggests that a combination of factors, biological and cultural, is responsible for the differences in aggressiveness between male and female. I should not wish this statement to be taken to mean that the male is born with a greater amount of aggressiveness—the evidence is, to me, quite clear that no one is born aggressive at all. I have discussed this subject in great detail in my book, *The Nature of Human Aggression.*[8] The fact is indisputable that the male tends to be more aggressive because he has a lower threshold for frustration than does the female, tending to respond with aggressiveness where under similar conditions the female tends to exercise more restraint. But this is undoubtedly socially conditioned: Boys, among other things, receive far less tactile stimulation in their preschool years than do girls.[9]

At nursery-school age, from three to five, boys tend to be more interested in things, while girls are more interested in personal relationships. Even at this age girls exhibit more responsibility and "motherly" behavior toward other children than do boys. Indeed, the evidence at *all* ages shows that the female is both socially more competent and socially more interested in human relationships than is the male. W. B. Johnson and Lewis M. Terman found that even in persons between seventy and ninety years of age, happiness for the woman was highly correlated with sociability, whereas in men the correlation was insignificant. In other words, in the basically most essentially desirable of human traits, namely, sociality, women at all ages notably surpass men. This difference and its significance will be discussed at length later in the present book; the difference is mentioned here because it gives some point to the female's manifesting from the earliest age a marked superiority in the most fundamental of all emotional qualities.

Professors Johnson and Terman, in a review of the studies that have been made on the comparative emotionality of the sexes, found that on the whole these studies agreed that the female was emotionally more "unstable" than the male.[10] This conclusion is incontestable and constitutes additional corroboration of the superiority of the female to the male. What males (even male professors) call "the emotional instability" of the female is simply evidence of the female's superior resiliency, her possession of a resource that permits her to absorb the shocks of life, to tolerate the stresses and strains to which she is subjected much more efficiently than the male. Scheinfeld aptly offers the analogy of a car equipped with soft, resilient springs and one with harder, firmer springs.

> The resilient springs (like the female's emotional make-up) would be more sensitive to all the bumps in the road, would give and vibrate more, but at the same time would take the bumps with less strain, prolonging the life of the car; the harder, more rigid springs (like the male's emotional mechanism) would not feel and respond to the minor bumps as readily but would cause more serious jolts over rough places and be more likely to result in an earlier crack-up of the car.[11]

In short, woman bends and survives, man keeps a stiff upper lip and breaks.

Emotionally unstable woman has been the support of emotionally stable man, I suspect, from the beginning of human history. Women have had to be emotionally well equipped to withstand the stresses and strains that in the course of a lifetime assault the mind and body not only of one person but at least of two. One of the principal functions of a wife has been to serve not only as a recipient of her husband's emotional responses to life's situations but also, unfortunately, as a scapegoat upon which her husband's frustrations expressed in unexpended aggressiveness can exhaust themselves, thus offering him the psychological relief from tension in the only place he can find it—his home. Were it not for this convenient arrangement, who knows to what new heights the frequency of mental breakdown in males might not have soared? One of the age-old functions of woman has been to provide man with a sympathetic ear into which he can pour his troubles; and woman has always stood by, with the touch of her gentle hands, the calmness, strength, and encouragement of her words, to bring balm and solace and rest to the weary, puzzled, and frustrated masculine soul. Woman has always been the firm rod upon which man can lean for support in time of need, and man has always needed woman. For man, because he is a male, needs a woman not only as a companion but also, upon occasion, to mother him; and a woman, because she is a female, sometimes needs to be a mother to her husband as well as to her children. Thus it is by nature that each ministers to the unique needs of the other.

But men have confused the natural complementary function and beautiful reciprocity of the sexes so that women, too, have become somewhat confused, and much pain and disorder in the world of human relations have thereby been caused. I do not mean that men never grow up to be anything except babies who are utterly dependent upon their mothers for survival, but I do mean that in their dependent relationships to their mothers they subsequently develop an interdependency in which a certain amount of reliance upon the female always fortunately remains. When such dependency functions at the adult level, it elicits those supporting responses from the female which constitute the interdependent relationship that is at the basis of all social functioning. It is highly desirable for the sexes to understand precisely how interdependent they are; but it is even more desirable that men should realize the nature of such *inter-*dependency and make life less difficult for women, and easier for everyone concerned, by making the necessary adjustments to the facts. The sexes need each other because they are precariously dependent upon each other for their conduct as healthy human beings. Interdependency is the human condition, and self-sufficiency usually winds up as insufficiency, which is the usual fate of the self-sufficient male. A bachelor is a poor fellow who has no one to blame but himself. Nature abhors a vacuum, but it abhors a bachelor more, and bemoans the fate of those women who (because of the incorrigible weakness of males for succumbing so much more frequently to the insults of the environment than females) fail to find a husband.

Constitutionally stronger and more resistant to disease than men, women are much better shock absorbers; that is, they are better able to handle the severe emotional and psychological stresses and strains of contemporary life. It is a striking fact that though admission rates to mental hospitals vary, on a sexual basis, from time to time, they are, on the whole, higher for men than for women. It is also remarkable that under conditions of siege and heavy bombardment, men break down much more frequently than do women. In an important study made during World War II, *Psychological Effects of War on Citizens and Soldiers* (1942), Dr. R. D. Gillespie reported that in the heavily bombed areas of London and Kent almost 70 percent more men broke down and became psychiatric casualties than women! Shortly after some of the heaviest bombings, the British Library of Information in New York published a bulletin entitled "Women Less Prone to Bomb Shock." It reported the results of a survey that showed that women respond to bombardment with much less emotional shock, hysteria, and psychoneurosis than do men. As Frank D. Long, who reported the survey, says,

> It may be true that women are more emotional than men in romance, but they are less so in air raids. Their protective instinct for those they love is actually a shield against the nerve-shattering effects of warfare noises. They perform the job in hand with calmer deliberation than men. Men get through the job all right, but they work in a state of mental excitement often consciously suppressed, which, in time, takes its toll.
>
> Women also recover under psychological treatment quicker than men. Part of the treatment is the re-telling of their experiences, and it has been found that women can recall details with greater ease than men and are willing to talk about them. Repetition in this way invariably tends to rob the experience of its initial horror, which is an important aid to complete recovery of normal self-control.

Reports from other parts of the war-scarred areas of the world are uniformly to the same effect.

Many attempts have been made to explain these facts away, but without success. It has been said that during wartime the strongest, youngest, and healthiest males are at the battlefront, that only the rejected, the sick, and the old remain behind, and that these would tend to succumb with high frequency to the shock effects of heavy bombings. The answer to this specious argument is that a normal distribution of physically healthy men past military age, middle-aged and older men, constituted by far the largest number of men in the London and Kent surveys. For concentration-camp data I know of no published figures, but it is the opinion of all those who had personal experience of such camps, and with whom I have discussed this matter, that women succumbed less frequently and withstood the rigors of the life more effectively than men. Here, again, it could be argued that women were better treated than men; however, that is not the general opinion.

The strength of the female constitution has been evidenced by famous and terrible tragedies such as those at the Donner Pass in 1846–1847, in which the party was imprisoned by snow for six months, at the end of which time there were 56.6 percent men dead and 29.4 percent women. In 1856 the walking, pushing, and pulling Willie handcart company, also on their way to Salt Lake city, was similarly distressed by snow for three weeks, resulting, at the time of rescue, in 24.9 percent males and 8.5 percent women dead.[12]

Knowing what we today do about the constitutional differences between the sexes, one would expect women to endure such conditions of stress better than men, and they do.

One of the best indexes of resistance to emotional stress is the suicide rate. Suicide has been described as a permanent solution to a temporary problem. Women don't seem to be as wholeheartedly interested in this permanent solution as men are. At all ages suicide rates are much higher among males than among females. In 1913 Eduard von Mayer showed that in the greater part of Europe, for every female who committed suicide three to four males did so. Louis Dublin and Bessie Bunzel, in their classic study of suicide, *To Be or Not to Be* (1933), found that in the United States the suicide rate reached the extraordinary figure of ten males to three females. These authorities remark that "suicide may be called a masculine type of reaction." These statistics remain remarkably unchanged throughout the world today. Most of the governments reporting to the World Health Organization as recently as 1995 found that suicides among men were two to five times as common as among women.

Even in suicide or attempts at suicide, men are more violent than women. Men resort to guns, hanging, and leaping from buildings, while women tend to rely upon the less painful devices, such as sleeping pills, gas, and the like. That women generally don't want to succeed at suicide is evident: Out of the one hundred thousand unsuccessful attempts annually made in the United States 75 percent are by women. The female's attempt often dramatically represents a desperate cry for sympathy and understanding.

Men are more impatient than women, and want to get things over in a hurry, presumably before reason sets in.

The evidence indicates that in all times and in all societies the suicide rates have generally been significantly higher for men than for women. Women value life more than men do. Men, we have already seen, are likely to resort to more violent means of solving problems than women, and obviously this fact doesn't render them the better solvers. Women look to more reasonable means for the solution of their problems, with heart and compassion, completely contradicting the myth that females are emotionally weak.

In the matter of who faces death with greater equanimity and genuine courage, Sergeant John Fiano, who for many years worked on death row at Sing Sing, is on record as saying, "Always, when there was more than one to be executed in one night, the weakest went first. The person with the strongest will goes last. In all my years at Sing Sing, women are always the last to go. They were much stronger emotionally than men."[13]

In studies of the fear of death that use self-rating scales, it has been found that women have a higher fear of death than men. This has been interpreted at its face value, but as Lester and Levene have pointed out, what may in fact have happened is that on these self-reporting scales men deny their fear of death, whereas women are more honest, or are more conscious of the fear of death than men. In an actual test, women show less fear of death, perhaps because they have less fear than men, or perhaps because, having faced the fear more honestly or consciously, they are able to cope with it more adequately.[14]

Medical men of considerable experience know that women bear pain much more uncomplainingly than men, and I have heard many surgeons remark that women make better patients than men. Writing in *The Listener* (London, 19 August 1966, p. 286), in an article entitled "The Relief of Pain," a "professor of neurology" writes, "There can be little doubt, for example, that women bear physical pain on the whole more stoically than men."

The Greeks, who were no more kind to their women than most men of other cultures have been to theirs, decided there was one disease that was peculiar to women, hysteria. They thought that the trouble began when the womb strayed from its place; hence they derived the name of the disease from the Greek word *hysteron*, meaning womb. For two thousand years women alone were, by fiat, declared capable of hysteria. It was not until 1887 that the great French alienist J. M. Charcot—one of the teachers, by the way, of Freud—showed that men, too, could suffer from "hysteria." Hysteria, which has been replaced by more contemporary language in the current psychological literature, was defined as essentially a chronic functional disorder of the mind, characterized by disturbances of the will, perversion of the inhibitory powers of consciousness, and partial arrest or hypersensitivity of the individual functions of the brain. Symptoms were described as ranging from simple nervous instability and attacks of emotional excitement, with causeless weeping or laughter, to convulsions, muscular contractions, disturbances of the circulatory system, paralysis, blindness, deafness, indeed, ailments affecting almost every organ of the body.

It was claimed by Drs. Eli Robins, M. E. Cohen, and J. J. Purtell[15] that hysteria in men differed from hysteria in women. They believed that men always stood to gain something by falling ill with hysteria, for hysteria was seen as an escape from something the victims were unwilling to face. Women suffering from hysteria did not appear to have anything nearly so tangible to gain from their condition, according to these investigators. The men could describe their symptoms crisply, but women were often vague, describing pains and aches all over, and commonly presented with twice as many symptoms as did the men. This differential expression of collection of disorders historically called "hysteria" in each sex is interesting, but the reason for our discussion of "hysteria" here is to record that for two thousand years it was considered an exclusively female disease, *and that for many years the evidence of its existence in males was denied.* Apart from its being a disorder limited to women, the condition gave quite a number of nineteenth-century medical men an opportunity to excise women's ovaries and to remove, by knife or cauterization, the clitoris in an attempt to cure the "disease."[16]

It seems difficult to believe that such drastic operations, in spite of all rationalizations by way of explanation, were altogether motivated by a desire to benefit the patient. Hysterical symptoms in women were described by Freud, and others, as conversions of repressed sexual wishes into psychophysical symptoms. Since the sexual involvement could hardly escape the attention of a perceptive nineteenth-century physician, it is not too difficult to surmise why it really was that the surgical attack upon the sexual organs was made, for nineteenth-century ladies were not supposed to be sexual at all. Men, it would seem, were avenging themselves upon women for having a womb and for having been ejected from it. But what is more to the point is that, while the statistics are unreliable, there is fair evidence that men were at least as often victims of "hysteria" as women, and possibly more often. Today psychiatrists and psychologists see the constellation of symptoms—those previously described as "hysteria"—in patients of both sexes.

Women are generally believed to be more "nervous" than men; and indeed, they do bite their nails and suck their thumbs more frequently as children than do boys, but this is, surely, a far superior way of expressing aggressiveness, dissatisfaction, and tension than is the boy's more intemperate method. The female, it has been found, beginning at a very early age, is more fearful than the male, and this may be evidence of her more highly developed sensitivity and general superior adaptation to her environment. Fear is a basic drive that assists the organism to negotiate its way through life with the maximum chance of survival. As long as the fear responses are within normal bounds, fear is a highly desirable emotion; it keeps one from rushing in where fools too often do not fear to tread. Lack of fear is often a deficiency of development which renders one heedless of dangers that more sensitive and more imaginative persons tend to avoid. The physical courage or lack of fearfulness so often admired is generally the result of an underdeveloped imagination. I do not refer to such irrational fears as those that many women have displayed, until very recently, of such creatures as mice. Such fears were very early learned and are for the most part being unrenewed by contemporary women. And yet much was made by earlier generations of such fears as evidence of the essential emotional instability of women!

Further evidence of the greater "emotional weakness" of women have been statements characterizing women as gossipy, superstitious, and more religious than men; greater prevaricators; that they rely on their intuitions for their judgments, and that they are moody and temperamental.

The response to the accusation of being gossipy is: Have you ever been a member of a men's club? Men, of course, never gossip: They simply investigate rumors. Of course, women gossip. But if women were to gossip more than men, it would be perfectly understandable. Human beings are born for communication. With their children away at school and their husbands away at work, women often begin to talk to themselves; but because that isn't altogether satisfactory, they talk to neighbors across the hedge or pick up the telephone and talk. Women talk to their husbands, when they arrive home, but the husband's desire is nothing more than to relax. In a man's view, when his wife talks with her friends it's gossip, whereas when he talks with other men he's "talking business" or "talking shop."

Women have *friends* with whom they can talk intimately; men have *acquaintances* with whom they cannot. Women, on the whole, probably do talk more than men; and one of the reasons for this, I suspect, is that women find speech to be the most readily satisfactory of all tension releasers.

There have been a number of studies that indicate that women do tend to be more superstitious than men; and this is not to be wondered at, for a woman lives, in many ways, a much more precarious psychological existence than a man. As Scheinfeld pointed out, chance has until only relatively recently played a much more important role in a woman's life. When she will marry, whom she will marry, what her future is to be—these and many other questions were often, and in some places still are, settled only by chance, which for many is another name for "Fate." No great harm can be done by subscribing to the superstitions that, so many persons surmise under such conditions, *may* have something in them after all. Under conditions of a similar sort, where chance plays a considerable role, as in gambling, sports, and war, men are not one whit less superstitious than women.

Women do appear to be more religious, more idealistic, and aesthetically more interested in spiritual matters than men are. Church attendance records, and the enthusiasm with which women throw themselves into the work of the church, bear testimony to their religious ardor. Professor Frederick H. Lund, in a study of human beliefs, found that women "were more confident of the practicability of the Golden Rule, more assured that a democracy was the best form of government, more convinced that the world came into existence through the creative act of a divine being, more ready to question the human origin of morals." The factors that make one religious are extremely complex; possibly some of the factors that lead to the belief in superstitions are involved, but quite frankly I believe these play a very minor role in the lives of women. Women, it seems to me, tend to feel rather more in tune with the universe than do men, largely because they are more sensitive to the world in which they live than men. Furthermore, while most men are able to talk with their wives and tell them their troubles, many women have no one else to talk with but a sympathetic friend or their minister or their God. Many people find God a substitute for an inadequate earthly father or husband; they devotedly offer their piety to a Heavenly Father in place of one they might have had on earth. Or if life with father and his counterparts has been too much of a failure, one can call on the Heavenly Mother. Consuelo Vanderbilts' mother, later Mrs. O. H. P. Belmont, the woman's suffrage leader, is said to have counseled a despairing young suffrage worker, "Call on God, my dear. *She* will help you." Then there is the matter of communication with the Creator, as well as with one's neighbors in the community of the church. Spiritual comfort can be more satisfying than the material comforts provided by a husband too busy earning a living, and when he isn't earning a living, occupied telling his wife what his troubles are without giving her equal consideration. Everywhere, women remain the pillars of the church, while men at best may be described as flying buttresses.

It will be said: Yes, but this is an exaggeration. Women do tell their husbands their troubles, and husbands do listen. My answer is that of course there are numerous wives who have husbands who make sympathetic and helpful listeners; but for every wife who has such a husband I strongly suspect there are a number who make neither sympathetic nor helpful listeners, and I suspect also that this is a factor, though certainly not the largest one, in the greater religiousness of the female. It is not so much a matter of hearing on the part of the male, as a matter of listening. Women, who are so much closer to the fundamental problems of life than men, are more sensitive to the needs of human beings than men. It is women who know better than anyone else that man cannot live by bread alone and that human beings are something more than slaves to the idea that men exist to earn a living and beat the other fellow to the mark. Men flatter themselves on being realists, on living in the present, and, like practical men, they go on repeating the errors of their predecessors.

Women, who live more profoundly in the present than most men manage to do, are idealists in addition to being far better realists than men, for they see not alone the present but the future as well. They do so because they are the creators of the future through their children. The true realists of any day are the visionaries (often described by practical men as being long on hair and short on sense); the visionaries who believe in improving the world as they find it and are unwilling to accept things simply because they are; the visionaries who have the wisdom to know the difference between the things they cannot change and those they can.

Woman is a more religious creature than man because she understands so much more than man how much there is in the world to be worshipped, and this understanding seems clearly to be a function of her maternal role whether she has ever had children or not. The truth is that, in the modern world, were it not for women the churches would cease to exist. There is not the least doubt that women are by nature maternal and nurturing, and that men are not, and that it is the essence of the maternal attitude toward life to be sensitive to the needs of others and to retain the wonder of the miracle of creation and of the miracle of love, the willingness of the heart. Such experiences and such wonderment are generative of the religious spirit. In this also, women display their superiority to men, believing as they do that the only true prayer is a good deed, and the only true religion is living a loving life.

Lund tells us that women show more interest in the aesthetic, the ideal, and in the mystic, and he thinks this may be due to woman's greater sensitivity, and to training. Children who are trained to play a musical instrument seldom, if ever, become juvenile delinquents. Common experience, in our culture at least, tells us that women are more interested in beauty than men are. Men sometimes say, when they wish to describe the peculiar delicacy of another man's sense of beauty, that he has a "feminine" sense. The "feminine touch" is something to which we all warmly respond. Indeed, the more closely a man's sense of beauty approaches the feminine, the less violent and the more harmonious in character he is likely to be. It is interesting to observe that during the last fifty years, with the development of the post-impressionist, nonobjective schools of painting, cubism, pointillism, vorticism, there have also gone many "arty" experiments. Women painters have been conspicuous because, while they have progressed with the times, they have kept their aesthetic heads and not gone to the violent extremes that have characterized so many experimental schools of painting. Marie Laurencin painted exquisitely beautiful canvases, and so did Georgia O'Keeffe, in a totally different style; even that delightful primitive, Grandma Moses, managed to avoid the contaminating influence of the machine age, painting rustic scenes with feminine ardor. The poetry and the novels of women usually show the same sensitivity to beauty, a beauty of a more loving, graceful, and humane kind than that which generally characterizes the work of male writers.

In art men express something of their sense of beauty and conflict; women, on the other hand, practically never use art as a vehicle for the expression of anything but love. When women try to ape men, their aesthetic sense becomes deformed, and they vie in toughness with the male writers, let us say, of the Hemingway school. These are not the feminine writers who will endure. The women writers who will endure are those who remain true to themselves, who are admired for the virtue of their own qualities and not for being like men. One thinks of the Brontës, Jane Austen, Elizabeth Gaskell, George Eliot, Mary Webb, Willa Cather, Virginia Woolf, Colette, Doris Lessing, Toni Morrison, and many others. The humanitarianism, warmth, wit, and moral earnestness that characterize the writings of these women grow out of a feeling for humanity based on love. It is this that gives their novels and other writings an enduring vitality and attractiveness. One may say of all these gifted women what Rosamond Lehmann wrote of three of them:

> They believed, all of them, that love is of paramount significance in human affairs; that what gives life dignity and importance is the amount of love expended in personal relationships; the amount in each individual of that quality without which the human specimen, in print or out of it, is apt to look both small and dull, a predatory fragment.[17]

It is not without significance that the first two great psychological novels of Japan and of the West should have been written by women, the Lady Murasaki's *The Story of Prince Genji*, completed about the year 1004, and Madame de la Fayette's *The Princess of Clèves*, which appeared in the year 1678.

Women have many firsts as innovators in literature.[18] Thus Marie of France, who flourished during the latter half of the twelfth century, is said to have invented the genre known as the Breton lay. Dame Juliana of Norwich wrote the earliest mystical prose autobiography (1342), and Dame Juliana Berners, the abbess of Sopwell priory, near St. Albans, wrote the earliest English treatise on fishing, *The Boke of St. Albans* (1486). Margaret Cavendish, Duchess of Newcastle, wrote her autobiography (1655) and a biography of her husband (1667) which was added as an appendix to her *Observations on Experimental Philosophy*, in addition to writing the earliest English prose romance, *The Blazing World* (1666). This remarkable woman was also the author of *211 Sociable Letters*, an epistolary novel, preceding Richardson's *Pamela* (1740) in the same genre by years. The Restoration playwright Mrs. Aphra Behn was also the author of the famous novel *Oroonoko, or the Royal Slave* (1688), which was distinguished, among other things, for its sympathetic view of blacks. The Gothic, or horror, novel was the invention of Ann Radcliffe whose *The Mysteries of Udolpho* (1794) is perhaps her most famous work. Mrs. Susannah Centlivre whose many plays were a great success, wrote, *The Wonder! A Woman Keeps a Secret* (1714), which furnished David Garrick with one of his best roles. Mary Shelley's *Frankenstein* (1818) was the first science fiction story, about a monster who ultimately kills the scientist who created him.

As Grace Shulman points out, women were leaders in the revolution that overthrew romantic flaccidity during the twentieth century. Harriet Monroe founded the magazine *Poetry* in 1912, and Margaret Anderson founded *The Little Review* in 1915. It was a woman, Sylvia Beach, who, in 1922, had the courage to publish James Joyce's *Ulysses.*

In the past, and to some extent persisting into the present, male critics of women's literary and dramatic works did not hesitate to draw upon their stockpile of misogynistic prejudices. Their views were well summarized by "the Great Cham," the incomparable Doctor Samuel Johnson, when he said, "A woman's preaching is like a dog's walking on his hind legs. It is not done well; but you are surprised to find it done at all." As Mary Ellmann has said in her luminous book on male critics anatomizing female writers, femaleness is regarded as a congenital fault, rather like Original Sin.[19] This view of femaleness owes a great deal to Judeo-Christian teaching. *Woman* still remains a term of opprobrium, a state from which the female of the species may achieve ladyhood through "good" behavior. Ah, the *ladies*, bless them—noblesse oblige. Nevertheless, "lady writers" still carries a full charge of stereotypes and clichés.

Some critics walk down the field after the battle and shoot the wounded. In condescending mood, what greater praise can such a critic bestow upon a "female writer" than to say that she has "a masculine mind." George Eliot passes, but only as a male impersonator. Virginia Woolf, however, fails abysmally. Mary McCarthy gets by on her "formidability," which, presumably, disqualifies her for being a *lady.* Ivy Compton-Burnett, "that big sexless nemesic force," as Anthony Burgess labeled her, also passes, but only just. Jane Austen, however, is far too genteel for the critic who requires brawn with his brain. For him "conversation pieces" will hardly do. The obsessive antifeminism of such critics constitutes a sorry commentary on both their critical integrity and their sensibility. Dostoevski dubbed them "these lovers of humanity—by the book." Like an impacted tooth that is unable to break through the gum, these critics painfully persist in pushing in the wrong direction.

Being a woman to the masculine critic has meant being shrill, hysterical, erratic, temperamental, and all those other female "infirmities" upon which men in particular are so expert. Compare with these the masculine qualities of verve, panache, dash, impulse, the exaltation of error. Men nobly investigate, while women gossip. "The little woman" of the past, according to the macho critics, is still a little woman even in literature. Women, according to them, are incapable of grasping subtle principles of conduct, large aspiration, bold errors, grand designs. The healthy vulgarity of man was contrasted with the anemic gentility of women; the daring of the heroic sex, with the timidity of the weaker sex.

Why is it that men, even intellectual men, sometimes still find it necessary to diminish women? Why must critics so often weave their misogynist prejudices into the fabric of their best judgment, which is what criticism is supposed to be? Are the usual critical judgments of women writers by masculine minds really worthy of serious critics?

One of the obligations of the genuine critic is to rise above parochial and tradition-bound ideas, to avoid looking at the creativity of others through the distorting glass of prejudice. When it comes to women writers, few critics ever managed to achieve such responsibility. What seems to have irritated some masculine critics was that women dare to write at all, recalling La Bruyere's words, "It is the glory and merit of some men to write well, and of others not to write at all." Must women write like men or ape some neuter model of what is arbitrarily considered acceptable? If style is the man, is it not also, surely, that of the woman, and at the very least, of the human being of whatever sex or inclination? And is there not at least as much to be said for the woman's angle of vision as for the man's? How rare it is to find a male critic praising a writer for his or her feminine qualities. And yet, it is these so-called feminine qualities that are the essentially humane ones. So-called because the qualities we call feminine are not biologically linked to one sex but are learned traits, the acquisition of which would greatly benefit most men, and especially critics.

Among the many tests that have been made of sexual differences, it has been found that girls, in general, do better than boys on tests involving aesthetic response to color, shape, and discrimination in pictures. In tests involving the classification of pictures according to prettiness, quite small girls do better than boys. In drawing it is found that girls include more detail than boys—yet another indication of the greater sensitivity of girls to their environment. Indeed, the best description I have ever heard of what an artist does when drawing was offered by a little girl. When asked what she did when she drew a picture, she hesitated for a moment and then replied, "Well, first I think, and then I draw a line around my think."[20]

Does anyone today really talk of women as being born prevaricators or born liars? In *Women and Men* (1944) Scheinfeld said, "The most common charge of wrongdoing which men level against women is that they are given to *lying* and *deception*."[21] Scheinfeld thought the charge based baseless, and so do I. He considered it to be yet another example of the application of the double-standard principle: When men lie it is not the same thing as when women do. I think that there is yet another factor at work here, namely, *projection*. It is the easiest thing in the world to project upon others the failings we are unable to face in ourselves. The mechanism is unconscious, and hence, in its consequences, all the more real. In an investigation on lying in relation to age, conducted over a period of eight years on 151 mentally competent men and women, Dr. Nathan Masor found that the men lied about their age in 21 percent of cases compared with only 10 percent of the women. However, when the women lied they stretched the bow appreciably longer than the men.[22]

Because women have had to use much tact and discretion and employ certain discreet devices in order to achieve their ends, men have concluded that women are not "straight dealers." This is to add insult to injury, for if there have been women who were not straight dealers—and no one would deny that there have no doubt been some—it has often been because men have forced them into that oblique approach. Most of their faults women owe to men, while men are indebted to women for most of their better qualities. Nowadays, one hears less of women's "trickiness" than one used to, for men seem to have developed a greater respect for women than their fathers had. Men sometimes claim that women make fools of them. This is quite untrue. No woman ever makes a fool of a man, she merely presents him with an opportunity to realize his natural propensities.

Women's intuition has been a favorite topic for a long time. Woman's intuition stood to her as reason stood to man, and was a proof of her greater emotionality. Shakespeare, in *Two Gentlemen of Verona*, makes Lucetta say:

> *I have no other but a woman's reason;*
> *I think him so because I think him so.*

And Shakespeare, who was himself among the most sensitively feminine of spirits, was a great understander and admirer of women. Indeed, as Ruskin noted in *Sesame and Lilies* many years ago, Shakespeare has no heroes; he has heroines only. The catastrophe of every play is caused always by the folly or fault of a man; the redemption, if there be any, is by the wisdom or virtue of a woman, and, failing that, there is none.

Woman's intuition, as everyone knows, is a true faculty that most women possess in a form far more highly developed than anything the random male ever acquires. It is a kind of sixth sense, an ability to listen in the dark, a capacity for picking up, as it were, vibration of every short wavelength almost as soon as they have been generated. James Stephens put it very nicely in *The Crock of Gold* when he wrote, "Women and birds are able to see without turning their heads, and that is indeed a necessary provision, for they are both surrounded by enemies." Being a woman, as Joseph Conrad remarked, is a terribly difficult task, since it consists principally in dealing with men. As Helene Deutsch put it,

> Woman's understanding of other people's minds, her intuition, is the result of an unconscious process through which the subjective experience of another person is made one's own by association and thus is immediately understood. The other person's subjective experience manifests itself in an external happening that is sometimes barely perceptible, but that in an intuitive person evokes by quick association a definite inner state; the conscious perception rapidly tames the inner reaction, incorporates the impression received into a harmonious series of ideas, masters the "inspirational" element, and translates it into the sober form of conscious knowledge. Since the whole process is very rapid, its second phase, that is, the intellectual elaboration, is barely perceived—everything seems to take place in the unconscious and affective element, because the conscious ingredient does not come to the fore.

What we see in intuition is not a logical concatenation of impressions; on the contrary, in each intuitive experience, the other person's mental state is emotionally and unconsciously reexperienced, that is, felt as one's own. The ability to do this will naturally depend on one's sympathy and love for a spiritual affinity, with the other person; and the extent of this spiritual affinity, for which the German language has the term *Einfühlung* (sometimes translated as *empathy*), depends on the richness of one's own emotional experiences, which underlie the "inner perception" or the ability to understand one's own feelings and psychologic relations and, by analogy, those of others.[23]

I subscribe entirely to Dr. Deutsch's admirable description of feminine intuition, and I agree when she says that women are able to identify themselves with other persons more effectively than men and that they are able to do so because of their more profound feeling for people. I do not know whether there exists a fundamental difference between the sexes in inborn potentiality for the development of intuition; I suspect there may be such a difference. I know quite a number of men who possess this quality, but they do not possess it in so highly developed a degree as most women. In any event, in men the capacity seems to become progressively atrophied so that by the time they reach adult age there is, in most of them, very little of it left. Women, on the other hand, receive every assistance for its development, for sensitivity to human relations is woman's special domain.

Not so long ago men had little difficulty in believing that witchcraft was largely a feminine accomplishment. Thousands of women were hung, drawn, quartered, and burnt at the stake. The average male, when he first encounters woman's intuition, is astonished; it seems to him like magic. After all, he hasn't said a word or in any way indicated to her where he has been and what he has done; yet she knows, and pierces his thin disguises with appalling accuracy! How can one keep anything secret from her? Well, just as gamblers will go on believing that they can win at their gambling, so will men continue to believe that they can keep secrets from their wives. But few men have secrets that their wives do not know. Woman's intuition is clearly a valuable trait, and its possession gives her a great advantage in the pursuit of life, liberty, and a reasonable facsimile of happiness. The great superiority it confers upon females can no longer be disputed by anyone. To be jealous of woman's intuition, and even afraid of it, is understandable; but it is to the advantage of everyone concerned to understand that the depreciation of the good qualities of others is not the best way of acquiring them oneself.

8

WAS IT TRUE ABOUT WOMEN?

When this chapter was originally written in 1945 as an article for *The Saturday Evening Post* (24 March) it was written in the historic present. The myths held about women then are no more true today than they were then. In other words, there were a large number of entrenched myths in circulation concerning women's driving and financial capacities. I have retained the chapter to some extent unaltered because it is revealing of the general atmosphere and falsity of the beliefs that were held about women in matters that men claimed added to proof of the inferiority of women. Prejudice was all. Perhaps no other beam in the structure of the male ego was so solidly mortised in place as the myth about women drivers. The mythology went: It's a woman driver—and if it wasn't that time, it was the last, and the time before that, and it will almost certain be the next time. Why were women believed to be bad drivers? Probably because, among many other myths, women were held to be incompetent at things mechanical.

In August 1938, the Keystone Automobile Club of Pennsylvania presented facts and figures to show that the woman driver was competent, careful, and less liable to accidents than the male. In that year women drivers in Pennsylvania numbered 492,934, or nearly one-fourth of the state's total of 2,086,127 registered drivers. In the six-month period for which motor fatalities were checked, it was found that the ratio of women drivers to fatal accidents was 1 to every 1,724 operators. On carrying the analysis further, the figures show 8.9 as many men as women drivers involved in fatal accidents in Pennsylvania. By 1951 these figures had risen to 8 percent and 12 percent respectively. In 1962 the crude death rate per 100,000 from automobile accidents was 31.5 for males and 1.2 for females. In 1966 this rose to 39.9 for males and 14.7 for females.

Men tend to drive a car as a means of self-expression, and tend to aim it rather than drive it, they tend to be competitive, and on occasion reckless, and are likely to take a dim view of the more careful manner in which women drive. Men tend to regard women's circumspection in driving as evidence of their lesser competence. It all depends upon the angle of vision. Most of us would prefer to ride with the careful driver rather than with the competitive one.

Women, on the whole, are thoughtful drivers. In a difficulty they will not hesitate to ask for help. Men are disinclined to do so, and rather than ask directions prefer to blunder on. Today when more than half the work force is made up of women, and many of those drive to and from work, there is no evidence that women are greater hazards on the road than men.

In April 1963, the executive officers of the American Automobile Association, who, according to the *New York Times* of April 19, 1963, said they were "tired of hearing long-disproved clichés" about women's driving abilities, came to their defense: Gilbert B. Phillips, executive vice president of the Automobile Club of New York, said that AAA data showed the average woman driver to be no better and no worse than the average man.

From time to time it is a very healthy practice to hang a question mark on some of the things we take most for granted and to take another look at the facts. The myth about the woman driver is generally cited to reinforce the argument that women are temperamental and emotional—too much so to make good drivers. Well, we have hung a question mark on this dearly cherished belief of the superior male, and we have found evidence that leads us to believe that the woman driver is largely a creation of the "superior" male or rather of the male who wants to feel superior; for males, let us remember, are concerned not so much with woman's inferiority as with their own superiority.

Many men are ready to admit that, as drivers, their wives are as good as, or better than, themselves. Though they are glad to admit that their own wives are practical, wise, and levelheaded, the same men persist in thinking that the opposite is true of women as a whole. They say that women can never balance their checking accounts, that they are as blind as bats in matters where money or common sense is involved, and that shopping with them is an agony because they are indecisive and can't make up their minds.

What men so often take to be feminine indecision and an inability to make up their minds is in reality an inverse reflection on the trigger thinking of men. Women, for example, tend to take time to think about what they want to buy; they are more inquisitive about the quality of the goods they purchase than men; and they are much more likely to engage in comparative shopping in an effort to obtain their money's worth. Women are aware that it is around them that the family is built and that the practical economic situation of the household is determined by the woman who runs it.

Women often handle the family finances. This should constitute a sufficient commentary on the rather moth-eaten myth that women are no good at managing the finances of the household. Few men would ever have yielded the management of household finances to their wives had they not been convinced that their wives could manage better than themselves, even though there may still be some men who ungratefully rationalize away this fact with the explanation that to yield is easier.

In the *Life with Father* era, the bills for drygoods, groceries, and clothing were supposed to be as unintelligible as Sanskrit to Mama and were paid by Papa as a matter of course. Nowadays, in millions of families, the woman pays all the household expenses including her husband's allowance. Out of the household expenses money the "financial lightweight" who shares her husband's bed and board is often still expected to see to it that the dry cleaning is regularly dropped off and retrieved; that the children get not only to the doctor and dentist for regular examinations, but to an ever-expanding array of enrichment activities; and that several palatable meals are available in a continuously changing delectable variety for man, child, and

dog. She is expected to keep on hand a complete supply of light
bulbs, to make sure that ginger ale and soda are always on tap,
and to keep herself and the children as well clothed as the family
next door, who may have twice the income.

Men joked in days past about chuckle-headed women who
thought that banks used red ink because it's such a pretty
color. Such jokes indicated what men thought about women's
ability to keep on the right side of the ledger. Many a man even
today has an exaggerated notion of the number of times his
wife's checks rebound from the bank; perhaps hazarding that
his wife's checks bounce ten to a hundred times more frequently
than his own. Yet, while in the years after the turn of the century
men did the bookkeeping for the banks of the country, nowadays
women have largely replaced men as our banks' bookkeepers.
Throughout the country, thousands of women bank officials are
acting in a supervisory capacity, and the figure is growing. Their
jobs range from chairing the board to heading departments.

It is inevitable that women play an ever larger role in banking
and in the investment world, since they have long been up to
the tops of their pocketbooks in ownership: In 1952, according
to a survey made by the Brookings Institution, women owned
almost half of all privately owned stock in large corporations.
Of the 6,490,000 owners, 3,260,000 were men and 3,230,000
women; men owned an estimated 1,763,000,000 shares, while
women owned 1,308,000,000. Fifteen years later, in 1967, these
figures had almost trebled in favor of women. Of the 18,490,000
shareowners, 9,430,000 were women and 9,060,000 were men;
as of January 1967, 51 percent of individual shareholders were
women; 3.2 billion shares, or 17.8 percent of the total, with an
estimated market value of $119 billion, were registered in the
names of women. Sixteen percent of the total adult female
population were shareholders, and of those 6.4 million women
shareholders, more than half were housewives. This same year
Muriel Siebert became the first woman to own a seat on the New
York Stock Exchange. She was the nation's first discount broker,
and the first woman to serve as Superintendent of Banks for the
State of New York.

By 1990 the change in the representation of women in every
branch of the world of finance was dramatic. For example, in a
field that was virtually completely closed to women, namely,

securities analysis, the range of industries covered by women—once limited to cosmetics, household products, textiles and apparel—today includes steel, small growth firms, engineering construction, gold mining, automobiles, quantitative analysis, and biotechnology. Janet Lewis suggested that women may have fared better in research than in other Wall Street fields because there success can come relatively quickly and be measured objectively, successes and failures are highly visible, and the work is less social, less competitive, and more individual.[1]

Women investment advisers and counselors have increasingly proved their mettle and earned the respect of their male competitors. Women continue to earn the respect of all their male competitors. A number of women have earned full partnerships in prestigious investment banking firms. In the middle levels of banking women have solidly established themselves in impressive numbers, and it is only a matter of time before they do so in top management positions.

In 1997, women held more than 10 percent of the total board seats of *Fortune* 500 companies, fully 84 percent of *Fortune* 500 companies had one or more women directors; 36 percent reported having two or more women directors. Companies with the highest percentage of women holding board seats (19-10%) included savings institutions, airlines, and computer software companies. The lowest percentages of women on the board were reported by the mail/package/freight delivery industry and the securities arena (3-5%).[2]

Statistics on women as business owners indicate that women are indeed making a substantial mark on America's economy. The more than eight million businesses owned by women contribute more than two trillion dollars annually into the economy, more than the gross domestic product of most countries. At the same time, employment growth in women-owned businesses exceeds the national average in most regions and industries. Interestingly, nearly three-quarters of the business owned by women in 1992 were in business three years later, compared with an average of two-thirds for U.S. firms in general.[3]

Today there is a genuine recognition that women constitute an important factor in the whole system of American business. The direction of women's development in the financial world has become quite clear.

9

THE INTELLIGENCE OF THE SEXES

A scientist does not set out to prove anything one way or the other; the scientist is interested in finding out what *is* and stating it. Perhaps it is this austere attitude toward the fate of the facts that has prevented scientists' findings concerning the intelligence of the sexes from becoming as widely known as they should be. What is found must be tested and checked by other independent scientists before it can be accepted.

In 1910 Helen Thompson Woolley, the first principal of Mount Holyoke College, in an article on test results wrote, "There is perhaps no field aspiring to be scientific where flagrant personal bias, logic martyred for the cause of supporting a prejudice, unfounded assertions, and even sentimental rot and drivel, have run riot to such an extent as here."[1] These frank remarks apply with even greater force to the findings relating to the thousands of so-called intelligence tests that have been administered since those words were written. The truth is that there can hardly be a field of science in which so many follies have been solemnly committed in the name of science, and so many unsound conclusions drawn on the basis of tests that do not in fact measure what it is claimed they measure. I wonder I never see Woolley's comments on intelligence tests quoted.

The principal error committed by the intelligence testers has been the assumption that their tests yield a quantitative measure of the biological determination of intelligence. Evidence today reveals that these tests measure, if anything, the background of information of the testee, plus the combined effects of socio-economic status and schooling combined with genetic factors passed through the alembic of a unique personality. While there is no known means of teasing out of this amalgam what is due to environmental factors and what is due to genes plus the individual history of the person, we do know that when the environmental factors are improved IQs go up, and that when they are depressed IQs go down.

Just as the broader significance of the sex chromosomes might have been understood much sooner if they had been discovered by a woman rather than by a man, so it may also be that because the basic work on intelligence testing was done by males (though it has since been very largely participated in by women) it was not considered necessary to do more than state the facts. But facts do not speak for themselves, and unless they are given a little assistance they have a difficult time getting established. In 1910 Helen Woolley listed less than half a dozen previous studies of psychological sex differences; today several thousand such studies are available. But it is one thing to report the findings set out in these studies, and quite another to say what they mean.[2] Fortunately, there is fairly common agreement among scientists on the meaning of the facts. This preamble is necessary because the facts obtained by so-called intelligence tests and other tests do not speak for themselves; indeed, when they are assumed to be speaking for themselves it is almost certain that the grossest errors of inference have been committed because of the many concealed factors that have probably affected the results as reported. For example, when one compares the intelligence scores of elementary school boys and girls it is found that the girls do better, on average, than boys. On the other hand, the intelligence test scores for high school seniors are, on average, higher for boys than for girls. What is the meaning of these findings? Do they mean that boys develop a higher intelligence than girls when they enter high school years? On the face of the scores alone this might be the conclusion, but were it to be drawn it would be erroneous.

The explanation is all in favor of the girls. In practically every high school in the land there is a much more rapid elimination of boys than girls. Boys whose schoolwork is unsatisfactory drop out of school and go to work, whereas girls tend to stay on. Furthermore, girls make a better adjustment to the school curriculum than do boys; the slower girls make much more of an effort to master their school problems, and generally manage to pass sufficiently well to stay in school, while boys under the same conditions tend to become frustrated and give up. But such facts should put us on guard against jumping to the conclusion that high school girls are thus proven to be more intelligent than boys, or rather that a sexual difference of a biologically determined nature is involved. It may be that such a factor is involved, but quite obviously, or perhaps not quite so obviously, certain social factors in the ways in which girls and boys are conditioned are also to be considered.

Where especially bright children have been selected for testing, another concealed factor may enter which works to the disadvantage of girls, namely, the effect of sex stereotypes on the teachers' judgments. Since girls are generally brighter than boys at school, a girl of high intelligence may simply be regarded as a good pupil, whereas a boy of similar intelligence may be judged as brilliant.

Allowing for this and similar concealed and selective errors in the interpretation of the results of intelligence tests, let us, before proceeding further, state what is to be understood by intelligence. Such a statement is not as easy to arrive at as one might think. There is probably not a single definition of intelligence in the psychological literature that would find agreement among authorities.

In defining intelligence, the concepts that occur most often in the writings of psychologists are the ability to deal with abstract symbols and relationships and the ability to adapt oneself to new situations. But these are obviously general definitions, for there are all sorts of abstract symbols, in mathematics, music, philosophy, logic, and so on. An individual may be excellent in one area of abstract symbols and poor in others. Adaptation to new situations will often depend upon a person's previous familiarity with the context of the new situation. A white man taken at random, however intelligent he might be in adapting himself to new situations in his home environment, would almost certainly behave less "intelligently" in situations completely new to him, say, in an indigenous culture. Indeed, such behavior has often been misattributed to lack of intelligence, whereas it is usually nothing more than a reflection of the cultural disorientation most of us exhibit in foreign surroundings. Therefore it should be clear that intelligence is very closely related to experience and that it can be defined only in relation to a distinctive cultural setting or environmental milieu.

Within our own cultural milieu, psychologists are generally agreed, intelligence in large part consists of verbal ability. But, of course, it is the quality of one's capacity for verbalization and linguistic development that is important in the evolution of intelligence. Here it may be noted that the way verbal thinking and language are organized appears to be dependent more exclusively on the left side of the brain in males, while in females both the left and the right sides appear to be involved. This may confer certain linguistic advantages upon the female compared with the male. Apropos of that, it is well known that females learn to speak foreign languages more quickly and accurately than males.

A short definition of intelligence is the ability to make the most appropriately successful response to the particular challenge. That involves thinking, which essentially is problem solving. A more detailed definition of intelligence is that given by Dr. George Stoddard in his book, *The Meaning of Intelligence.*

> Intelligence is the ability to undertake activities that are characterized by (1) difficulty, (2) complexity, (3) abstractness, (4) economy, (5) adaptiveness to a goal, (6) social value, and (7) the emergence of originals, and to maintain such activities under conditions that demand a concentration of energy and a resistance to emotional forces.[3]

Possibly the only one of the attributes in this definition that requires clarification is the emergence of originals. By this Stoddard means simply the capacity for the discovery of something new; and it is included in the definition of intelligence not because it is an inevitable outcome of high ratings in each of the other six attributes, but because of its special place at the upper end of any valid distribution of intelligence. To what extent do males and females differ in the frequency with which they exhibit such traits?

Here it should be pointed out that IQ tests have no scientific value whatever, they do not measure intelligence, what they measure is really information, no more, no less.

Remember that the material that goes into a so-called intelligence test will, to a certain significant extent, be environmental background, past and during the testing itself, health, psychological state, language, and understanding, all of which will influence at any time what is meant by intelligence. It should be emphasized that IQ tests do not measure intelligence, but rather offer an utterly distorted statement of reaction to tests that invariably fail to take into account the schooling and socioeconomic experience, not to mention the life history, of the individual. In a long history of critical studies of this subject, the most recent and most devastating is Elaine and Harry Mensh's *The IQ Mythology: Class, Race and Inequality*.[4] I have also addressed these issues in the sixth edition of my own, *Man's Most Dangerous Myth: The Fallacy of Race* (1998).[5]

IQ tests not only do not measure intelligence, but rather serve to falsify and obscure what should really be understood by intelligence. Whatever intelligence is, if it can be called by a single term, it is much more complex and extensive than a single concept that can be measured and described in a so-called quotient. Hence, comparisons of the differences between the sexes in IQ tests are invalid and should not in any way be trusted. A refreshing challenge to traditional conceptions of intelligence is the work of Howard Gardner of Harvard's Graduate School of Education. His research has led him to conclude that there are at least seven areas of intelligence competence. These multiple intelligences are relatively independent of one another. They are (1) linguistic—sensitivity to the meaning and order of words; (2) logical-mathematical—ability to handle chains of reasoning and recognize patterns of order; (3) musical—sensitivity to pitch, melody, rhythm, and tone; (4) bodily-kinesthetic—ability to use the body skillfully and handle objects adroitly: athlete, dancer, surgeon; (5) spatial—ability to perceive the world accurately and recreate or transform aspects of that world: sculptor, architect, painter, surveyor; (6) interpersonal—ability to understand people and relationships: politician, salesman, religious leader; (7) intrapersonal—access to one's emotional life as a means to understanding oneself and others: therapist, social worker.[6]

Gardner's findings make a good deal of sense. He is the first to agree that his theory is not writ in marble, but he has also shown that it has much evidence, drawn from many sources, in support of it, and that it is certainly subject to modification as research continues. I have presented it here because it seems to me that it would constitute a far better assessment of a person's "intellectual" abilities than present tests are capable of achieving, especially judging sex differences. Such sex tests have yet to be made. When they have, I believe they will be found to be more accurate and useful than our current tests in revealing that all studies concerning the comparative differences in intelligence between the sexes have been "barking up the wrong tree." However, even in the interpretation of tests based on Gardner's intelligences, vigilance will continue to be necessary against falling into the customary error of neglecting to consider the individual's socioeconomic and schooling history, not to mention the many other jokers in the pack.

For example, Dr. Deborah Weber of the Department of Psychiatry at Children's Hospital Medical Center in Boston suggests that rate of maturation rather than gender may be responsible for some of the observed differences in mental abilities between the sexes. It is well known that females mature earlier than males. Weber found that early maturers tend to score higher on verbal tests, while late maturers do better on spatial tasks. A sample of eighty early and late maturing girls and boys was studied. When the subjects were rated along a continuum of maturation, gender made no difference. Early maturers, regardless of sex, scored better on verbal than on spatial tests. Tested for right or left brain lateralization, Weber found that the late maturers were more left-brain lateralized for speech than the early maturers. Weber suggests that rate of maturation rather than sex-related behaviors may play an important role in the organization of higher brain functions.

In what follows I shall set out the facts relating to sex differences in intelligence as they have been arrived at through the standard IQ tests which are so open to criticism. I do so in order that the reader may be able to judge for him- or herself what those differences have been found to be by means of those highly flawed tests. Throughout the following presentation of the facts, let us always bear in mind the differences that exist in the social environments for males and females, the differences to which they are called upon to adapt themselves. Because the facts are so numerous and complex it will be clearer and more helpful to the reader if I set out those facts in simple, brief sentences. In setting out the IQ findings I have relied entirely upon the admirable presentation of them by Professor Ann Anastasi of Fordham University and the Psychological Corporation. In her classic book, *Differential Psychology*,[7] she gives, among many other findings relating to individual and group differences in behavior, a quite comprehensive survey of the scientific findings concerning the intellectual functions of the sexes.

We may as well be prepared for what we are going to find—the cumulative effect of the repeated shock may in this way, for some males, and perhaps even for some women, be assuaged; namely, that with the exception of the tests for arithmetic, mathematics, mechanics, and mazes, females achieve significantly and consistently higher scores on the intelligence tests than males.

- At the ages of two, three, and four the average IQ, as tested by the Kuhlmann-Binet test, is higher for girls than for boys.
- From school age to adult life females obtain a significantly higher average rank on intelligence tests than males.
- On tests designed for testing the intelligence of Army inductees during World War I, the Army Alpha test, New England rural women attained a significantly higher average than the men.
- From infancy to adulthood the female superiority in verbal or linguistic functions is consistent and marked.
- Girls of preschool age have a larger vocabulary than boys.
- Girls on the average begin to talk earlier than boys.
- Girls begin to use sentences earlier than boys and tend to use more words in sentences.
- Girls learn to read earlier and make more rapid progress in reading than boys.
- Girls have few reading difficulties compared with the great number of reading disabilities among boys.
- Girls excel in speed of reading, tests of opposites, analogies, sentence completion, and story completion.

- Girls do better than boys in code-learning tests.
- Girls show a highly significant superiority in handling linguistic relations, as in the test requiring them to construct an artificial language. (Here the subject is given a short vocabulary and a few grammatical rules, and is then required to translate a brief passage in English into the artificial language.)
- Girls learn foreign languages much more rapidly and accurately than boys, a difference that is maintained throughout life.
- Girls excel in most tests of memory. They do significantly better on tests of picture memories and such tests as copying a bead chain from memory.
- Girls tend to excel in logical rather than in rote memory, especially when the content of the test favors neither sex. The suggestion is that logical memory depends more upon verbal comprehension than upon anything else, hence the superior achievement on logical-memory tests of the female.
- Women are characterized by a more vivid mental imagery than men.
- Girls excel, on the whole, in general school achievement as measured by achievement tests and school grades.
- Girls do better than boys, on the whole, in those school subjects that depend largely upon verbal ability, memory, and perceptual speed.
- Boys do better in those subjects that depend on numerical reasoning and spatial aptitudes, as well as in certain information subjects, such as history, geography, and general science.
- Insofar as school progress is concerned, girls are consistently more successful than boys. Girls are less frequently held back, more frequently advanced, and promoted in larger numbers than boys.
- In school grading, girls consistently do better than boys, even in those subjects that favor boys.
- Girls obtaining the same achievement test scores as boys consistently had higher school grades than boys.

At the school ages, but not in the preschool age range, boys do better than girls on spatial and mechanical-aptitude tests.

But a cultural factor is suspected as operative here, because boys do no better than girls in the preschool years on such tests, and it seems obvious that they depend upon the special kind of information that helps them in these tests and that is not culturally offered to or encouraged in girls. Furthermore, boys do much better in these tests than they do in the more abstract tests of spatial relations, upon which both sexes may be equally uninformed.

Boys are found to do better than girls on block counting from pictures, directional orientation, plan of search, tests of form boards, puzzle boxes, assembling objects, pencil-and-paper mazes, mechanical comprehension, arithmetic problems and arithmetic reasoning, ingenuity, and induction.

On the Army Alpha tests boys excel significantly in only three tests: arithmetic reasoning, number-series completion, and information. In arithmetic computation girls do better than boys, but they do not do as well as boys in solving arithmetic problems and in arithmetic reasoning.

As far as intelligence scores and other indications of what we call intelligence go, the conclusion is clear: Girls, on the whole, do better than boys on whatever it is that the intelligence tests and other tests "measure." The only things in which boys do better than girls are mathematics, arithmetical reasoning, and mechanical and spatial aptitudes; and the evidence indicates that cultural factors play a significant role in assisting boys to make a better showing in these areas of knowledge—for it is largely upon knowledge that, it is suspected, the superior achievement of boys, on the average, is based. That this is so is indicated by the girls' increasingly doing as well as boys on those tests in which boys ritually excelled.

It is well established that females start developing *in utero* at a more rapid rate than males and that this acceleration in the rate of growth is maintained by the female throughout childhood and up to the age of seventeen and a half years. It has been suggested that the acceleration in physical growth in girls is also accompanied by an intellectual acceleration, in which case boys and girls of the same chronological age cannot be compared with one another. It would be necessary to make the comparison on the basis of psychological or developmental age rather than chronological age. But such a procedure would seriously distort the results obtained by giving the boys an advantage of anything from a year to almost two years in training and general environmental experience. The fact is that intellectual acceleration in girls has not been directly demonstrated, and all that we know about the relationship between physical and mental factors is against the influence of physical maturation on intellectual development. Intellectual development is obviously far more dependent upon kind and quality of environmental stimulation than it is upon slight differences in physical development. And this is the critical point: What the intelligence tests measure is to a large or an appreciable extent the response that a particular person with a unique history has made to the environment in which she or he has been conditioned, the response made through the alembic of the individual's special history of experience to the test designed to measure "intelligence."

It should, then, be obvious, that before one can pass judgment on the intelligence of one group as compared with another it is necessary to afford that group equal opportunities for the development of intelligence. It need not be reiterated here that boys and girls do not enjoy equal opportunities for the development of intelligence. Boys and girls live in different social environments, different achievements are expected of them, and they are called upon to play very different roles from earliest childhood. If girls do not have opportunities equal to boys' for the development of intelligence, neither do boys have opportunities equal to girls' for the development of intelligence. Each sex has different kinds of opportunities; these different kinds of opportunities are not comparable. Hence it is, under the circumstances, impossible to answer the question of the biological quality and development of the intelligence of the sexes, because the biological potentials for the development of intelligence have been so markedly and differentially influenced by the constant operation of factors of a social nature based on differences in the cultural attitudes toward the sexes.

One thing, however, is strikingly and significantly clear, and that is that intelligence, as it is defined and expected of each sex, is, on the average, something in which females of preschool and school age do better than males, with the exception of the mechanical, spatial, and mathematical reasoning tests. This does not necessarily make girls superior in intelligence to boys, but it does make them superior to boys in terms of what the intelligence tests measure, with the exceptions named. In other words, where the opportunities are afforded them and where they receive the necessary encouragements, girls generally do better than boys. Where boys receive the more favorable environmental stimulations and encouragements, they do better than girls. The evidence strongly suggests that if boys and girls received equal environmental stimulations and encouragements, they would do at least equally well on whatever the intelligence tests set out to measure.

In short, the age-old myth that females are of inferior intelligence to men has, so far as the scientific evidence goes, not a leg to stand upon. Indeed, by present tests and standards of measurement girls, on the whole, do better than boys. At school they make better adjustments to conditions than boys and better satisfy the requirements of the definitions offered at the commencement of this chapter than boys do. The conclusion cannot be avoided that girls of school age are, on the whole, more intelligent than boys of school age. The fact is, whatever it may mean, that on entering school at the age of five years the average girl's mental age is two years ahead of that of the average boy!

Thus far our discussion has been focused largely on the intelligence of preschool children and children of school age because most of the intelligence tests have been carried out with children and are both revealing and important. What now of the intelligence of adults? Here the wise and thoroughly considered words of Stoddard may be quoted:

> It is futile to attempt a thorough exploration of sex differences in the later ages, in terms of the contents of present-day group or individual tests. In future, having defined intelligence with a heavy saturation in the abstract, having prepared tests with high ceilings, and with full reach to complexity and originality, all in total disregard of any found or estimated differences between the sexes, we may then apply these new tools of measurements to the sex problems indicated.[8]

However, such tests have not yet been devised, and until they have been I think most of us will agree with Stoddard that it is futile to compare the intelligence of the sexes, *on the basis of present-day intelligence tests,* with the expectation of learning anything about the fundamental nature of the genetic basis of the intelligence of either sex. Such tests as have been made on adults—and there have been many—parallel the findings that have been made on schoolchildren. The same holds true for males and females at college.

Even so, the tests tell us quite a number of things: They tell us, for example, that there is no evidence to suggest that the female adolescent and adult are genetically inferior in intelligence to the male; they tell us that the factor of social experience is a major one in influencing the development of intelligence, for most females in their middle teens begin to evidence an increasing preoccupation with matters that are not measured by the usual tests, and tend to become less and less interested in the content of such tests. It is at this stage that the boys begin to pull ahead on the tests; and it is at this stage that most girls begin to think seriously of marriage, while boys begin to think in terms of earning a living. The one prepares for the requirements of a wife, the other for the expected requirements of a breadwinner. At this point in their lives the goals and aspirations of most boys and girls are utterly different, though they are directed toward similar ends. When, therefore, the average male ends up with more information at marriage than the female at marriageable age, it is highly probable that this does not mean, as it is frequently said to mean, that the female stops growing mentally at eighteen while the male continues to grow, and that this difference is due to a genetic difference between the sexes. Rather it means that while the male goes on acquiring the experience and information that intelligence tests are alleged to measure, the female turns to more domestic interests that the tests do not measure.

Girls in high school and in college frequently discover the disadvantages of being "brains." Many boys tend to avoid such girls. Bright girls are, therefore, often reluctant to appear as bright as they really are. As the 1955 report of the Commission on the Education of Women, *How Fare American Women?*, showed, "the intelligence quotients and grades of girls in high school become lower when they consider that successful academic work militates against their popularity and femininity." The same holds true for many college girls. Summarizing the evidence, Professor Howard Moss, in his book *Comparative Psychology* (1946), wrote: "In human beings, it has appeared to be a universal fact that, other things being equal, there is a negligible difference between males and females in cognitive capacities. And the findings in subhuman species have been similar." If anything, the difference is in favor of the female.

As John Gibson has remarked, "Trying to evaluate the overall intelligence of the sexes with the standard IQ tests is a little like trying to measure a ball of mercury with a yardstick."[9] Hence, more oblique approaches to the solution of this problem have been attempted. Humor, it has been determined, is a remarkably accurate index of intelligence. With this in mind psychologists at Wesleyan University and at Smith College investigated several hundred men and women from both institutions. They were exposed to extremely funny to utterly pointless jokes. The results were very illuminating. The men found all the jokes much funnier than the women did, and gave them higher ratings. The women showed far greater discrimination. They were unamused by the poorer jokes, but rated the really funny ones higher than the men did. In view of the high correlation between a sense of humor and high intelligence the women in these tests scored considerably higher than the men.

Studies carried out at both Duke University and at the University of London uniformly agree that women are far better judges of character than men—yet another evidence of women's higher problem-solving abilities. Indeed, as Henry James remarked in his story *In the Cage*, "The cleverness of men ends where the cleverness of women begins."

With marriage and children, women continue to grow in intelligence; especially in the kind of intelligence that is of the greatest importance for the survival of the human species, the intelligence of the heart, I think it can be shown that women far outdistance men. The one field in which it has long been established that males do better than females is mathematics, but here, too, recent studies have unequivocally shown the double-bind situation in which girls normally find themselves. They receive mixed messages—on the one hand to be career women and on the other to be wives and mothers, or to devote themselves single-mindedly to a demanding subject like mathematics. Added to this are the effects of the self-fulfilling prophecy that wreaks havoc upon women's chances of excelling at mathematics: the still widely-accepted belief that some biological factor prevents them from doing well at math.[10]

A later study, conducted by Professor John Ernest of the University of California at Santa Barbara, concluded that societal rather than genetic factors more adequately explain the differences in mathematical achievement between men and women. The sex differences in mathematical achievement, Ernest writes,

> are the result of many subtle and not so subtle forces, restrictions, stereotypes, sex roles, parental-teacher-peer group attitudes, and other cultural and psychological constraints which we haven't begun fully to understand. Our studies confirm the hypothesis of the sociologist Lucy Sells that mathematics is a 'critical filter' tending to eliminate women from many fields, from chemistry, physics and engineering, to architecture and medicine. This conclusion lends greater import and urgency to this study.[11]

With the advent and growth of the women's movement, and the entrance of so many women into the workaday world and the professions, a revolutionary change has occurred in the outlook of women. Today women are freely entering virtually every field that was formerly closed to them. The accomplishments of women in these fields have given young women the confidence and motivation to go out and do likewise. One of the results of this is to be seen in the decreasing differences in conventional IQ test scores, the best scores being shared equally between boys and girls, and the frequency with which girls are graduating at the top of their high school, college, army and naval academy classes.

In conclusion, it needs to be said that there are many intelligences that constitute the mind of every normal person, and that under an optimum life experience and education the quality of these intelligences would develop to a degree which is seldom reached today in a world in which most of us are more or less the wreck of what we ought to have been. It is not geniuses in a technologic-scientific and socially cubistically dilapidated world, but people who exhibit the highest form of intelligence whom we should most value, those who are able to love, to work, to play, and to use their minds soundly. Finally, let us remember that it is not statistical averages that should immediately concern us, but individual human beings who, whatever their sex, ethnic group, or religion, constitute the wealth and signature of humanity. Like the concept of race, the concept of IQ is a snare and a delusion which narrows the definition of humanity.

10

WOMEN AND CREATIVITY

Why is it that there have been no great composers among women, no great logicians and philosophers, so few great poets, musical instrumentalists, painters, scientists, inventors, technologists? Have not women, from the earliest times—or at least during the last few hundred years—been employed in kitchens to which they have not, by their own invention, contributed (so it is usually said) a single gadget? Is it not because they are lacking in the kind of genius that appears to be more abundantly distributed in the male sex?

This sort of reasoning constitutes a begging of the question, for it implies that there is an inborn kind of genius that probably occurs more frequently among men than among women. There exists no evidence for such an inborn limitation of the potentialities for genius in women. There is not the least reason to suspect that the genes for genius are in or limited to the Y chromosome.

Indeed, it is very much more likely that if such genes exist (which is extremely doubtful), they are present on the X chromosome, and that a female, because of her two X chromosomes, would be likely to receive a double dose of such genes; whereas a male, because of his single X chromosome, would receive but a single dose of them. Brain research seems to show that women do receive a double dose of such genes.

Every dispassionate investigator of the subject has agreed that woman's comparative lack of accomplishment cannot be entirely due to her not having enjoyed such opportunities, as in music, the arts, philosophy, spiritual leadership, invention, and science; yet until recently their accomplishments in these fields have been far from startling. Why have there been so few outstanding representatives of the female sex in these fields? There are many reasons.

The tradition that women are unable to do as well as men in anything requiring the use of the mind is a very ancient one—

Seek to be good, but aim not to be great,
A woman's noblest station is retreat.

These famous words, written by Baron Lyttleton (1709–1773) in his poem *Advice to a Lady* represented the kind of debilitating pabulum that women were sedulously fed by almost everyone, virtually all the days of their lives. The truth is that if it is continually being reiterated that the individual belongs to a group that has never achieved anything and never will, and that everything ever achieved in the world has been accomplished by persons of another kind; if you tell that person that it is useless to attempt to provide an education, or more than the rudiments of one, because she wouldn't be able to take advantage of it; if you make laws that prevent her from owning property, as well as laws that assign her to an inferior position in the hierarchy of statuses; if you exclude her from all activities except those limited to the menial tasks of domesticity and executing the will of her superior in looking after children; and if you conduct yourself as if you were her natural lord and master, you will succeed, have no doubt of it, in convincing her that such is the natural order of things. You may, in fact, succeed to such an extent as to engender a doglike fidelity and an utter devotion to the principle that dog is dog and master is master, each occupying the station to which God and nature have called them. As Rousseau aptly remarked, "Slaves lose everything in their chains, even the desire of escaping from them; they love their servitude as the companions of Ulysses loved their brutishness."

We shall not ask the question: What does one expect of dogs other than complete loyalty? But we shall ask: What does one expect of any person under such conditions? Does one expect sights set as high as the privileged ones of society? What should this person aim to achieve? At what level should her aspirations operate? What goals does she set herself? Obviously, her sights are not set because she isn't permitted the instrument; or if she is, it has no sights, and her goals and aspirations are focused almost exclusively upon pleasing her master. Since the master is so much concerned with superiority, the diminished stature of the menial—who is always at his service—is very satisfactory, especially when the menial acknowledges her inferiority in innumerable subtly flattering ways; and come weal or woe, the inferior will help to maintain the *status quo*. And although the menial may sometimes experience the goadings of doubt and occasionally feel dissatisfied with her lot, so to think and feel is to partake of forbidden fruit, to eat of the tree of knowledge, which is prohibited.

Master and menials. Men and women. It is written in Genesis 3:15–17, that the Lord God said unto the serpent:

> And I will put enmity between thee and the woman, and between thy seed and her seed; it shall bruise thy head, and thou shalt bruise his heel.

> Unto the woman he said, I will greatly multiply thy sorrow and thy conception; in sorrow thou shalt bring forth children; and thy desire shall be to thy husband, and he shall rule over thee.

> And unto Adam he said, Because thou hast hearkened unto the voice of thy wife, and hast eaten of the tree, of which I commanded thee, saying, Thou shalt not eat of it: cursed is the ground for thy sake.

In I Corinthians 11:3 it is written: "And the head of the woman is the man." And again in I Corinthians 11:7–9:

> For a man indeed ought not to cover his head, forasmuch as he is the image and glory of God: but the woman is the glory of the man.

> For the man is not of the woman; but the woman of the man.

> Neither was the man created for the woman; but the woman for the man.

And finally I Corinthians 14:34:

> Let your woman keep silence in the churches, for it is not permitted unto them to speak; but they are commanded to be under obedience, so also saith the law.

> And if they will learn anything, let them ask their husbands at home; for it is a shame for women to speak in the church.

It is said in I Timothy 2:11–15,

> Let the woman learn in silence with all subjection.
>
> But I suffer not a woman to teach, nor to usurp authority over the man, but to be in silence.
>
> For Adam was first formed, then Eve.
>
> And Adam was not deceived, but the woman being deceived was in the transgression.
>
> Notwithstanding she shall be saved in childbearing, if they continue in faith and charity and holiness with sobriety.

In Ephesians 5:22–24 it is written,

> Wives, submit yourself unto your own husbands, as unto the Lord.
>
> For the husband is the head of the wife, even as Christ is the head of the church: and he is the savior of the body.
>
> Therefore as the church is subject unto Christ, so let the wives be to their own husbands in everything.

In I Peter 3:1 it is written,

> Likewise, ye wives, be in subjection to your own husbands; that, if any obey not the word, they also may without the word be won by the conversation of the wives.

And in I Peter 3:7 the husband is enjoined to give honor to his wife, "as unto the weaker vessel."

There shall be enmity between the serpent and woman and between man and woman, and woman shall be a sorrowful creature, over whom her husband shall rule; and he shall not listen to her because she is easily deceived; but she shall learn in silence and subjection, and neither teach nor attempt to usurp authority over her husband, but remain in silence. "Every woman," said the Fathers of the early Church, "should be ashamed of the thought that she is a woman." The early Church Fathers popularized, and their followers perpetuated, the idea of loving God by hating women.

These ideas from the Old and New Testaments, as well as the early commentaries on them, have had a baleful influence in determining the attitudes of the sexes toward each other. The ideas expressed in the passages above are much older than the Old and New Testaments; these books merely enshrined doctrines that were already old when they came to be written.

The passages in Genesis were probably written some nine hundred years before those in Timothy, and in the interval no love seems to have been lost. The profound contempt for woman that these passages sanction is accentuated by the account of the disdainful and irregular manner of her creation from a rib of her lord and master, compared to which even the lower animals were created in a regular and proper manner. And then, to cap it all, all the misfortunes and sorrows of humankind are ascribed to the credulous folly and emotional nature, the unbridled appetite, of this lowly appanage of man—Eve, the first woman, wife, and mother.

It is with some justice that Madame de Tencin, Montesquieu's mistress, was prompted to remark, "From the way he treats us, it is easy to see that God is a man."

It is interesting to note that the biblical account of the creation of woman is paralleled by similar stories among some indigenous and other peoples in many parts of the world.

In his *Vindication of Married Life*, Martin Luther, echoing the thoughts of St. Paul, writes of that "stupid vessel," woman, over whom man must always hold power, for:

> Man is higher and better than she; for the regiment and dominion belong to man as the head and master of the house; as St. Paul says elsewhere: "Man is God's honor and God's image." Item: Man does not exist for the sake of woman, but woman exists for the sake of man and hence there shall be this difference, that a man shall love his wife but never be subject to her, but the wife shall honor and fear the husband.

Where such misogynist views of women prevailed, and where women were forced to make the necessary accommodations, there was absolutely no encouragement toward achievement in the private preserve of the master. In fact, not only was such encouragement forbidden, but any attempt on the part of the menial to usurp the authority of the master was considered an infringement of the law, for which exemplary punishments were prescribed. Women who made themselves conspicuous in some "unwomanly" manner were often in danger of being treated as objects of derision, or of disparaging remarks, and in numerous other denigrating ways. In the year 415 A.D., Hypatia, the Alexandrian neoplatonist philosopher and mathematician, renowned for her learning and eloquence as well as for her beauty, was brutally murdered by a band of monks, said to be at the instigation and encouragement of the Archbishop St. Cyril of Alexandria (see Charles Kingsley's *Hypatia,* London 1843). Women were encouraged in the practice and preservation of womanly virtues, to know their place, which was in the home, and not to aspire to be anything other than what by nature they were designed to be. "And if they will learn anything, let them ask their husbands at home." The weight of this tradition and practice is still so pervasively with us that even today the vast majority of women do not approach anything like the same encouragements and opportunities for achievement as men. And just as it is true of intelligence, so it is true of achievement that unless each sex is afforded equal opportunities there can be no means of knowing whether there are any essential inborn differences in their potentialities for achievement. On the other hand, when imme-morial tradition "proves" and the present "knows" that women are inferior to men, and that women are all the things that they have customarily been said to be, and when so many women as well as men consider these beliefs to be true, the incentive to achieve on the part of all but a very few women is not likely to be great.

Among the principal reasons why women do not have as many achievements of the kind that men have attained are the following: (1) For the greater part of their history most fields in which men have excelled have been closed to them; (2) in fields in which women were admitted they were not permitted to enter on an equal footing with men; (3) or, having been admitted, they were not encouraged to excel, were actively discouraged, or were not noticed at all. Women weren't even permitted on the stage until the seventeenth century; by far the greater proportion of them couldn't read or write when their husbands could; and when, in the nineteenth century, women first really began to express themselves through practically the only means available to them, namely, the novel, they sent their manuscripts to the publisher under men's names—Currer Bell (Charlotte Brontë), Ellis Bell (Emily Brontë), Acton Bell (Ann Brontë), George Sand (Aurore Dupin), George Eliot (Marion Evans)—for what woman could write? What man ever chose to send *his* manuscript to a publisher under a feminine pseudonym?

Women have been the oppressed race of the "superior" masculine world for many millennia; as an "inferior race" they have been deprived of their privileges, the right of every human being to enjoy those opportunities, equally with all other human beings, which would enable them to realize their potentialities to the optimum degree. This statement does not, of course, imply anything so idiotic as that men should be given the opportunities to give birth to babies, or that they should enjoy the freedom to suckle babies, and that women should be free to grow beards with mustaches, but what it *does* imply is that men and women should be given equal opportunities to realize their natural potentialities within the social milieu. These opportunities have never been fully afforded women or men; but if they haven't been fully afforded men, they have been afforded women to an even lesser extent. Even today, when there are now more women in the professional specialty occupations than there are men, discrimination still exists.

Women have always been treated as the inferior "race" by the masculine world. Everything that has been said by racists about blacks has been said by men about women: that they have smaller brains, less intelligence, are of limited abilities, unclean, incapable of achievement, lacking in creativity, and so on. The parallel between sexism and racism is deadly. The same impediments to self-fulfillment that have traditionally been placed in the way of blacks have been operative for a much longer time in the case of women. In the eighteenth century men claimed that no woman had produced anything worthwhile in literature, with the possible exception of the Greek lyric poet of the sixth century B.C., Sappho. Since women had failed to do so up to that time, it was argued, it was a fair assumption that they would never do so. But within the first half of the nineteenth century the supremacists were to be proven wrong, for women writers of genius commenced the break into the literary world: Jane Austen, Elizabeth Gaskell, Ann Brontë, Charlotte Brontë, Emily Brontë, George Eliot, George Sand, and Elizabeth Barrett Browning. And they were followed by such distinguished writers as Emily Dickinson, Mary Webb, Virginia Woolf, Edith Wharton, Willa Cather, Edna St. Vincent Millay, Pearl Buck, Doris Lessing, Sigrid Undset, Selma Lagerlauof, Grazia Deledda, Nadine Gordimer, Mary McCarthy, Toni Morrison, and many others. No one any longer doubts that women can write, and that what they have to say is worth reading. Nevertheless arguments are still heard to the effect that relatively few women have achieved greatness in the fields in which men have excelled.

Even at this late date how many women enjoy the same opportunities as men to become great scientists? Although in all fields women receiving the doctorate are brighter than their male counterparts, and there are no differences in their productivity, the durability of women on the job is often greater than that of men. Nevertheless, their rate of promotion and their salaries still tend to be somewhat lower.[1]

As the editor of *Science*, Philip H. Abelson, stated in an editorial, "There has been massive discrimination against women in academia." And he pointed out that while in 1972 only about 2 percent of women were full professors in our major universities, women obtained 12 percent of the doctorates annually awarded.[2]

For centuries it was quite impossible for women to even think of entering into activities regarded as the exclusive preserve of men. It was taken for granted that women could never succeed in any "male" occupation. Since the occupations were by definition *male,* it was hardly conceivable that any woman would even dream of entering them. Even though the citadels of male privilege have to some extent been breached, full equality has yet to be achieved. Discrimination against women is still a factor very much to be reckoned with.

During the greater part of the nineteenth century, the medical profession continued its tradition of excluding women from its ranks. The first woman to receive a medical degree and a license to practice medicine was Elizabeth Blackwell (1821–1910) in the year 1849; her sister Emily (1826–1910) followed, and also graduated as a doctor. Both women overcame many rejections, and ultimately worked together to emerge triumphantly from the ordeal to make splendid innovative contributions to medical education for women. These included medical schools for women, and hospitals and infirmaries, both in America and England. It was not, however, until the late 1870s that women in Europe were admitted to medical schools in somewhat larger numbers.

In 1854 Florence Nightingale (1820–1910) in England, and Clara Barton (1821–1912) in the United States, organized the first nursing units to serve the injured and the sick in army camps and on the battlefields of their respective countries. Each founded the Red Cross organization of her country, and pioneered in sanitation and hygiene. Nevertheless, despite these and other widely applauded achievements, women continued to be largely barred from medical schools.

To this day, while planned home births are increasing, there are only about 30 nurse-midwife programs in medical schools, and the medical establishment remains especially opposed to home birth care—midwives—in spite of admirable records of benefits to newborns and mothers. This is also true of family birth centers, all of which have been brought into being and administered by women. Such centers frequently provide much needed related treatment and education for young people. Benevolence, it would seem, in a male-dominated world, emanates more spontaneously from women then from men. Another orthodox citadel of masculine infallibility is the view that babies should be born in a hospital, and that the whole process of pregnancy and birth should be in the hands of the obstetrician.

To this it should be said that birth is neither a disease nor a disorder, despite the mandate by the medical profession that women must have their babies in hospital. Prenatal check-ups of the pregnant mother should, of course, be the rule both for the welfare of the baby and the mother. As for "delivery," babies may be "delivered" in fairy tales, but in reality the birth of a baby is due to the combined work of baby and mother, while the father should be participating in the memorable event by providing the comfort that his helpmeet needs so much. The birth of a baby is the most dramatic and thrilling event a family can enjoy. It is not a medical emergency. Relating to all this should be the obstetrician, in the event that his or her expertise is needed. Understandably, it is asked by some women, "What if there is an emergency?" The answer is that preparation for such a contingency could be taken care of by regular check-ups during pregnancy, and that in a well-ordered society, most untoward developments during childbirth could be prevented at a cost considerably less than the cost of training a soldier for combat.

Now that medical schools have become trade schools, and medicine an industry, a complete reorganization of both medical education and the practice of medicine is imperative. What is needed are technologists with a heart, caregivers who care for the patient; lovers of humanity, of the person, able to love others more than one loves oneself. Then we shall have achieved genuine health.

Music and painting are most frequently cited as two arts in which women have been engaged for several hundred years. During that time there have been many male musicians of genius, not a single female composer of any note, and a few instrumentalists of the first quality. If it is said that there were no incentives for women to excel in these arts, one may ask whether there was any incentive for them to excel in singing, for there have been many great women singers, as all the world knows. Ever since the first mother sang her infant to sleep, song and chant have been universally associated with women. Lullabies and lieder, dirges and laments, have from the earliest times naturally been a gift of women. The first songs the male learns are most often learned from women. There is, therefore, a long and acceptable tradition of woman as a singer. Her voice can produce effects that no man's can, and these are beautiful and colorful. Hence, we may be reasonably sure that song is one natural capacity in which women from the earliest times have been allowed their freedom. The nurturing of women singers in our culture may represent the persisting practice of an immemorial tradition.

In musical composition and the public performance of music, however, it is a different matter. Sophie Drinker, in her book, *Music and Women*,[3] has shown that women have not been musically creative in our culture owing to the historical causes that brought about a nonpermissive environment for the woman musician. The music of our culture was originally indissolubly bound to organized religion and limited to church use. Women were officially debarred from playing any part in the religious ceremony and so became automatically cut off from the main source and inspiration for original creativity in music. Nuns, who occupied a specific place in the hierarchy, composed only liturgical and extraliturgical music and then only within the limits of the few opportunities offered them. Drinker points out:

> When men and women freed themselves from the heavy restrictions placed upon the free use of music by the churchmen and began to use music apart from ritual and liturgy, women were *theoretically* able to function again as musicians. But the leaders in music were still those connected with, or employed by, religious officials, and according to the established custom of over a thousand years, were all men. Effective musical education and training were still in the church. Since the

supply of male musicians was sufficient, women were not in demand but were expected rather to patronize and perform men's music. Furthermore, even though ecclesiastical authority waned, authority in church, state, educational system, and home remained largely in the hands of men. And it was an authority reinforced by the religion that women were spiritually and intellectually inferior to men.[4]

Whoever would have thought of employing a female court musician? What woman would have dared offer herself in such a capacity? Why are there so few popular female jazz bands? Is it because the level of musical performance is so high that no woman could achieve it? One may doubt whether there would be many persons who would care to sustain the argument. Certainly no one would who had heard Phil Spitalny's all-woman orchestra. Numberless women have played and do play every one of the instruments one finds in the largest orchestras, and play them well. The fact is that a jazz orchestra of women simply doesn't present the right *decor*. Women prefer all-male bands, but they have no objection to the woman often attached to such orchestras, who sings a few numbers. Nevertheless, a few all-women symphonic orchestras have appeared and braved the entrenched prejudices of the sexes. Izler Solomon, the first conductor of the first all-woman symphonic orchestra to appear regularly on the air, in a statement published in the *New York Times* of 29 September 1940, said, "It is perfect nonsense to say that women are inferior to men in the world of music. In many instances they are better than men. Women are more sensitive and are apt to have a finer perceptive reaction to phrasing." In the same newspaper, on 26 October 1946, Hans Kindler said of women musicians: "Their ability and enthusiasm constitute an added stimulant for the male performers. . . . They were a veritable godsend to most conductors during the war years. The National Symphony has re-engaged its fifteen women players." And Leopold Stokowski said, "I find that women are equally as talented as men." On the other hand, Sir Thomas Beecham, the English conductor, announced that "women ruin music." He said, "If the ladies are ill-favored the men do not want to play next to them, and if they are well-favored, they can't." Jose Iturbi has held that women can never be great musicians. When he was associated with the Rochester Symphony Orchestra, he refused to accept female graduates from the Eastman School of Music as players in the orchestra; hence the inaccesibility of the world of music to women.

What does seem to be sufficiently well known is that in the history of every great male composer, from Bach to Beethoven, Haydn, Mozart Mendlessohn, Handel, Tchaikovsky, Schumann, and Mahler, a woman has played an important role in nurturing his genius. This was the theme of a book published in 1880 and written by George Upton entitled *Women and Music*. Here is a passage from his opening pages.

> The attachments of love, the bonds of friendship, the endear-ments of home, and the influences of society, have played an important part in shaping the careers of the great composers, and in giving color, form, and direction to the music. In all these phases of life, genius has more than once sat at the feet of beauty and executed her behests; and more than one immortal work of music may be traced to the calm, patient, steadfast love of woman in the quiet duties of home-life. Few students of music know the effects of these subtle influences.[5]

Upton then goes on to suggest an answer to the question, Why have there been no great composers of music? Conceding the point, he writes that

> Music is the highest expression of the emotions, and that woman is emotional by nature; is it not one solution of the problem that women does not reproduce them because she herself is emotional by temperament and nature, and cannot project herself outwardly, any more than she can give outward expression to other mysterious and deeply hidden traits of her nature? The emotion is a part of herself, and is as natural to her as breathing. She lives in emotion, and acts from emotion. She feels its influences, its control, and its power; but she does not see these results as man looks at them. He sees them in their full play, and can reproduce them in musical notation as a painter imitates the landscape before him. It is probably as difficult for her to express them as it would be to explain them. To confine her emotions within musical limits would be as difficult as to give expression to her religious faith in notes. Man controls his emotions, and can give an outward expression of them. In woman they are the domin-ating element, and so long as they are dominant she absorbs

music. Great actresses who have never been great dramatists may express emotions because they express their own natures; but to treat emotions as if they were mathe-matics, to bind and measure and limit them within the rigid laws of harmony and counterpoint, and to express thcm with arbitrary signs, is a cold-blooded operation, possible only to the sterner and more obdurate nature of man.[6]

It is an interesting explanation, but though times have changed in many respects, there still exists a wall of prejudice against the admission of women to positions in which they would be free to develop as composers.[7] I think there can be little doubt that given the appropriate opportunities, women's creativity as composers would at least equal that of men.

Compared with the male, the female still finds it difficult to obtain employment as a musician. If she plays the trombone or the bassoon, she stands much less chance of securing a position than she would were she to play the harp, piano, violin, cello, or organ—in short, women have seldom been motivated to compose for much the reasons we have suggested. With time and the changing definition of sexual roles, women composers may cease to be a rarity. There have been some women who have been brilliant performers on various instruments: Maddalena Lombardini, the eighteenth-century violinist; Clara Schumann, the virtuoso pianist, who was also a not inconsiderable composer (the wife of Robert Schumann), in order to get her works performed before nineteenth-century audiences had to do so under the name of her husband. Most of Fanny Mendelsohn's compositions were published under the name of her famous brother, Felix. The Venezuelan Teresa Carreno was not only the greatest woman pianist of the nineteenth century but also a distinguished opera singer, popular composer, and composer of her country's national anthem. Myra Hess was undoubtedly among the most distinguished contemporary pianists, as was Wanda Landowska the most eminent harpsichordist, and Midori one of the finest violinists of our time. Until her retirement in 1957, Nadia Boulanger was the world's most renowned teacher of composition.

Though there have been a fair number of others, no one can tell how many brilliant women musicians there have been who never reached eminence because they were denied the necessary encouragement. With the exception of singing, the striking disparity between the number of men and the number of women who have achieved great distinction in music remains, but perhaps we now understand a little more clearly some of the possible reasons for this disparity.

Of women as painters John Ruskin said bluntly, "No woman can paint." But Angelica Kauffmann in the eighteenth century, Elizabeth Vigee-Lebrun in the eighteenth and nineteenth centuries, Rosa Bonheur in the nineteenth century, Mary Cassatt in the nineteenth and twentieth centuries, Suzanne Valadon, Berthe Morisot, Marie Laurencin, and Georgia O'Keeffe in the twentieth century belie his Olympian remark. It should be added that after seeing the battle pieces of Elizabeth Butler (1850–1933) Ruskin magnanimously granted that they were every bit as good as those being painted by her male contemporaries. Nine women painters of distinction have just been mentioned, but in every country there have been many extremely able women painters. In every national or international exhibition of painting there are usually present several paintings by women to which any man would be glad to put his name.

In the 1976 Los Angeles Country Museum of Art exhibition, "Women Artists 1550–1950" (which I attended), the work of eighty-four women painters, chronologically arranged, were exhibited. The catalog of the exhibition constitutes an admirable reference work and tribute to an eye-opening host of painters.[8] Paintings long attributed to the masters David, Tintoretto, and Frans Hals were shown to have been painted by women; Constance-Marie Charpentier in the first case; Marletta Tintoretto in the second; and Judith Lyster in the third. The seeming disparity in the number of women who have attained distinction in painting as compared with the number of men who have done so has considerably narrowed. Germaine Greer has discussed this subject splendidly in her book, *The Obstacle Race*. Following a brilliant examination of the conditions under which women were historically caused to live, Greer summarizes her findings as follows:

> There is then no female Leonardo, no female Titian, no female Poussin, but the reason does not lie in the fact that women have wombs, that they can have babies, that their brains are smaller, that they lack vigour, that they are not sensual. The reason is simply that you cannot make great artists out of

egos that have been damaged, with wills that are defective, with libidos that have been driven out of reach and energy diverted into neurotic channels. Western art is in large measure neurotic, for the concept of personality which it demonstrates is in many ways anti-social, even psychotic, but the neurosis of the artist is of a very different kind from the carefully cultured self-destructiveness of women. In our time we have seen both art and women changing in ways that, if we do not lose them, will bring both closer together.[9]

There have been more than a dozen distinguished women sculptors. Harriet Hosmer (1830–1908) was the best known American sculptor of her time. She was most famous for her *Puck*, now in the Smithsonian Institution, and for her *Zenobia*, the warrior queen of Palmyra, now in the Metropolitan Museum of Art. Another American sculptor of great originality is Louise Nevelson (1900–1988). Among the many well-known works of Barbara Hepworth (1903–1975) is the Dag Hammarskjold Memorial at the United Nations in New York.

Perhaps the most gifted of all women sculptors was the young Frenchwoman Camille Claudel (1864–1943). Claudel began modeling in clay when she was a child. By the age of twenty, when she went to work in Rodin's studio, she was already a marvelous sculptor. For some fifteen tumultuous years she shared life with Rodin as pupil, model, partner, and lover. During this whole period, while collaborating with Rodin on many pieces, she resolutely maintained her own originality and independence as a creative artist. That period was one of the greatest creativity for Rodin. It was generally believed among their friends that the change in Rodin's character and in his work was due to Claudel's influence. It is also believed that many of the works created in the studio during these years, and subsequently attributed to Rodin were in fact by Claudel. However that may be, judging from the works that remain, there can be little doubt of her genius. In recent years there have been several exhibitions of her sculpture, articles, books; and at least one motion picture, *Camille Claudel*, released in 1990, has been made of her life and work.[10]

Why, it may well be asked, was full recognition of Camille Claudel's genius so late in emerging from the obscurity to which she was consigned by the fame of Rodin? The answer would seem to be that, first, she was a woman, and, second, before she could become widely known, her creative life came to a terrible end. She had looked forward to Rodin making her his wife; this he would not do, although he genuinely loved her. Because of a longstanding commitment he felt bound to marry his housekeeper, Rose Beuret. Years of violent bickering eventually led Claudel, at thirty-five, to leave Rodin. A severe nervous breakdown followed, which rapidly grew into a raging paranoia and cruel disintegration. During this period she destroyed every one of her sculptures she could lay hands on. In March 1915 Camille's brother, Paul Claudel, the distinguished poet and dramatist, was reluctantly forced to have his beloved and much admired sister confined to an asylum. Here she spent the next twenty-nine years of her life, hoping for the liberation which came only with death. She died from a stroke in 1943 at the age of seventy-nine. A 1905 moving and wonderful appreciation of Claudel's sculpture by her brother Paul is reprinted in Reine-Marie Paris's book, *Camille*, moving and generously illustrated with photographs of Camille's sculpture.

In literature, women during the last century and a half have achieved a quality that puts a number of them in the very first rank with the best of men. Fanny Burney, Jane Austen, Charlotte Brontë, and George Eliot are, by general consent, considered supreme among English novelists. Mary Webb is thought by some to belong in their company and most people would rank Virginia Woolf. Not many are likely to question the judgment that there have been few journalistic writers in any day who have been as able as Rebecca West.

In the United States such women novelists as Edith Wharton, Willa Cather, Pearl Buck, and Toni Morrison, the latter two Nobel Prize winners, have achieved great distinction. In Scandinavia, Sigrid Undset, Nelly Sachs, and Selma Lagerlof have been awarded Nobel Prizes for their outstanding work as novelists. In Italy, Grazia Deledda received the Nobel Prize as a novelist, and in Chile, Gabriela Mistral received the Nobel Prize for poetry, and Nadine Gordimer, South Africa, the Nobel Prize for literature. And, of course, there is Sappho of antiquity, and there are Elizabeth Barrett Browning, Emily Dickinson, Marianne Moore, and Edna St. Vincent Millay, among poets.

Ever since women were first allowed upon the stage in the seventeenth century, there has been an unbroken succession of actresses of genius. From Mary Betterton, Anne Bracegirdle, and Nance Oldfield in the seventeenth and eighteenth centuries, to Rachel (Elisa Felix, 1821–1858), Sarah Bernhardt, Duse, and Ellen Terry in more recent times, women have excelled as actors. Here, indeed, is a field of accomplishment in which women have received every encouragement, and in which they have done surpassingly well. Possibly there is here an obvious moral to be drawn.

In science, a field demanding all the qualities that have traditionally been regarded as supremely those of the male, women, in spite of many continuing obstacles, have at least gained a foothold. We have already noted that in physics and chemistry we have the double Nobel Prize winner Marie Curie; in physics Marie Curie's daughter Irene Joliot-Curie, also a Nobel Prize winner. Another Nobel Prize winner in physics is Marie Goeppert-Mayer; in chemistry, Dorothy Hodgkin, and in physiology and medicine the Nobel Prize winner Gerty Cori. And another, Rosalyn Yalow, in medicine, and in genetics Barbara McClintock. We have also previously noted that the highest scientific academies are now beginning to open their doors to women, and the English Royal Society, admission to which constitutes the highest scientific honor it is in the power of the English scientific world to bestow, already has a sprinkling of women among its Fellows. In the United States a trickle of women have been admitted into the National Academy of Sciences. When, in May 1991, only six out of the sixty new members elected to the academy were women, one of those elected, Dr. Susan E. Leeman, a neuroscientist, remarked, "I think it's a disgusting percentage . . . It's amazing." In an admirable article by the Pulitzer prize-winning *New York Times* journalist Natalie Angier, it is clearly shown how discrimination still limits the progress of women in science. While women are entering the ranks of science, social barriers, invisibility at the top, unequal pay, intellectual bullying and the understandable reluctance of women to join the fray, are barriers still very much in place in this man's world.[11] While women constitute 51 percent of the U.S. population, only 22 percent of scientists and engineers in the labor force are women. Within science and engineering, half of the women in these fields choose to receive their degrees in social sciences, while only about 33 percent choose mathematics and physical sciences, and 15 percent select engineering as their career path.[12]

In spite of such discouragements women are bravely continuing to enter the various branches of science with a view to pursuing scientific research as a career, and are receiving bachelor's degrees in numbers similar to men in the same fields.

In my own field, anthropology, some of the most original and path-breaking work has been done by women, and among the outstanding names in the field of anthropology that of the late Ruth Benedict, author of the classic *Patterns of Culture*, and of the dynamic Margaret Mead will always occupy an honored place.

In the realm of behavioral field studies the real breakthroughs were all achieved by women, Jane Goodall in the study of chimpanzees, Dian Fossey on gorillas, and Birute Galdikas on the orangutan. Where men had gone into the wild armed with guns, the women went in armed with nothing more than goodwill, tact, and delicacy, and succeeded in making many new discoveries where generations of men had failed.[13] Another striking case in point is Shirley Strum, an anthropologist who studied wild baboons under natural conditions, and found that they were very much more congenial creatures than the male anthropologists who had observed them at a safe distance made them out to be. Her account of the reaction of other baboon watchers to her discovery that her baboons were neither aggressive nor male dominated, but cooperative and family oriented, is illuminating. Her views were met with hostility and disbelief, apparently because she set out before the "male-dominant" field workers facts which challenged their own "observations."[14] Most interesting in this connection is the work of Margaret Power, a Canadian anthropologist, whose book, *The Egalitarians*, challenges the orthodox view that chimpanzees are naturally aggressive, dominance seeking, and fiercely territorial.[15] Power conclusively shows that all reports from natural non-artificially fed field studies are of nonaggressive chimpanzees living peacefully in nonhierarchical groups, on home ranges open to all. These reports have been ignored and downgraded by most of the scientific community, who failed to perceive that by artificially feeding the animals they studied they substantially altered the conditions of their lives.

Can it be that male anthropologists sometimes have difficulty in freeing themselves of their gender prejudices? What Power has achieved is the construction of a model of an egalitarian form of social organization, based on a fluid role relationship of *mutual dependence* between many *charismatic* chimpanzees of both sexes and other more *dependent* members. This highly and necessarily positive *mutual dependence* system is characteristic of both (undisturbed) chimpanzees and (undisturbed) humans who live by foraging, like gatherer-hunters, who do not have to wait for relief of their hunger. Margaret Power has opened up a view of foraging societies that will have a fundamental and refreshing effect upon anthropological science.

In the field of psychiatry, of interpersonal relations, and psychoanalysis, much highly original and important work has been done by women. I mention some names that come to mind: Theresa Benedek, Charlotte Buhler, Helene Deutsch, Anna Freud, Frieda Fromm-Reichmann, Karen Horney, Melanie Klein, Clara Thompson, Phyllis Greenacre, and Alice Miller.

In the field of social work the outstanding name is that of Jane Addams; indeed, the whole modern social-work movement from its inception to the present day has been almost wholly a development brought about by women; and so have the pre-school and kindergarten movements. It is not, we may suspect, by chance that when women in medicine choose to specialize they tend to choose such lower paying specialties as internal medicine, pediatrics, psychiatry, obstetrics, and anesthesia.

There are, of course, many excellent women doctors in the other branches of medicine; but women do not enter these as frequently as the others mentioned, not because of the predominantly masculine grip on cardiology, surgery, radiology, and the like, but because it would seem women physicians are happier when they can provide the support of their personalities, their sympathy and understanding, as well as their wisdom and skill, to their patients. The technical accomplishment of a cure or a surgical procedure does not constitute their greatest reward, as seems to be the case with the male. The male is interested in the performance of a task, in the solving of a problem; the female is concerned also with its human meaning and with ministering to the patient's need in the context of that meaning. The female doctor knows what the male doctor so seldom remembers: The care of the patient begins with caring for the patient. A survey of medical school applicants offers an interesting glimpse into the differences in attitudes held by men and women entering the profession. Male applicants place a higher value on "prestige and salary," while women choose more often "helping people" as their motivation for selecting a career in medicine.[16]

It is not so much the treatment of symptoms as of their underlying causes that characterizes the good caregiver. The doctor tends to focus on disease, the caregiver focuses instead on health, on prevention.

It took a woman to do what no man had done before, for it was Florence Nightingale who introduced humanity into the handling and nursing of wounded soldiers. Following her arrival in the Crimea, an army major wrote, in scorn of women's knowledge of hospital work, that the first thing she had done was to order two hundred scrubbing brushes! But in spite of the hostility and the scant encouragement, she initiated the organization of the first war hospital at the battlefront; and, indeed, it was she who succeeded in contributing most to making the nursing profession what it is today. It surely could have been predicted that this was one profession that women would make their own, for it is essentially the profession of caring. In the United States, Clara Barton (1821–1912), the "Angel of the Battlefield," who cared for the wounded during the Civil War, who helped gather identification records for the missing and the dead, and in 1881 founded the Red Cross in the United States, was also responsible for securing the important amendment providing Red Cross relief in catastrophes other than war.

Inventions by women have never been more than 2 percent of the total accepted in any one year at the United States Patent Office. I do not know what the proportion may be for other countries, but I doubt whether there are any in which it exceeds that of the United States. As for the typical masculine comment that women have contributed not a single invention to ease their lives in the kitchen, the answer may be that women have been so busy using, among other things, the gadgets invented by men that they have had no time left for inventing anything themselves. Lilian Gilbreth has pointed out that "men often have good ideas about housework chiefly because they don't like it much. The engineers sometimes say that they are careful to observe the laziest person in the plant. He is the one who thinks up the short cuts." In any event, a more than one housewife has remarked, the most useful domestic gadget ever invented is a husband.

The law and the ministry until recently made little appeal to women, and most churches actively discouraged them by refusing them ordination. Professions such as engineering and architecture have attracted a fair modicum of women. Of the more than 609 federal judges in the United States in 1979, 28 were women. Altogether, in the various courts of the country, about 200 women held important judicial posts. As in most professions traditionally dominated by men, the numbers are changing, albeit slowly, as more and more women join their ranks.

Many names of women could be cited who have done distinguished work in almost every branch of human endeavor. It is not, however, my purpose to make out a case for women as creative workers, even if it could be done; on a numerical basis alone one would not expect women to excel in as great numbers as men. The important fact is that in spite of the great discrepancies in the numbers engaged, many women *do* excel. Therefore the probabilities are high that it is not a biological incapacity that is responsible for women achieving "excellence" less frequently than men. Quite obviously there is nothing on the X chromosomes of women that debars them from attaining great distinction in any branch of human endeavor.

But how can we say this, someone is bound to ask, since there are innumerable fields in which women have not attained great distinction? Undoubtedly this is true, but one can be reasonably safe in saying that such fields are the ones in which women have not been engaged in as large numbers as men, and most certainly not for as long a period. Writing on this subject some hundred years ago, the great English humanist J. M. Robertson settled the argument with the following *responsum ad hominem*: No Englishman has yet written a great symphony or a great opera, and no American has yet written a great symphony, great opera, or great tragedy: Is it then reasonable to suppose that no Englishman or American is genetically capable of doing so? I leave the question to be answered by those who may feel they are competent to say whether or not any Englishman or American has done so. If adequate opportunity and stimulus are provided, great works will be created. Have women ever been provided with such opportunities and encouragements over an adequate stretch of time?

At the time when the male is preparing for that period in his life when his creativeness is likely to be at its highest, the female is turning in a totally different direction: toward marriage and a family. During the years spent in childbearing and child rearing, not to mention the enervating domestic chores that family life entails for so many women, whatever other creative abilities she may have had tend to fall into desuetude. There is no opportunity or stimulus to develop and exercise one's creativity. Were the male required to do all that the average woman has always been expected to do, how much would he achieve? Most males consider it a calamity when they are called upon to perform for a few days the domestic chores with which their wives deal virtually every moment of the day, year in and year out.

A commentary on some men's understanding of women's work is provided by a communication received by Dr. Alice Chenoweth which she quotes in an article in the *Journal of the American Medical Association*, 30 January 1960,

> Some years ago I was asked to answer a letter addressed to the 'Health Department' from a mountain man. It read, in part, as follows: 'Dear Sir: I am writing to ask your advice. I want some personal advice and not just some little papers or pamphlets.' He went on to say that when his wife had given birth to their first and second children she had got up in a day or two and begun helping him in the fields. Then he related what happened to her in each successive pregnancy—her third, fourth, and fifth; her sixth ended in a miscarriage. By the end of the first page she had had nine pregnancies. In her tenth she had a convulsion, then followed her eleventh, twelfth, and thirteenth. And now she was pregnant for the fourteenth time. She didn't want to do anything except lie around all the time. He didn't know whether she was getting lazy or not. He had heard when women had grown children they liked to sit down and let their children wait on them. The letter ended with the question, 'Can it be that my faithful wife don't want to help me anymore?'

A woman usually enters upon an occupation with a somewhat different attitude from that which characterizes a man. Most working women regard their work outside the home as important but secondary, or at best, unless they are career women, are committed to both a job and to the family. Such divided allegiance is not what men feel. Men regard their work as primary. Men make their occupations whole-time jobs, a way of life; their jobs take possession of them. Women do not have the same capacity for dissociation characteristic of men. Women think of marriage, home, and family as integral parts of their entire lives. Men are able to dissociate the family from their work and lead two separate existences, employing much greater concentration upon their work than upon their families. A woman's life is first and foremost bound up with that of her family, with her husband, her children; or if she hasn't a family of her own yet, with the hope and expectation of one.

Consider a typical situation in the professional field. The profession of medicine, for example, will bring the point out, as it were, in high relief. In medicine today, it is more likely than not that a woman will marry, and she is more likely than not to continue her career. It is, however, less than likely that she will have children, or that, having them, she will continue a fulltime profession. In fact, two-thirds of women doctors with active practices have children, and therefore limit their work hours. To some extent this is a factor in the disparity of earnings between genders in the medical profession.[17]

The responsibility for young children is the dilemma with which women in most professions are to a greater or lesser extent faced. The male, however, with his uncanny faculty for detaching his mind from his heart, his reason from his emotions, his work from his home, is seldom confronted with such a quandary. For him work and home are two utterly different worlds, so that when he arrives home it is, in large measure, to a totally dissimilar way of life, with new terms and symbols and relationships. The working male doesn't have the same kind of problems that the working female has. He is able to devote all of himself to his work when he is at it, for traditionally the male stakes his whole career upon his performance; a woman rarely does. For the most part women are busy creatively living the life that men can only paint or write about. Because women live creatively, when they write, as they so ably are increasingly doing, they bring an added dimension of humanity to their writing that makes, for example, the novels of Jane Austen, Virginia Woolf, George Eliot, and Toni Morrison among the most distinguished in the English language. Women create naturally, men create less sensitively.

Great gifts in a woman's mind and character, great achievements made by women, do not usually take the form that brings recognition and fame. Her medium is humanity, and her materials are human beings. Her greatest works remain unsigned, and fame and recognition are bestowed upon the work and not upon the artist. In a stirring address delivered at the tenth National Woman's Rights Convention, at the Cooper Institute in New York on 10 May 1860, Elizabeth Cady Stanton (1815–1902), a leading founder of the Women's Rights Movement in the United States, stated the case beautifully:

> In marriage either party claims the right to stand supreme, to woman, the mother of the race, belongs the scepter and the crown. Her life is one long sacrifice for man. You tell us that among womankind there is no Moses, Christ or Paul—no Michael Angelo, Beethoven, Shakespeare, no Columbus or Galileo, no Locke or Bacon. Behold those mighty minds so grand, so comprehensive—they themselves are *our* great works! Into you, O sons of earth, goes all of us that is immortal. In you center our very life, our hopes, our intensest love. For you we gladly pour out our heart's blood and die, knowing that from our suffering comes forth a new and more glorious resurrection of thought and life.

But in the masculine-dominated world, creativity in women can hardly be allowed a place. This is well illustrated by the story of the scholar who insisted that Shakespeare's plays had been written by Queen Elizabeth. The Scots minister Dr. Hugh Black challenged him. "Surely," he scoffed, "you don't believe a woman could have composed such masterpieces?" "You miss my point entirely," replied the scholar. "It is my contention that Queen Elizabeth was a man." Creative women, in the sense in which men usually understand the term, have frequently been childless. Let the reader make a survey of the creative woman of history and ask how many of them have been mothers. It is of interest to note that many women "become" creative after their children have grown up, and they are relatively free to pursue their interests. Such women are beginning to create in fields which were once considered the sole prerogative of men. The world of men is highly competitive, and women traditionally simply haven't been competitors. For millennia they were not allowed to compete with men; a woman's place was in the home, and women have from the earliest times been encouraged to look to the home and children as the fullest possible realization of their lives. If they were employed in any way, they usually regarded their employment as secondary to the most important business in life, that of having a family. Whereas men have concentrated most of their energies upon their work, most women have distributed their energies in the service of men. Men have never suffered from housemaid's knee. If men have been able to achieve as much as they have, not a little of their achievement has been due to the support that their women have given them, an achievement in great part due to the very home that the male is so effectively able to dissociate from his work! Support is another word for love, and love is woman's domain. Woman's concentration is on love first and only secondarily upon work, profession, achievement, and competition.

The explanation of the disparity in achievement of men and women is that, in addition to the barriers that have been erected against them, women have simply not been as interested for themselves in the kind of achievement upon which men place so high a premium. Hence, even if from the very beginning men and women had enjoyed full and complete equality, there would still have been a larger number of men than women in almost all fields of accomplishment. Because of this difference of interest I believe that there may always be some disparity in these types of creativity between men and women. I am not saying that women could not do as well as men if they could be interested in doing what men do, for there is every reason to believe that they could; all I am saying is that women, because they are women, are more interested in relationships, in which they can creatively love and be loved. As long as this remains the true genius of women, the world will be safe for humanity. On the day that women begin to outstrip men in the fields of worldly achievement, the human race will have to take its temperature. But I do not think that day will ever come, *not* because women aren't as intelligent or as well endowed with genius as men, but because women will increasingly tend to realize their intelligence and their genius in the most important of all areas for human beings—human relationships.

11

THE GENIUS OF WOMAN

AS THE

GENIUS OF HUMANITY

Woman is the creator and fosterer of life; man has, for the last half-dozen millennia at least, been the mechanizer and destroyer of life. The fact that men cannot have babies and suckle them, nor remain in association with their children as closely as the mother, has a profound effect upon their subsequent psychological development. Altogether apart from the psychological influences due to sexual physiological differences, the mother-child relationship confers benefits upon the mother that are wanting between father and child.

The maternalizing influences of being a mother have, from the very beginning of the human species, made the female the more humane of the sexes. The love of a mother for her child is the basic patent and model for all human relationships. Indeed, to the degree to which we approach in our relationships with others the love of the mother for her child, to that extent do we move more closely toward the attainment of genuine humanity. The mother-child relationship is an interdependent one. The interstimulation between mother and child is something the father misses, and he suffers from the want of it. In short, the female in the mother-child relationship tends to be more considerate, more self-sacrificing, more cooperative, more altruistic, and more involved than the male.

The female thus acquires, in addition to whatever natural biological advantages she starts with, a competence in social understanding that is usually more responsive to human need than the male's. The tender relationships that exist between mother and child belong to a unique order of humanity, an order in which the male may participate as a child, but from which he is increasingly caused to depart as he leaves childhood behind. Not so the female, whose practice in the art of human relations continues throughout life; and this is one of the additional reasons that enable women to perceive the nuances and pick up the subliminal signals in human behavior that men usually fail to perceive. The very words *sensitive* and *tender* are seldom parts of the male's vocabulary, or applied to his behavior.

Because women are unselfish, forbearing, self-sacrificing, and maternal, they possess a deeper understanding than men of what it means to be human. Women live the whole spectrum of life; they do not think in terms of achromatic black and white, "yes" and "no," or in terms of the all-or-none principle, as men are inclined to do. Women don't settle matters of life and death by saying, "Put him up against a wall and shoot him." They are inclined to say, rather, "Give him another chance." Women are more ready to make adjustments, to consider the alternative possibilities, and to see the colors and gradations in the range between black and white. By comparison with the deep involvement of women in living, men appear to be only superficially engaged. Compare the love of a male for a female with the love of the female for the male. It is the difference between a rivulet and a great deep ocean. In Byron's words:

> *Man's love is of man's life a thing apart*
> *'Tis woman's whole existence.*

Men, the world over, lack the depths of feeling which seem natural to women, most of all of what it is like to be pregnant, to give birth and love the child. Anyone who has ever observed the joyful expression on a mother's face when she sees her baby, no matter how painful or prolonged the labor and the birth may have been, can never forget or find Words adequate to describe it, the jubilance and the triumph together with the, powerful need to nourish the newborn's dependent needs are all there in her face. In a male dominated world obstetricians have not understood the nature of the relationship between mother and newborn and the vital importance, for example, of breastfeeding in directly conferring enduring physiological and psychological benefits upon mother and child, thus perpetrating a great hoax upon the public and an incalculable cost to the individual and society, not to mention innumerable other failures.

Few men understand women as they really are, living instead by the institutionalized ignorance of women in which they have been conditioned. Many years ago an Ethiopian woman eloquently threw some much-needed light on the subject when she explained to anthropologist Leo Frobenius,

> "A woman's life is altogether different from a man's. God has ordained it so. A man is the same from the time of his circumcision to the time of his withering. He is the same before he has sought out a woman for the first time, and afterwards. But the day when a woman enjoys her first love cuts her in, two. She becomes another woman on that day. The man is the same after his first love as he was before. The woman is from the day of her first love another. That continues so all through life. The man spends a night by a woman and goes away. His life and body are always the same. The woman conceives. As a mother she is another person than the woman without child. She carries the print of the night nine months long in her body. Something grows into her life that never again departs from it. She is a mother. She is and remains a mother even though her child die, though all her children die. For at one time she carried the child under her heart. And it does not go out of her heart ever again. Not even when it is dead. And this the man does not know; he knows nothing. He does not know the difference before love and after love, before motherhood and, after motherhood. He can know nothing. Only a woman can know that and speak of that. That is why we won't be told what to do by our husbands.[1]

Women love the human race; men behave as if they were, on the whole, uncomfortable with it. Men act as if they haven't been adequately loved, as if they had been rejected, frustrated, and rendered hostile. Becoming aggressive, they say that aggressiveness is natural, and that women are weak and inferior because they tend to be gentle and unaggressive! But it is precisely in the capacity to love, in their cooperativeness rather than aggressiveness, that the superiority of women is demonstrated;[2] for whether it be natural to be loving and cooperative or not, as far as the human species is concerned, its evolutionary history, its destiny, its very survival, are more closely tied to the capacity for love and cooperation than to anything else.[3]

It is in this, of course, that women can realize their power for good in the world and make their greatest gains. *It is the function of women to teach men from the moment of birth how to be human.* Women must not permit themselves to be deflected from their function by those who tell them that their place is in the home, in subservient relation to man. It is indeed, in the home that the foundations of the kind of world in which we live are laid, and in this sense it will always remain true that the hand that rocks the cradle is the hand that rules the world.[4] And it is in this sense that women must assume the task of creating men who will know how to participate in the process of making a world fit for human beings to live in. The greatest single step forward in that direction will be made when women consciously assume the task of teaching their children to be, like themselves, loving and cooperative.

Having been made to feel inferior to men all their lives, it seems only natural to expect many women to react to the feeling of inferiority, that the male-dominated world has produced in them, with behavior calculated to demonstrate that they are as "good" as men. It has been sagely remarked, "any woman who wants to be the equal of a man lacks ambition." By such behavior women do themselves and the world a disservice. Women do not have to, and should not, compete with men. They should not compete with anyone, any more than men should. Women and men should cooperate. That is what they are naturally designed to be, and that is what they are born to do. The function of women in relation to men is not to outdo men but to do for them what women alone are capable of doing; namely, to prepare them while they are children for the responsibility of being good, mentally healthy human beings.

Men must fully and sympathetically understand that it is not their occupation that is the most important, but that it is the occupation of the woman, the mother, that is the most important and significant in the world. Men must understand that if anyone is competitively handicapped in this connection, it is not the female but the male. But why speak of handicaps? Only to clarify them. Men have made women feel that childbearing and childrearing are handicaps that prevent women from competing with men. The most important occupations in the world handicaps! Alas! And yet this piece of nonsense, wrongheaded and stupid and awful as it is, has caused some women, particularly in our own time, to react with an overweening desire to compctc with mcn in their own fields, on their own ground, in order to prove their equality. How wrongheaded both attitudes are! Neither man nor woman should ever work in order to compete. Nor should women continue to measure themselves by male standards. To do so is to proceed in an utterly misleading direction. A thorough understanding of the differences between male and female, while leading to a promotion of the female, also leads to a promotion, not a demotion, of the male; for men, through better understanding, will be enabled to realize their potentialities quite as fully as women. This is an area in which both men and women can work together most cooperatively and creatively, in getting to understand each other better, in learning to think jointly, and in contributing to each other's happier development. As the distinguished American naturalist William Emerson Ritter (1856–1944) wrote in his last book, *Darwin and the Golden Rule*, "It appears to me certain that a major factor in hastening the socialization of the male will be his getting a deeper insight than he seems ever to have had into the real nature of the female in relation to the whole sexual, domestic, communal and political complex."[5]

Both men and women must clearly understand the significance of women's performing the role of mothers, of women's bearing, giving birth to, and being largely responsible for caring for and helping the child to fulfill itself. This, we now know, is the most important of all the tasks that any human being can be called to perform for another. Indeed, the findings of contemporary scientific investigations in this area have shown that no less than the future of humankind depends upon the manner in which the task is carried out. By virtue of the female's being biologically equipped to bear and nurse children, she stands in the most fundamental relationship it is possible for one human being to stand in relation to another, namely, as the support and sustainer without whom the child could not survive during its first nine months in the womb, and thereafter in only a deformed sort of way, unless a person can be found who will perform the functions of a mother. The function of the mother is to love her child. That statement contains all that it would be necessary to say on the subject were it not that a large number of persons in our culture do not understand the meaning of love. It is here that a note of caution must be sounded.

The women's movement has done magnificent work, though there are some extremists in it who argue that those who plead the need of motherhood, and who emphasize the importance of mothering in the first few years of the child, are engaged in a conspiracy to perpetuate the servitude of the female. Some women in the movement are apparently desperately in need of enemies, for even in the face of the abundant evidence they continue to maintain that a good daycare center can do just as well as a mother.[6] *Some* mothers, no doubt, and even better. But for the genuinely loving mother—and that is the only kind of mother who matters—there can be no substitute, whether she be biological or surrogate. When a baby is born, a mother is born too. It is a false view of "liberation" to believe that motherhood is a role from which women should be liberated. Liberated from what to what? From the oppression, discriminations, and injustices from which they have suffered, most certainly. But if women ever come to believe that they will be freed from the necessity of being mothers to their children, and that being a mother is somehow inferior to being a career woman, they will have betrayed themselves, and revealed how profoundly they have been brainwashed into accepting the mythology that males have imposed upon them. For the truth is that being a mother is the most important career anyone can be called upon to follow.

Women can and should enter any occupation or profession they choose. But when they become mothers they must realize that they have entered the most important of all occupations and professions combined, for what can be more important than the making of a loving human being? The demeaning references made by some in women's movement to women who choose to focus on family rather than career indicate how dangerous some of these female "chauvinists" may be. The needs of children are not incompatible with the rights of women, and any attempt to secure such rights at the cost of those children imperils all our rights. To see the child as an object rather than as a person is to reduplicate the offense that men have for so long committed against women. Women have a right to decline to have children, but if they do have them, they cannot abdicate that role in shaping their future. When Dr. Spock said, "I myself would say it is much more creative to rear and shape the personality of a fine, live child than it is to work in an office or even to carve a statue," women's liberationists may jeer him, as they did at their Political Caucus meeting in Washington in July 1971, but who else would disagree?

As Ian Suttie put it in his splendid book, *The Origins of Love and Hate*, "Any social factors therefore which stunt the character-development of women, contract her interests or lower her prestige with her children will interfere with her function of promoting the maturation of her children and their independence of herself."[7] And as Suttie goes on to show, disturbances in the maternal capacity to love constitute the major cause of mental illness, in the child and in the mother.

What is love? "Fool," exclaimed Sir Philip Sidney, "said my Muse to me, look in thy heart and write." But were any scientist to do so, his colleagues would almost certainly object. So let me, in plain English, and basing my answer on the interpretation of scientific findings, define love as the state of responsiveness to others during which we communicate to the other by demonstrative acts, to be tenderly regardful and wholeheartedly involved in satisfying the basic behavorial needs of the other. It means behavior calculated to confer survival benefits upon the other in a creatively enlarging manner. Not merely to enable them to live longer, but to live more fully realized than they would otherwise be. It means to communicate to them your profound involvement in their welfare, such that they can depend upon your being there to minister to their needs, to give them all the supports, sustenance, stimulations, and encouragements they require for their growth and development as warm, loving human beings. It means to communicate to them that you will be there whenever they have need of your answering to their need, that you will never commit the supreme treason of letting them down when they stand in need of you, but that they can depend upon you whenever they need you. That is love.[8] And that is what women, when they are not confused and rendered overanxious or turned into social workers in their own homes, have given or attempted to give their children. Where they have successfully been able to give such love to their children, the personality of the adult shows its effects, even though many other elements have entered into the making of that personality. Such a person will be capable of entering into meaningful relationships, of loving others, and of cooperating with them, living a life perfectible through love—by demonstrative acts of involvement with one another; and loving others more than one loves oneself.

Unfortunately, in many cultures, including our own, the natural capacity of women to love their children is made to express itself in a social matrix that often distorts and nullifies it, with resulting serious consequences to the development of the personality of the child and the person into which he or she will grow.

The most important thing in the world for a developing human being to enjoy is love, unconditional love. Fathers are parents, too, and their love for their children is important; but when everything has been said and done the love of the father does not compare in fundamental importance with the love of the mother for her child. Indeed, so long as the occupational roles of the parents in our society remain what they are, no one can ever take the place of the mother, or someone who acts as a loving mother.

If men continue to impose their views upon women as to how a family, a society, and a world should be run, and if women continue to act as the executors of men's will, the world will remain in the unhappy plight in which it finds itself at the present time; however, together, men and women can remold that world nearer the heart's desire by recognizing that the best way to make loving, cooperative, harmonic, and nonhostile human beings is by being so toward children. Men can help women make better men, as well as better women, by permitting women to realize their potentialities for being human to the fullest. The most satisfactory way in which men can serve themselves in this connection is by supporting them in their needs to fulfill their potentialities for loving their children.

The best way of remaking the world is not by changing the world but by changing the people who make the world the kind of place it is, by making human beings out of people. Unfortunately we have changed the environment more rapidly and more substantially than we have changed ourselves. Each of us must ask ourselves what we are doing that is really creatively relevant to the world in which we are living. Almost everyone will agree that there have been more geniuses for being human among women than there have been among men.

The true genius of women is the genius for being human, for being loving. In our materialistic age, because we have placed far less value upon the qualities for being human than we have upon those for accomplishment in the arts, sciences, and technologies, our values have become confused, undeveloped, and we have almost forgotten what the true qualities of love are. Surely the most valuable quality in any human being is the capacity for being loving and cooperative. We have been placing our emphases on the wrong values, and it is time we recognized what every man and every woman, at the very least subconsciously, knows: the value of being loving and the value of those who can teach that better than anyone else.

I hope I shall not be taken for an anti-intellectual when I say that intellect without humanity, without love, is not good enough, and that what the world is suffering from at the present time is not so much an overabundance of intellect as an insufficiency of humanity. Consider men like, Lenin, Stalin, and Hitler, as well as a sizable number of others, at the moment still respectable (allegedly elected by the people), whom I must forbear to mention. They are the extreme cases. What these men lacked was quite obviously the capacity to love. What they possessed in so eminent a degree was the capacity to hate and to be unforgiving. It is not for nothing that the Soviet Communists attempted to abolish the family and masculinize women, while the Nazis made informers of children against their parents and put the state so much before the family that it became a behemoth that well nigh destroyed everyone who was victimized by it.

What the world stands so much in need of at the present time, and what it will continue to need if it is to endure and grow in happiness, is more of the maternal spirit and less of the masculine. We need more fosterers of life and fewer wreckers of it. We need more persons who will love and less who will hate, and we need to understand how to teach them to do so; for if we do not try to understand we shall continue to flounder in the morass of misunderstanding that frustrated love creates. The tendencies to love with which the infant is born are frustrated, and frustrated love results in estrangement and aggression. Hatred is love frustrated. That is what too many men suffer from, and what an insufficient number of women recognize—at least too many women behave as if they fail to recognize it.

Let us remember that in the United States every fifteen seconds a woman is assaulted by her husband or boyfriend, and that one-third of the emergency calls to the police are made by battered women, and that the battered-woman syndrome is now a clinical entity. Many children are battered by their care-givers, be they parents, single parents, or boyfriends.

What many women have learned to recognize is that the much-bruited superiority of the male isn't all that men, so loudly advertising their own wares, have claimed it to be. The male seems to be neither as steady nor as wise as women have been led to believe. But on this subject there appears to be a conspiracy of silence. Perhaps women feel that men ought to be maintained in the illusion of their superiority because it might not be good for them or for the world to learn the truth. In that sense this book might have been entitled *What Every Woman Knows*. But one can't be sure that every woman knows it. What one can be sure of is that many women don't appear to know it, and even that there are many women who are horrified at the thought that anyone can possibly entertain the idea that women are anything but inferior to men. And there is the hostility of women toward their own sex, reflected in 18th century Lady Wortley Montagu's remark, "It goes far to reconcile me to being a woman, that I reflect that I am thus in no danger of marrying one." This sort of thinking did no one any good.

The world is in a mess. Men, without any assistance from women, have created that mess, not because they have been failed by women but because men have never really given women a chance to serve them as they are best equipped to do, namely by teaching them how to love their fellow humans. Women must cease supporting men for the wrong reasons in the wrong sort of way and thus cease enabling men to marry them for the wrong reasons, too. "That's what a man wants in a wife, mostly," says Mrs. Poyser in *Adam Bede*, "he wants to make sure o' one fool as 'ull tell him he's wise." But women, as James Stephens wrote, are wiser than men because they know less and understand more. Serving as natural mirrors, they have helped men reflect to twice their natural size. It is time that men learned the truth, and perhaps they are likely to take it more gracefully from another male than from their unacknowledged betters. It is equally important that women learn the truth, too, for it is to them that the most important part, the more fundamental part, of the task of remaking the world will fall, for the world will be remade only by helping human beings to realize themselves more fully in terms of what their mothers have to give them. Without adequate mothers life becomes intolerable, and Mother Earth becomes a battlefield upon which fathers participate in the slaying of their young and are themselves diminished. Old soldiers never die. Young ones do.

Though men have had a long tenure in mismanaging the affairs of the world, it is time that women realize that men will continue to run the world for some time to come, and that women can best assist them to run it more intelligently and more humanely by teaching them, when young, what humanity means. Thus men will not feel that they are being demoted but rather that their potentialities for good are greatly increased. What is more important, instead of feeling hostile toward women, they will for the first time learn to appreciate them at their proper worth. An old Spanish proverb has it that a good wife is the workmanship of a good husband. I am sure that even in Spanish societies it is no longer true. For of one thing we can be certain: A good husband is the workmanship of a good mother. The best of all ways in which men can help themselves is to help women realize themselves. In this way both sexes will come for the first time fully into their own, and humankind may then look forward to a happier history than it has thus far enjoyed. It was Matthew Arnold, that man of great sensibility, poet and critic, who, more than a hundred years ago, said, "If ever the world sees a time when women shall come together purely and simply for the benefit and good of mankind, it will be a power such as the world has never known."

The genius of woman is the genius of *humanity*, the ability to love others more than one loves oneself, and love, humanity, is the supreme form of intelligence. Humankind must learn to understand that all other forms of intelligence must be secondary to the developed humane, compassionate intelligence, for any form of intelligence that is not primarily implanted into a matrix of humane feeling and understanding is the most dangerous thing in the world. The clever can never be too clever when they are governed by the desire and the ability to think of the welfare of others even before they think of their own, for so to think and conduct oneself is to serve oneself better than one may in any other manner. It is that kind of intelligence that the world stands most in need of at the present time. It is that kind of intelligence that the world will always stand in most need of. It is that kind of intelligence with which women are so abundantly endowed. It is that kind of intelligence that it is their destiny to teach the world.

12

Mutual Aid

In this book I have had to deal with certain myths about women, myths that have grown hoary with the ages, and I have had to set out the facts. The facts, for the most part, completely controvert the myths, and the facts prove that, on the whole, the advantages are unequivocally with the female. This conclusion alone will be sufficient to elicit the sympathetic interest of most women and bring them rallying, even more devotedly than ever, to the side of their men, which is precisely as it should be. Men need women more than men need men. This is not to say that women don't need men; they do very much but not as basically, pressingly, as men need women; for just as a child needs the love of a mother if it is to develop healthily, so a man needs the love of a woman to maintain him in good mental and physical health. For his complete and adequate functioning he is more *dependent* upon such love than a woman is. In such a fundamental human situation women will not dream of considering themselves as anything but helpmeets to men. One can only wish that men would more profoundly understand what the medieval English poet Geoffrey Chaucer so well expressed almost six hundred years ago.

For this ye know well, tho' I would in lie,
In women is all truth and steadfastness;
For in good faith, I never of them sie
But much worship, bounty, and gentleness,
Right coming, fair, and full of meekéness,
Good, and glad, and lowly, I you ensure,
Is this goodly and angelic creature.
And if it hap a man be in disease,
She doth her business and her full pain,
With all her might him to comfort and to please,
If from his disease him she might restrain:
In word ne deed, I wis, she woll not faine;
With all her might she doth her business
To bring him out of his heaviness.
Lo, here what gentleness these women have
If we could know it for our rudéness!
How busy they be us to keep and save
Both in hele and also in sicknéss,
And always right sorry for our distress!
In evéry manner thus show they ruth,
That in them is all goodness and all truth.

Of course we do. But why in the name of goodness we men have done so little about this knowledge, and left it until so late, perhaps constitutes a commentary on our lack of understanding of ourselves.

We have been scared and we have been confused, and we have had to live within the framework of the male-dominated society into which we have been born. Something of the truth of Chaucer's words every man knows—which is a good point of departure on the rewarding journey of learning to know more—why Chaucer wrote a *Legend of Good Women* but no *Legend of Good Men*. And in "Tales of Melibeus," in *The Canterbury Tales* (1380?), he asks the rhetorical question, "What is better than wisdom. Woman. And what is better than a good woman," And answers, "No-thing." We are with Chaucer. Men can help women, and women can help men. Men should help women; women will help men, anyway.

The sexes are interdependent in a manner so biologically fundamental, their functions are so basically reciprocal, and they are so delicately related to each other, that any failure in adjustment between them is likely to have serious personal and social group consequences. Perhaps it need not be emphasized that such lack of adjustment has been characteristic of the greater part of humankind for a very long time, and that the consequences have been more than unfortunate. Just as the lack of adjustment between mother and infant may do irreparable harm to the mental health of the infant, so the lack of adjustment between the sexes has done damage to men and women and their children, and to the societies they constitute. Men cannot keep one-half of the human race in subjection and expect to escape the havoc they thus cause in themselves.

The tragedy is that modern men are caught in the web of a tradition they never made—a tradition that came to them as part of their social heredity but that they most often believe to be part of the biological order of things. But if men were conditioned in the truth, if they were afforded opportunities for studying and learning the facts, and if they were brought up in a society that hung question marks on antiquated traditions and on ideas that have been taken for granted, they might successfully disentangle themselves from the web of false traditional beliefs concerning women as well as themselves.

People have deep investments in their own illusions.

It is, however, not only a matter of disentangling oneself from the entanglements of the old and fallacious ideas and practices, but a question also of adjusting oneself to a new conception of the relations between the sexes. In these tasks women and men will have to work together; they will *need* to cooperate; and by doing so they can free each other from the shackles that have bound them for so long. By working together in harmony, men and women will confer the greatest benefits upon each other and upon the whole of humanity.

These are nice sentiments; but now let us proceed to a discussion of the rationale, the scientific basis for such ideas, so that readers may judge for themselves how well founded such recommendations are.

First I should like the reader to understand something of the basic meaning of social relationships; this done, we may then proceed to the discussion of the practical significance of the facts for the improvement of the relations between the sexes. It is a convenient academic device to start with the simplest types of organisms in order to show students as clearly as possible the main facts about an organism's functioning. I shall follow this procedure here. Remember, we are interested in the nature of social relationships.

If, under natural conditions, we observe a simple one-celled organism like the amoeba, we shall generally find it in association with other amoebas. Now, if we look at a number of amoebas long enough under a microscope we shall find that when the single amoeba has reached a certain size it begins to duplicate itself, that is, to reproduce. By studying the process of reproduction carefully, we will find that the nucleus of the amoeba, the central structure that contains the chromosomes, divides into two, and that the new nucleus flows into the protoplasm to the side of the maternal nucleus. There it remains with the protoplasm while certain other changes are going on, still quite within the same maternal cell membrane. Any changes induced in the protoplasm will mutually be responded to by both the maternal cell and the daughter cell that is coming into being. Whatever affects the one affects the other. There is a complete exchange of physiologically necessary substances between the maternal and daughter cells while they are still within the same cell membrane. There is a complete interdependent relationship; one is dependent upon the other.

Every living thing comes into being originally in this fundamentally similar interdependent manner. It is in the process of origin of one living thing from another, in the biologic relation of interdependency that the reproductive process constitutes, that the fundamental meaning of social relationships, of social life, is to be sought and understood. It is, indeed, in the pattern of interdependency that has been described for the single-celled organism that the significance of social relationships in the most complex of many-celled organisms is to be understood, for interdependency, no matter how complex the organism or how simple, is the basic pattern of the social state. Indeed, the earliest source of social drives may be perceived as an outgrowth of the original biologic interdependent relationship between genitor cell and offspring cell in the process of reproduction. Physical relatedness evolves to a much higher order of psychological complexity, but whatever the origin of relatedness, interdependency is the social condition that characterizes all living organisms, that is, responsiveness between organisms, or interactive behavior.

The social state is the process of interaction between organisms during which they confer survival benefits upon one another. In other words, social relationships are an extension and amplification of the physiologic relations obtaining between maternal organism and offspring. The suggestion is that apart from the very nature of protoplasm itself, which is cohesive, both maternal organism and offspring in the process of reproduction undergo an intensification of their physiologically cohesive or interdependent energies, with the result that the offspring experience strong impulses of attraction that cause them to remain in association with the organism or organisms of the same kind; while the maternal organism, as a consequence of the reproductive process, finds that her own tendencies for social aggregation are intensified and focused upon the needs of her offspring.

With rare exceptions, throughout the whole kingdom of life organisms are found in association. Excluding, possibly, certain insects, if one ever finds a solitary animal in nature it is either only temporarily dissociated from its social group or something else is wrong. In fact, when any living creature begins to isolate itself from the group, and tends to remain isolated, one can be certain that something is awry, or else that such behavior is actually conferring survival benefits upon the group. In short, social interaction and responsiveness is a well-nigh universal concomitant of life. Cooperation, not conflict, is the law of life.

Some years ago, as reported by Professor Chauncey D. Leake, president of the American Association for the Advancement of Science, a group of distinguished American scientists, following a fruitful conference of several days, formulated the following principle: "The probability of survival of a relationship between individual humans increased with the extent to which that relationship is mutually satisfying."[1] This is, of course, a special case of the more general principle: "The probability of survival of individual or groups of living things increases with the degree with which they harmoniously adjust themselves to each other and to their environment."

These principles apply to all human relationships without exception, and with particular force to the male-female, husband-wife relationships.

When we examine the manner in which these principles actually work in all individuals and groups, we find that the benefits conferred upon those mutually participating are striking. In addition to the great psychological benefits conferred, it has been found that in human beings every physical system of the body is benefited as well. Psychosomatic medicine and psychoneuroimmunology bear living testimony to that truth.[2] It has been found in recent years that children do not grow properly if their socio-emotional relationships are disturbed. Dr. Ralph Fried of Cleveland published a most impressive study on the subject, and workers in Canada and elsewhere independently made the same discoveries. May it not be that the psychosocial subjection in which women have been kept for many millennia has some connection with their greater sickness rate? Response to an unrelenting depressing environment is often expressed in chronic or frequent illness. When, however, organisms live together under cooperative conditions they contribute to one another in such a way as to enrich what can only be described as the fa-ulty to live.

To love thy neighbor as thyself is not only sound ethics but perfectly good biology; but even sounder than that is the principle to love thy neighbor even more than you love yourself, to live as if to live and love were one. The most immediate relationships in which this principle can best be applied are those of husband and wife, parents and children. If parents would learn what is known about these matters, and apply the knowledge in their family relationships as all of them, I am sure, would be more than willing to do if they possessed that knowledge, the greater part of the world's human problems would be solved, for it is in the home that human beings are formed, and it is human beings who mold the world according to the kingdom that is within them. We must understand that it is in the nature, dominantly in the nature, of human beings to be cooperative, to want to love and be loved. It is not in the nature of human beings to be aggressive and hostile. Aggressiveness and hostility are the responses of an organism that is frustrated, that has been thwarted in its expected satisfactions of love; such an organism, in many cases, turns to aggression in order to attract, to compel toward itself the love it seeks. Hostility arises when the organism feels itself both frustrated and threatened.[3]

It is only very recently that we have learned to understand these things as scientists; men of religion, prophets, seers, poets, and philosophers have understood them for thousands of years, while the remainder of poor struggling humanity has painfully striven to climb the ladder of their high ideals. But it has not been given to many to ascend beyond its lowest rungs. The source of much of man's difficulty has lain in the fact that for the greater part of humanity the struggle for survival has been an unremittingly hard one, in the course of which men have been forced into ways of life that hold the promise of being of benefit to themselves though they may be inimical to the interests of others. Such behavior is learned, it is not innate.

When people first began to grow into the ways of urban civilization, about twelve thousand years ago, and began to exploit each other as commodities, the ability to obtain the advantages that an urban civilization made possible a new standard of "success." Success was now no longer seen as being a good, cooperative member of one's society, but as the achievement of the money and the power to increase the material comforts of life. Though spiritual success was not denied as a possibility, as something toward which one might strive, the success that received increasing attention was material success.

The progress we flatter ourselves as having made since prehistoric times has been great, but in a very real sense it has meant a progress at the cost of many of our humane values. Our progress has been concentrated upon things, while spiritual values and our preoccupation with the truly good life have been allowed to lag, even to fall into desuetude. It sometimes seems that for every step forward we have taken in science and technology, we have taken one backward in morality; for every step forward we have taken in material civilization, we have taken backward in moral development. Hitler's extermination of millions of human beings, the dropping of atom bombs, government terror, fascism, communism, war, the competitive relation of man to man, all these things and much else appear to be evidence of a very real and serious deterioration of man as a moral human being. It is not that prehistoric humans lived in a Golden Age, as some thinkers have believed, but it was almost certainly not nasty, brutish, and short, as Thomas Hobbes imagined. However, of one thing we can be virtually certain: People were far more interested in one another's welfare than people of the Western civilizations of the world are today. Had this not been so, no human group could have survived to the present day.

The principal disorders of Western civilization today may be traced to the development of the competitive way of life in an increasingly competitive industrial world. However, it was not until the eighteenth century that it acquired a terrifying momentum that has accelerated with dizzying speed during the last two hundred years. The Industrial Revolution revolutionized the lives of the greater part of Western humankind; though it brought great benefits it also brought great disasters in its wake. Commerce, it has been said, through competition, is the lifeblood of a nation. All things compete, erroneously said the Darwinists. Evolution and the progression of species come about, it was argued, by means of a struggle for existence, through competition, and by the selection for survival of the fittest competitors. Society, opined the sociologist Herbert Spencer, mirrors the struggle for existence that is constantly going on in a state of nature. War is natural and good, said the generals, because it delivers the only just verdict on the fitness of nations to survive. You've got to be a go-getter, says the American creed, because if you're not, somebody else will go out and get what you want, and deprive you of the victory. You must get the highest marks, be first, be out in front, because this is a competitive world and the race is to the swift, and you've got to be a football hero to make a hit with the beautiful girls—even if it means breaking the leg of another player who is known to have a bad knee, or stepping on his hand and crushing it deliberately because he belongs to a minority group, or resorting to conduct that outrages every tenet of decency and sportsmanship. It's Civilization; Man's Own Show; Rugged American Individualism, you know. Well, America has made some progress, not because of competition, but in spite of competition, because people have frequently gotten together and done things. Competition is the striving of people against each other in order to attain the same goal. Greatest progress has been made when they have striven *together* to attain the same goal. But cooperation and competition have been sadly confused and intermixed, and the resulting disorder and its effects are nowhere better seen than in the United States, the land in which the competitive spirit is most highly esteemed!

The United States is one of the few countries in which it is possible to apply the term "aggressive" to a person in a flattering way. We like our men to be tough; we don't like our boys to be sissies because they've got to go out and fight for themselves. The tragedy is that many women have been trapped by this rough masculine doctrine into teaching their children to be competitors. Mothers will even bargain with their children for love that should be unconditional and the birthright of every child: "Junior, if you don't eat your cereal you won't make the football team, because you won't develop the necessary muscles, and Mama won't love you." In this, and in many other ways, Mother bargains with Junior for her love. Perhaps no American mother has uttered just those words, but most of us know from innumerable experiences that many mothers convey the essential meaning of such words to their children. Margaret Mead has appropriately called this bargaining type of love "conditional love." Junior must be a greater success than his father was, and, of course, Mary must do better for herself than Mama did. At the same time the children will receive an ethicoreligious training, in which they are told on the one hand that they must love their neighbors as themselves, and on the other that they must go out and compete with them. Yes, on Sundays you may fall upon your knees, and upon your neighors during the rest of the week. This is very confusing, and to most children, particularly adolescents, disturbing. Are adults hypocrites? Do they believe what they *say* or what they *do*? Quite rightly, children decide that adults believe what they do, not what they say. And so they go out and do likewise. In this way the vicious circle is perpetuated. The nationally cooperative organism is taught to be competitive, even though the ideals of the religion to which she or he may have been exposed teach cooperation, with a resultant internal conflict that is never successfully resolved.

Cooperation and competition are not mutually reconcilable drives. Either you are a cooperator or you are a competitor; if you are both, then you are in a state of disoperativeness, disconnectedness, of confusion, unreconciled and in conflict with oneself. And this is the state in which most members of Western civilization find themselves; this is the state that is essentially identified with the masculine spirit, the masculine role in society; this is the state from which men need to be weaned.

At a critical time in the development of their children mothers learn to reject the love of their sons, a love which the sons offer unconditionally but which mother cannot wholly accept. Unconscious, half-conscious, or conscious anxieties about incest, mother attachments, or fear of making the boy too soft cause many mothers to make the little rejections of their small sons' love, an experience which for the child constitutes a traumatic deprivation and frustration. The father's participation in this process in the form either of an unconscious or of a conscious jealousy of his son's place in the affection of his wife, complicated by the little boy's jealousy of his father, adds to the boy's feeling of privation and frustration and contributes to his store of aggressiveness and hostility. Clearly, the mother-son relationship is a particularly delicate one and requires the most sympathetic and gentle understanding.

If to be tough and crude and crass and competitive is to be a man, and if to be gentle, tender, kind, considerate, and cooperative is to be a sissy, then in the name of all humanity let us have fewer men and more sissies! But why grant the confused the solace of their own confusion or fall into their confusion by using their terms? What they contemptuously refer to by the term *sissy* constitutes the qualities usually associated with the female; and no man can bear the imputation of resembling in any way the "inferior" sex. But those very feminine qualities are the essential qualities of humanity—gentleness, kindness, thoughtfulness, and cooperativeness—and insofar as men have departed from these qualities they have departed from the true path of humanity. By this I do not mean to suggest anything so absurd as that it would be a good thing for humanity if men became women! I *do* mean to suggest that if little boys were helped to be gentle, kind, thoughtful, and cooperative, they would easily become so in their own masculine way. And in that endeavor, fathers as well as mothers can help. If fathers will themselves place a little less emphasis on being rough and tough, and more on being gentle, tender, and kind themselves, particularly in relation to their wives, their sons will observe, and do likewise, and humanity will be bound to make great advances in the right direction.

We have to understand that what any society considers to be the gender roles of masculinity and femininity are mainly arbitrary. Male and female are terms that refer to biological sex, *not* to gender sex. A biological male may by gender role be feminine, and a biological female may by gender role be masculine, and each may be all the gradations in between. A survey of the societies of the world shows that the vast majority of them are organized by and around males rather than females, and that statuses and roles are subject to this male dominance. Based on the biological differences between the sexes men have erected a superstructure of expectations, obligations, rights, and duties that they call statuses and roles. These gender roles are quite arbitrary, and their determinance by men has led to every conceivable discrimination by them against women. The long-entrenched dominance of the asymmetric gender roles in most societies has so solidified them that they have come to be accepted by almost everyone as expressions of the laws of nature. It is, for example, in the Western world generally believed that gender is a biologically, a genetically determined status. The fundamental error committed here is that gender is confused with sex. Sex is biologically determined; gender is to a great extent learned, and often plays a significant role in influencing adaptability.[4]

The species trait of *Homo sapiens* is educability, flexibility, and malleability, and adaptability, and it is particularly important at this critical period in our social development to understand that fact, to understand what it means to be human. What is to be comprehended is that within the limits of what is possible human beings are capable of learning anything. That whatever the biological or physiological components that enter into sexual behavior, sexual status, and sexual gender, their character, form, and expression are functions of the interaction between genetic potentials and the environments in which those potentials undergo development. What the evidence indicates is that every-where in human societies sexual behavior, gender, and yes, even society itself, are influenced not by genetic potentials, *but by the action of the individual's learning experience upon those potentials*. It is what society does with the genetic potentialities, and not what genetic potentialities do with society that creates human institutions. The genetic potentialities are possibilities and within the range of those possibilities culture can do virtually anything with them. In short, with the exception of the reproductive roles, sex roles and the roles of sex are what we choose to make them. And what we need to do in the socialization of the young is to humanize those roles to function in loving relationships with others, rather than in tyranny and exploitation of one sex by another, and of children by parents (however well meaning). And this, I believe, each of us can at least approximate, if we would but make the effort.

I thoroughly agree with Carolyn Heilbrun who, in her book *Toward a Recognition of Androgyny,*[5] has pointed out the dangers of an ideal of masculinity that emphasizes the characteristics of competitiveness, aggressiveness, and defensiveness. By placing such men in positions of power, we have greatly endangered our survival and ensured such tragedies as Vietnam and will continue in the brutalizing environment of the *man*made world.

The traits that men have called *feminine*—gentleness, tenderness, loving kindness—are human traits, and they are the very traits that males need to be conditioned in and develop if they are ever to be returned to a semblance of humanity.

The important thing for men to understand is why it is desirable to be kind and cooperative. The brief answer to that "why," which has been set out at greater length in the preceding pages and elsewhere, is that it is to the advantage of everyone to be so. To be cooperative means not only to confer survival benefits upon the cooperators but also to enlarge their capacity for living; it means the production of harmony, health, wealth, and happiness; it means to restore to human beings their ability to love, to work, to play, and to think—their mental health; and it means an end to conflict on the interpersonal plane and on the international plane, by being conciliatory, nonconfrontational. Someone has defined civilization as the process of learning to be kind. That is precisely what we need to do—to become more civilized, to learn to be kind; and that kind of civilization is a race between a loving education and catastrophe.

It is not sufficient for men to be kind to their children, which as yet they are from being: They must be kind to their wives also, to all women. Men need to understand that the principle of cooperation, like charity, begins at home, and that the best place to begin anew with the development of their own characters and their children's is in their relationships with their wives.

The husband-wife relationship is the proving ground of character. No less an authority than Balzac remarked that marriage is the best school for a man's character that was ever devised. For both sexes, marriage should be a continuing, and the best, part of one's education for living. It should be a mutual exchange of experience and stimulation contributing to the greater creative growth and development of each, of supports and assistance, of mutual working out of problems, of sharing and preparing for the requirements of parenthood and of being human in a world at war with itself. Above all, marriage should be based on friendship and mutual respect. And in the present state of the relations of the sexes I should add that on the man's part it should be accompanied by a sense of responsibility and obligation to his partner.

Men should feel it one of the obligations of marriage to make available, as far as it lies in their power, all the assistance they can to help their wives be more effectively what they desire to be. Men must realize, more profoundly than they seem to have done so far, what it is to be a domestic slave; they must learn that a woman should not be exclusively required to be her husband's maidservant, laundress, cook, concubine, nurse, and governess to the children, spending the first quarter of a century of her married life so employed, and the next twenty-five years recovering from the effects of bringing up the children, still unrelieved of her other duties. A woman is a person in her own right who wants to be, and should be, treated as something more than the good companion who happens also to be one's domestic slave.

Men are altering their attitudes toward women, and have been doing so for more than a hundred years, but their attitudes must undergo this final change; namely, that where they may have retained any doubts about the right of women to complete equality as a human beings and as citizens they must shed their doubts and freely acknowledge women have that right. And this means not only constitutionally and before the law but in all human relationships on the interpersonal plane. The first large-scale step in the cooperation of men with women will be achieved when men stop denying women their natural right to be what they want to be. It is a debt that men owe women, and payment is long overdue. The accumulated interest on the debt is enormous. Women don't expect to be paid the interest, compound or simple; which is all the more reason men should assume the obligation to discharge their debt and pay at least some of the interest by cooperating to the fullest in helping women to achieve complete emancipation from their long period of subjection to the supremacist male.

As men aid women to emancipate themselves, so will women aid men to emancipate themselves from the confusion that has prevented them from realizing the best that is within them. Mutual aid is the principle by which all human beings must live if they are to live most efficiently and most happily. Women will not assist men in the dual task of emancipating women and emancipating themselves if they continue to play the role of clinging vines or half-men. Let women be themselves. In human relationships it is much more important to *be* the right person than to expect others to be so.

In a hostile, warring world women alone preserve the understanding of love. It is time for them to realize this; it is time for them to take the world back into their arms so that once again men may know what it means to live within the bosom of the family. Men can afford to be magnanimous; they can, in justice, not be less. Women must have the wisdom to recognize that justice is on their side, and to be generous they could not be more; for women owe it not only to themselves, but to men, to their children, to civilization, to realize themselves, to be what it is in their nature to be, and not be content to remain what they have in so many cases become. Women play a very large role in determining the behavior of men toward themselves. Women must, therefore, take thought, and grasp the opportunity that is offered to help their men to help them achieve equality.

A democracy is as strong as it weakest links, and among the weakest links is the position of woman. It was Abraham Lincoln who said: "As I would not be a *slave*, so I would not be a *master*. This expresses my idea of democracy—whatever differs from this, to the extent of the difference, is not democracy." What is the extent of the difference between women and men in our democracy? The answer to the question will provide us with something of the measure of the changes that must be brought about—changes largely in the status of women—before we can speak of having a full democracy. Men and women must become partners in the greatest of democratic enterprises—the making of a democratic world; and a democratic world can be made only by persons who are themselves truly democratic. To label oneself democratic is not enough: One must *be* democratic.

Neither peace nor equilibrium can be achieved in a society in which the relationships between the sexes are out of balance. Most women and men wish to see a balance achieved, but they don't know quite how to bring it about. How is one to deal with innumerable little and big problems that must be solved before progress can be made? Women are discontented with their lot— not all of them, but enough to constitute for them and for society a very real problem. Men feel that all is not well, and that something ought to be done about it—but what? Perhaps as Elizabeth Wordsworth, the first principal at Lady Margaret Hall at Oxford wrote,

If all the good people were clever,
And all clever people were good,
The world would be nicer than ever
We thought that it possibly could.

But somehow 'tis seldom or never
The two hit it off as they should,
The good are so harsh to the clever,
The clever so rude to the good!

So friends let it be our endeavour
To make each by each understood;
For few can be good like the clever,
Or clever, so well as the good.

13

CHANGING TRADITIONS

Discontent is the mother of progress. Necessity is the mother of invention. And since discontent is almost a necessary condition of the life of the average educated woman of our day, progress and invention in the area of woman's place in the world are inevitable. Major changes have already occurred, such as the number of women in the work force and the professions. Others will continue to occur at an accelerating rate. The important thing is to see that we don't make too many mistakes; though we should avoid precipitancy we should not worry too much about wrecking the machinery of traditional social organization by exceeding the speed limit of rational inquiry; there need be no concern on that score, for we can expect the inertia of tradition to continue to some extent in the great tradition of tradition; namely, to act as a governor upon those who may be inclined to accelerate beyond the speed limit.

At this point it is very necessary to say some things that may rile some feminists. Friends, I hope, can be frank; let enemies be cautious. While the feminist movement has done much good by strenuously promoting women's rights in many ways, it has to some extent demeaned the family, and the unsurpassably important role of mother, wife, and child, and slighted the issue of individual choice. There are, however, clear signs that these attitudes toward the family are changing, and that we may predict calmer weather. The educated woman in the Western world finds herself faced with a peculiarly complex dilemma. She is educated to appreciate and to contribute to the world in which she lives in a much broader capacity than that of wife and mother. She wants to be a good wife and mother, but she also wants to participate in a significant manner in the work of the world outside the home. She subscribes completely to the view that the home is the most influential environmental factor in the molding of the human personality. She wants the love of her husband and children and the shared responsibility of making good human beings of her children, but she also feels that she has capacities and abilities that cry out for exercise and for the discipline of applying her mind to some useful purpose outside the home. But how can she be a good mother, a good wife, a good homemaker, and have a job outside the home too? I don't know whether anyone has ever given the answer to this question which I shall shortly attempt. I can only express the hope that its simplicity will not be too startling, or that it will not be thought too silly or impractical.

There still exists a general feeling that the married woman worker constitutes something of a problem. A married woman, it has been traditionally held, is the wife of her husband; her duty is to minister to his needs and those of their children. The husband's duty is to provide for the family; it is the wife's to look after the family. Many married women, and particularly those who have enjoyed the benefits of a college education, find the traditional view of the occupational roles of husband and wife too one-sided. Certainly, a wife should fulfill the obligations that are traditionally expected of her, but she has a right to expect her husband to do this in partnership with her. She should also have a right to a life of her own. If a married woman wishes to work, she should, when the conditions are appropriate, be free to do so, but her first responsibility should be toward her children, and this means staying at home and caring for them for at least their first half-dozen years. Many women have been sold a bill of goods by a vociferous minority of individuals in the women's movement, who have rejected the evidence of the importance of the mother's role in closely nurturing her children. These individuals are quite untroubled by the scientific evidence that has enriched our understanding of the indissolubly necessary bonding and mutuality, the attachment, that must develop between mother and child. Why? Because it is fundamentally necessary for the health physical and emotional development of the child.[1]

Motherhood is a privilege and the most important *of all the occupations in the world*. It is not something that can be relegated to someone else or to a "quality" day care center. There is no such thing as a part-time mother. For a married woman to be gainfully employed outside the home is in no way incompatible with her being a good wife and a good mother, and were the conditions essential for a happy family life—enjoyment of parenthood, of mothering, and also of fatherhood—made routinely available, this would be a far healthier society than it is today. We shall make some practical suggestions toward this end a little later in this chapter.

The changes that have been proceeding during the last fifty years in the occupational roles of women may come as a great surprise to many who read these pages. The proportion of U.S. families with both spouses in the labor force increased from 11 percent (almost 3 million couples) in 1940 to 22 percent (more than 7.3 million couples) in 1950. In 1997, more than half of the nearly thirty million U.S. families with children under the age of 14 were headed either by two working parents or a single working mother. In that same year, more than 60 percent of mothers with children under the age of six were in the workforce, and 76 percent of women with school-age children were similarly employed outside the home. Women comprised 46 percent of the total labor force in 1997, and according to the U.S. Department of Labor, jobs for women will account for 59 percent of total labor force growth by the year 2006. Fifty-nine percent of all women over the age of sixteen are labor force participants; this percentage increases to nearly 70 percent when for women between the ages of twenty and fifty-four.

These statistics reflect and give point to a major social and human revolution the importance, character, and consequences of which can hardly be overemphasized. It is a revolution which continues to bring about profound changes in the ways we think about ourselves and in the arrangements in which we order our lives and those of our children and other dependents. In short, something of a reorganization of society as we have known it, beginning with the family, is indicated. While it is true, as an ancient Greek remarked, that foresight is the last of the gifts granted by the gods to man, it is easy to see that the changes in family structure and functions due to the presence of millions of women in the work force will require completely new approaches to the challenges they present. The Department of Labor, the universities, and every possible private agency, new and old, ought to be engaged in planning for the New Age that is upon us, the Age of Partnership, of Cooperation, of Attachment.

It should be clear that we are already faced with a crisis that will not go away, but which will increase in intensity at an accelerating rate unless we put in place a public policy that satisfactorily meets the needs of parents and children in a land which only dimly perceives that a problem exists. The crisis, the problem, is: How do we meet the needs of everyone involved in the families of working mothers? In talking and writing about the problem which faces the working mother especially, namely, the freedom to work and at the same time take care of the child, the importance and primacy of the child somehow tends to get lost in the debate. What must always be the primary consideration is the wellbeing of the child. Whatever arrangements may be made for the future, it is well to remember that there is no substitute for a loving mother, not even a loving father, for fathers are unable to breastfeed their children, and breastfeeding should be available to every child for at least a year, preferably longer, for the benefits of the child as well as the mother.[2]

Most authorities agree that children under three are better off with their mothers at home. Yet it is working mothers with child-ren under three years of age who constitute the fastest growing segment of the work force. Many of these women will be employed in service or other positions during nonstandard hours, meaning they will work a schedule different from the traditional nine-to-five schedule. By the age of three, children need the experience and friendship of other children and people, and day-care centers can provide such opportunities. Until we have put in place those far better arrangements which I am about to suggest, we have to do what we can, as interim measures, with the following: maternity leave up to full pay for several years; paternity leave for a period to be determined according to the requirements of the situation; modulated working hours for parents; childcare arrangements in the workplace; childcare services in nursery and public schools; private care centers; childcare centers; family day-care homes; federal guidelines for childcare standards, registration, and licensing; before- and after-school programs; babysitters and the like—all should be as accessible as are our public schools in every community. These should be basic requirement, and this is where enlightened minds, and women in particular, must become so politicized, who by their organization and relevant pressures will bring about these necessary changes. Such arrangements should be fully supported by the government, as in Sweden, where the government encourages women to work, and their work force participation rates are nearly equal to those of men. In Sweden more than 90 percent of women twenty-three to fifty-four years old are in the work force. Were government-financed child-care systems so widely accepted by the public to be instituted here, more women would undoubtedly choose to work here.

Women today are in a privileged position. They have it in their power, by virtue of their indispensable presence in the work force in numbers which exceed those of men, to begin the rehumanization of society. Feminism has been more than good news, and for its accomplishments, in spite of some early errors, elicits our praise, but what is needed as a next step is a humanism. Women are now strategically well placed to bring the power of their numbers to bear upon the proper agencies, to make their voices heard and attended to, always remembering that some people are not so much hard of hearing as hard of listening. Toward this end one of the principal changes due to be made is the correction of the crazy sexual disparity that exists in the legislatures of the land, from federal to state and community. In this land in which there are always more women than men, and in which women live, on the average, six years longer than men, Congress is still shockingly short of equal female representation.

Let us here once more recall the words of Matthew Arnold: "If ever the world sees a time when women shall come together purely and simply for the benefit of the good of mankind, it will be a power such as the world has never known." More than a hundred years have passed since Arnold made that ringing pronouncement, and if it is to be realized it will only be by the politicalization that women seem to be ready for as the twentieth century draws to a close. Girls as well as boys must be taught to understand that politics is life, and encouraged to look forward to serving their country, not in the armed forces, but in the forces that will make arms a thing of the past, where in addition to work force and family, they will be equipped to serve their country at every level of government so that they may help to bring about a world of encouragement and opportunities for cooperative fulfillment.

We must learn to elect our legislators on the basis of their qualifications, first and foremost, as humane beings, with programs designed to solve problems and the knowledge and courage to work for the replacement of outmoded and wasteful institutions. This alone will require a complete reconstruction of the electoral system, and this especially is where women can play a major role. But that is a big subject that can hardly be dealt with here. Such changes will require a complete overhaul of our so-called educational system, which will function not as an array of instructional institutions but as truly educational enterprises, deigned to teach our children *how* to think rather than *what* to think, to develop that compassionate intelligence that will always put people before blueprints. Where teachers will be esteemed for what they are worth as educators, the acknowledged legislators of the world, and as such paid the highest salaries of any profession. This will, of course, require the training of such teachers for the privileged roles they will be called upon to play in the education of children from preschool to college—where every child's individuality will be recognized as a matter of course and be encouraged to grow and develop at his or her own rate, where the first qualification of a teacher will be the ability to love, and where children will learn to love by being loved. In the conduct of such a program it will become customary for parents and teachers to meet regularly to help each other in furthering the welfare of the child. Teachers, standing *in loco parentis*, will lay the groundwork that will enable the child in later years to become a loving parent. Where parenthood, the care of children, the most important of all the arts, replaces parentage, the perfunctory discharge of an onerous and restrictive obligation.

In this connection it is more than imperative to re-examine the grounds upon which we marry, the folklore, of loving that reduces tenderness to a physical act, a theatrical performance, or worse, a technical exercise. The modern myth of romantic love, for all its sweetness and light, has received mixed reviews in recent years. While it continues to dominate the popular imagination and to saturate the establishment media, it has repelled and exasperated a growing host of critics ranging in style from cool academics to overheated advocates. In the prevailing critical view, love of the romantic variety is not merely a fragile foundation for marriage but a dangerous potion when taken seriously. If these criticisms seem harsh, the statistical shambles of modern marriages which start out long on passion but short on understanding or even acquaintance—more than 50 percent of marriages in the United States end in divorce—speak for themselves. Both marriage and the family are clearly at a crossroads.

The attacks on the family from left and right—feminists, liberationists, communalists, and others—have certainly done nothing to strengthen the family. The mainstay of the criticism has been that the family is an antiquated institution for the exploitation of women in the unremitting service of their husbands and children. The criticism is justified; the family as an institution will have to be reconsidered. Clearly the future will see the acceptance of a variety of family types, and these will each present their own problems; in all these matters and many more, women have a fundamental role to play.

At this point it would be interesting to inquire what the effects are upon the family when the mother becomes a working woman. Of course, no generalized answer to cover all cases can be given. Such studies as we have that throw any light on the subject point uniformly in the same direction. The married woman worker has generally learned to systematize her housework so well that she experiences no difficulty. In one study, made in Philadelphia, over 62 percent of the working mothers maintained either that there had been no effect on the quality of their household management or that their housekeeping had actually improved. Many of these working mothers had learned the value of order and routine so well that their homes, in these respects, would compare very favorably with the best-run homes of non-gainfully employed housewives. Similar results are reported in a British study.

But what of the effects upon the children? As the figures given above show, many mothers don't leave home to work until their children are six or more years old. Even so, the children will generally not be at home without their mother for more than two or three hours. They get out of school at three or three-thirty, and mother returns after five. Mother would not see significantly more of her children, except at the very end of this period, even if she stayed at home. It is perhaps not difficult to understand why the working mother is often happier with her children than the mother who, having become progressively fatigued and exhausted with the routine chores of the day, awaits the return of the children from school with some trepidation. Feminists have claimed that the loneliness of the average housewife, when husband and children are away, would compare unfavorably with the kind of stimulation that the working mother receives from her workaday experience with the outside world. But this opinion is not supported by the finding of the polls on the views of working women. In 1981 the Harris poll found that 44 percent of working women felt that their working outside the home had negative effects, while 37 percent felt that their working outside had had positive effects, 14 percent felt that it had had no effects, and 5 percent were unsure.

A working mother may, however, work too hard, and she may be in no state to resume the cares of a household upon returning from work. Of course, this is highly undesirable, and no mother should engage in exhausting work. It is unnecessary to deal here with the exploitation of women as cheap labor, unequal pay for the same job, and discrimination against women workers. These practices are slowly losing ground, but unfortunately have not been completely eradicated. They are regrettable, and an unfortunate reflection upon the character of many employers.

Thus far, all I have attempted to do in this chapter is to show that more and more women, and particularly married women, are working, and will continue to do so, outside the home. It is a trend that no one can halt: The married working woman is here to stay. For the most part she works for the same reason that the married man does: to support the family.

During World War II the Women's Bureau of the Department of Labor conducted a study among 13,000 working women employed in all sorts of industries. More than half the married women planned to continue working in peacetime. Among the reasons they gave were: to support themselves and others, 57 percent; to save money in order to help buy a home or educate children, 21 percent; because they liked to, and because of the independence that working gave them, 22 percent.

Now, compare the statements of the unmarried women: 86 percent of the single women planned to continue working in peacetime, and of these 96 percent gave as their reason support of themselves or others; 2 percent were saving for a special purpose; and only 2 percent said they worked because they liked doing so.

In other words, after a taste of domesticity, one-fourth of the women who looked forward to marriage find a job outside the home a refreshing experience. There can be little doubt that increasing numbers of married women will continue to do so— and for much the same reasons that men do: It gives them a change, much needed stimulation, the acquaintance and friendship of persons one would otherwise never have known, the sense of doing something that is contributing to making the world move on its axis.

Men have seldom, if ever, considered the domestic activities, the homemaking of women as "work." In spite of the fact that they may have heard of the old saying "Women's work is never done," or similar observations, which can readily be dismissed as "old wives tales," they go steadily on in the belief that it is the "breadwinner" who works while his wife has a comparatively easier time. However, should the homemaker for some reason become incommoded and the stronger male is forced to take over his wife's duties, he is ready after three or four days for an ambulance or early retirement.

Men escape the chores of domesticity, seeing neither their wives nor their children for the greater part of the day. There are still some men who consider it an affront to their ego when their wives suggest that, for a change, they would like to savor the experience of the outside workaday world. A man is traditionally the support of the family—so the story goes. But women have been working for ages—on the land, in agricultural and industrial cooperatives, taking in piecework in the home, and the like— and in this way they have helped support the family. Until the advent of machinery many women of poorer families, even in large urban centers, helped to support the family. It has largely been a middle- and upper-class prejudice, now rapidly losing ground, that women shouldn't work. It is an issue upon which, after the children are sufficiently grown up, fewer men would quarrel with their wives than would have done so not so many years ago.

It is an interesting fact that while men will take every opportunity of emphasizing that it is a mother's task to look after the children, they will neglect to observe that a father is a parent, too, and that his responsibility to his children is no less than his wife's. Father usually relieves himself of the responsibility for the care of his children on the ground that practically all his time is consumed in the process of making a living; and having satisfied himself (if no one else) on this point, he complacently feels that everyone understands. But nobody understands—least of all himself. Making a living should not be a way of life, but a way of earning a living. The fact is that, in general, men don't enjoy domestic responsibilities and would do almost anything to avoid them. The traditional dispensation that enables them to get out of the house for the greater part of the day, and thus escape the incubus of domestic chores, is worth any sacrifice. Not that the average man doesn't love his home and family—but he loves dishwashing, laundering, changing diapers and baby clothes, cleaning the house, and making the beds less.

Certainly, the American husband is a great help around the house, and he's a fine fellow. But even so, they may be accused of running away—from their responsibilities as husbands and fathers; of vacating the privilege of participating fully in the growth and development of their families; of running out on the most rewarding experience of life, the molding and making of the character of another human being, in the process of which the husband and wife provide the life they brought into being with the skills and techniques for a loving human being.

When men abandon the socialization of their children to their wives, a loss is suffered by everyone, but perhaps most of all by themselves. For what they lose is the possibility of personal growth that the stimulation of bringing up one's children affords. Pearl Buck has put what I want to say so beautifully that I should like to quote her.

> It is perfectly true that women do not see enough of men here, and that the children suffer from the lack of influence of men

upon them in home and school. But men lose more. They lose very much when they relegate home and children to women. They lose fun and the excitement of growing, developing life— life which they have had a part in creating. But they lose something deeper than that. They lose touch with source of the life itself, which is deep in the very process of living with a woman and the children a man has created with her. When he lives not there but in his office, in his work, among other men, he is strangling the roots of his own being. If he can comprehend fully the one woman and can help her to comprehend him, they are both fulfilled. When they enlarge the mutual comprehension to include children, then the universe is within their grasp and they cannot be disturbed. They have life in their time.[3]

"They have life in their time." In our time, however, most men miss this quintessential experience of life, or partake of it fitfully. Next to the loss of mother love, it is the greatest loss a man can suffer; and in a very deep and significant sense it may be said that no man who has failed to take an active part in the "rearing" of children ever develops as a complete human being. Somehow women do not seem to suffer in quite the same way as men do from the effects of such privation, but suffer to some extent they do.

What, then, is the working man to do? After his arrival home is he to spend the remainder of the children's waking time with them? Should he spend a good part of his weekend with them? And what of the working mother? Should she do likewise?

It will be generally agreed that such cut-and-dried apportionments of time do not represent the best possible thing for the children; yet for some time to come many children, after they have passed the age of early childhood, will receive little more of their parents' time. I suggest that, granting the importance of parents for the development of good mental health, some better arrangement could be conceived whereby parents and children might enjoy a greater amount of time together. Our society would do well to consider the effects of the changing roles of parents, and to plan for the future in the light of these trends. I have a suggestion to make that, though at first it would involve certain practical difficulties and readjustments, would, I believe, solve many of the problems that bedevil both women and men and seriously affect our society. It is, otherwise, a very simple idea—too simple, I will be told, I'm sure.

I suggest that for married persons the working day be limited, on a voluntary basis, to half the normal working hours, that is, to four hours a day. Such an arrangement would immediately make it possible for each of the parents to spend not only a great deal more time with their children but with each other, and would result in other untold benefits to our society. It is not being suggested that such an arrangement would auto-matically produce these effects. In the majority of cases, one may speculate, it would greatly help. Working hours could be arranged so that husband and wife could work the same hours, either in the morning or in the afternoon, or one could work in the morning and the other in the afternoon, or stagger the hours whichever way was found most suitable. Thus at least one of the parents would be at home a good part of the day, or both of them would. Alternatively the presence of one parent throughout the day could be ensured simply by arranging alternative working days for each parent.

Making more time available to young parents would not in itself solve any problems; it is not time but the uses to which one puts it that are important. I am assuming that educational changes paralleling the changes here suggested will have occurred which will prepare young parents to put their new inheritance of time to healthy constructive uses. Wisely used, the bounty of increased time would make the solution of innumerable family problems so much easier; it would contribute substantially to the solution of the problem of leisure and assist our whole society to take on a less tired, less feverish look.

It has been calculated that no one in our society need work more than three hours a day in a five-day working week. All the work, and more, that is done today on a full week's employment could be done on a three-hour-a-day week of five workdays. I think we will eventually arrive at such a workday, but I am not suggesting it now. I am not suggesting that the five-day working week or the eight-hour day be abolished; such arrangements may be retained for unmarried persons and for all married persons on a voluntary basis. I am suggesting that as soon as women and men marry they be given the privilege of working only half a day, say a total of four hours each of the five days of the week, or alternatively if they wish only three or two-and-a-half days a week. When children arrive, the mother should not work for at least two years, and preferably six years, but should devote herself to her child and home; the husband should have the freedom to work no more than half a day or the reduced day week during this period and thereafter. Women and children could, indeed, have life in their time. And I see such working and family arrangements as these, as well as other benefits, as the product of the approach of the sexes toward a better understanding of each other.

I am quite aware that the four-hour working day or the reduced day week will be dismissed by many as impractical and that it will be greeted by others with derision. I should like to remind any such readers that many of the impracticalities of yesterday are the realities of today. Not so long ago many workers were laboring sixteen and eighteen hours a day, while the twelve-hour working day has been reduced to an eight-hour day, and in some cases to a six-hour working day. There were those who thought that the introduction of such short working hours would ruin our economy. The best answer to them is the economic history of the United States.

Let us be fair and try to see whether the suggested four-hour working day or reduced-day week has any merit at all. No one could expect it to be put into practice on an extended scale and all of a sudden, as it were; but do let us try it on a small, experimental scale, in various parts of the country and under varying conditions, and let us fairly judge the results. If the results are satisfactory, let us extend the four-hour working day for married couples. If the results are unsatisfactory, let us drop the whole idea. I am willing to predict that when it is tried and examined, workers who have had a four-hour working day or reduced workweek to look forward to will, on the whole, be found to be more efficient than those who have to contemplate the traditional working week. Anyone who has had any experience in such matters will, I think, agree. In considering the balance of incentives to work, students of industrial life have uniformly found that the most important factor in a worker's efficiency is contentment or happiness at work. In this, as in so many other matters, the secret of contentment or happiness lies not so much in doing what one likes as in liking what one ought to do.

The advantages of the four-hour working day and the three- or two-and-a-half day week are innumerable and far-reaching, the effects of such an arrangement could alter the face of our whole civilization and contribute to the improvement of human relations in the most effective and wholesome of ways. It would give men and women, for the first time in their lives, the time they have never enjoyed for doing something constructive about human relations. It would give them the time for fulfilling the primary function of life: *living*. As it is, most people haven't sufficient time to live, having become as they have, hostages to their work.

I conceive that the most important function of the four-hour day or reduced day week for family couples is to make more time available for the parents, and particularly the father, to be with their children and with each other. Even if one parent works in the morning and one in the afternoon, each will be in a much more fresh and happy state of mind than either would be at the conclusion of an eight-hour day. One could easily fill a large book by setting out the advantages of the four-hour day or reduced workweek, and I hope someone will do so. I do not, however, think that the advantages need be enumerated here; the reader, in reflecting upon the proposal, will readily see many of them. Once having granted the desirability of trying the experiment, a way must be found to make it a reality. In certain groups where conditions are favorable, as among teachers and in academic groups, such an experiment would be quite feasible. In the business world special arrangements would have to be made in order to conduct such an experiment. Indeed, the first steps in this direction will probably be taken by an enlightened private industry. And there is no reason why a movement for a four-hour working day for the married couldn't get under way. I am convinced that genuinely civilized living will not come about until, among other things, the four-hour working day or some-thing akin to it is available to everyone.

The development of these ideas—namely the choice employees may make, with the support of their employers, toward a more flexible work schedule—is very promising, and goes by the name of *flextime*. The reports, as of 1999 on flextime experiments thus far are highly favorable, and it is to be hoped that flextime will become a widely established practice.

In general, evidence has long indicated that no mother should abandon her child for a job before the child is six years old. Experts at the 1950 Midcentury White House Conference on Children and Youth agreed in its fact-finding report that such abandonment was undesirable. They said: "It may well be questioned whether most mothers can, without undue strain, carry a full-time job and still give responsive and attentive care to the physical and emotional needs of small children. The first six years have been shown to be crucial years for the child, who would seem to need a substantial share of the mother's time and attention during this period." Hence, short of the four-hour working day or the reduced hours or days a week, or flextime, I can see no satisfactory way of solving the problems of the mother of the preschool child, of the mother who wants to be a mother to her child and who also wishes to work outside the home. But until the four-hour day or some such working day arrangement comes into being, such mothers will have to resort to mother substitutes, nursery schools, and day care. These can never be adequate substitutes for a mother who wants to be a mother. Men as well as women must learn to understand these facts.

As men begin to understand women's true value, and abandon the myths they have traditionally inherited, they will come to view their relationship to women as a partnership conferring mutual benefits, as well as benefits upon all who come within the orbit of their influence. The freeing of women and increasing respect for them will mean the freeing of, and increasing respect for, men. Men need not fear that women will be transformed into men or that men will turn into women—there are certain biological arrangements in each of the sexes that will effactually prevent such development. On the contrary, each of the sexes will for the first time function as completely as it has hitherto functioned incompletely, for each of its members will have, for the first time, a full opportunity to realize themselves according to their own nature and not according to the "nature" that has been forced upon them.

What do the schools teach concerning the sexes? Largely what is taken for granted. But the schools could be a most powerful influence in readjusting the sexes to each other in the light of our newer knowledge and of the great benefits that will accrue from the application of our knowledge. Such facts and ideas as I have set forth in this book should be a matter of staple discussion in our schools and colleges and evaluated for what they are worth. From the very beginning children of opposite sex should be educated to understand each other; they should not be left to pick up the traditional myths they find so freely floating about in their culture. The essential human state is harmony, cooperativeness; our culture has managed to produce a complex separateness and lack of understanding between the sexes. Much effort will be required to break down this separateness, but I know of no better way to accomplish this than by education—the education of the sexes *for* each other, not in opposition to each other.

An ounce of example is worth a pound of precept any day. But in view of the probability that the examples will be rather slow in developing, education concerning the sexes will always remain necessary. The sooner we begin teaching the facts— and not only the facts, but the practice of their implications in human relations—the better.

The climate of opinion concerning the status and the relations of the sexes in recent years has undergone so favorable a change that the idea, for example, of a woman running for the presidency of the United States is no longer inconceivable. This marks a distinct advance. It is commonly acknowledged that the women who have been appointed or elected to federal and state positions have, even by male standards, done well. Indeed, American women in general have done extremely well, and this in itself constitutes one of the greatest tributes that one can pay to American men. Men have the women they deserve.

During the more than half a century of expanded research on the mother-child relationship since the Midcentury Conference of 1950, the findings of its contributors have been fully confirmed and widely extended. What is pressingly needed is that our government should make it possible for women to breastfeed their children for what has been shown to be a minimum amount of time, namely a year or as much thereafter as seems necessary or agreeable to both mother and child. The results that would accrue from the institution and encouragement of such a reciprocal relationship, would greatly benefit not only mother and child, but also the family and society. Since 1935 the Social Security Act has provided financial aid to families with dependent children, the old, the disabled, are made through Medicare payments, to all whose monthly incomes fall below state-specified levels. We must be grateful for such programs, but they all could stand much improvement by more attention to the needs of the child.

It is the warm embrace of the home, that haven from which we begin and are shaped by our parents, the family beyond all else, that provides the benison of love—that wonderful facilitator of all that the child will be as a warm, loving human being.

We hear much today of the breakdown of the family, of "dysfunctional families," of the lost extended family, that nourishing institution that flourished not so long ago, in which the benefits of parents, maternal and paternal grandparents, often great-grandparents, aunts and uncles, as well as teachers and playmates, provided a "togetherness," love, and awareness, discipline, and a primary education in human relations. Kinship meant an affinity, the proximity of multiple caregivers in the shared involvement in the welfare of the children, an enduring bequest that lasted a lifetime.

The mobility of Americans is such that physical and social disconnection between the members of the family and friends has become the order of things. In his novel *Howard's End* (1910), E. M. Forster makes a telling point by occasionally introducing into his narrative the phrase "only connect." It is very effective in underscoring the unconnectedness, the disabling effects, the social codes of the period, produced in thwarting communication between relations and friends, frustrating human feeling. The upper and middle class Victorians, alas, understood very little concerning the importance of love in caring for children, with consequences that led to the "cold fish syndrome," the inaccessibility of the Englishman, a dehumanization syndrome, a psychopathy ranging from mild to serious disorder.

When everything has been said and done on the subject, what will always remain are the biologically and socially formative influences of the mother on the child. As a Middle Eastern saying has it, "Since God could not be everywhere he created mothers." Modern civilizations have yet to recognize the fact that women are the creators of humanity. The evidence of archaeology and anthropology has revealed that this was probably the common belief of humankind up to about six thousand years ago. After that, invaders from the north, by their violence and the subordination of women, put an end to egalitarianism, and replaced it with male domination, androcracy.

The considerable scientific evidence that is now available proves without doubt that the involvement between mother and child is indispensable for the healthy development of both. That involvement should actively last from conception to the end of their lives. The truth and wisdom of this should help women to bring about those changes, which will, beyond all else, restore the mother and the child to each other, and so a renewed humanity. In the new-found chaos in which we are living, women are our last best hope.

Full restoration of egalitarianism will, of course, take time; however, the signs all point in the right direction. At this time thousands of women with children have no alternative other than to work in order to help maintain the family. This is at a cost that is unfortunate for everyone concerned, as well as to the community as a whole. Such a state of affairs produces an inescapable maladjustment, an instability, a lack of interpersonal relationships, connectedness and an enfeebled integration into the bonds of society. This unhappy state, suffered by many others for similar reasons, is known to sociologists as *anomie,* an alienation of the individual, a widely diffused unease. People recognize that a problem exists, but few understand how serious it is.

As the pediatrician Dr. T. Berry Brazelton has observed, "We are paying a terrible price for our nation's inattention to the increasing stresses on children and families." He went on to identify teenage violence, suicide, drug abuse, alcoholism, and pregnancy, as "obvious signals that our children are growing up with hidden anger, and self-destructive impulses."

There have been many conferences, monographs, articles, newspaper reports, and interviews with mothers faced with the problem of having to work and be caring mothers. The toll it takes upon their lives, as well as upon their children, is writ clear upon their faces. As one mother said, "being a parent is the greatest responsibility society can bestow on me, yet it's a terribly squeezed part of my life." Such women wonder how they can be good mothers, and work in order to support the family, as well as meet all the other demands placed on them, and perhaps even enjoy a moment for rest, and some time for themselves.

The serious effects the working mother and child suffer have been revealed in many scientific studies, but no government agency has been engaged enough to address the problem with the action it calls for. It is curable. The cry from the heart has been heard but gone unheeded. The causes and disturbing effects of anomie on the family constitutes a challenge that should become a major concern of government. Because it is women who are the most deeply involved in the personal struggle of combining home with employment, it will be mostly up to women to use the power that they possess, namely the *franchise*: the right to vote in local, state, and national elections, to bring about the changes which will free them and their children from the ravaging handicaps they now suffer. The call to action was loud and clear then, it is even more so today.

It is estimated that women cast more than one-half the ballots in national elections and yet full constitutional rights are not yet theirs. One of the most notable ways in which women can exercise their influence is through the ballot, principally by helping to elect to the legislatures of the land men and women who are sympathetic to their cause. Of the 540 members of congress as of June, 1999, only 65 (12.03%) are women. This can scarcely be called proportional representation. It is up to women to change this state of affairs; and it cannot be too emphatically stated that unless they exert themselves to bring about a fairer representation of their sex in Congress, no one else will. The government of this land, of every land, needs the brains, the ability, and the understanding of women. It should be a self-imposed obligation upon women to take politics more seriously than they have in the past. Women have an important contribution to make to their society, and one of the best ways to do so is through politics. Let it be remembered that politics is the complete science of human nature, the science through which human nature is ordered. If the world is to be remade, human nature will have to be remade, a task in which women must always play the leading role.

Who is to remake the world? It is a proper question to ask in a book of this sort, which has been written not simply to throw some light on the relations between the sexes with especial reference to man's injustice to women, but as part of the larger task of helping human beings to understand themselves better, to understand more fully how they came to be the way they are now, and what they can do about changing the conditions that make men and women function as unhappily as they frequently do at present. Who is to remake the world? Those who begin remaking the world by remaking themselves; those who will help future generations remake the world nearer the heart's desire by assisting to free the next generation, and the generations to follow, from the myths upon which their parents were bred; those who will make the truth available to the next generation in a humanizing way. They will do so not simply by stating the facts but by incorporating them into the lives of those who are to be the future citizens of the world in a vital and meaningful manner.

Women are already exercising a considerable influence in the realm of political and social action, an influence that is so conspicuously for the good, that one can only hope women will enter both the governments of their states and of their country in larger numbers than they have so far done. Not only their communities, their states, and their country need their help; the world also needs it. I have seen the ideas and action women have to offer in a multiplicity of different roles, and I have found them good. I recommend them to the attention of my fellow men, and particularly to those women who are wanting in sufficient faith in their own sex.

In the field of education women are being admitted in greater numbers as teachers in the colleges and universities, where, it is to be hoped and expected, their verbal abilities will reduce some of the dead weight of boredom that has afflicted so many campuses for too many generations! Pernicious academia is at present largely a disorder due to years of academic masculine inbreeding. But discrimination against women teachers at the higher academic levels is in many ways becoming a thing of the past.

Perhaps when the sexes have developed a better understanding of each other, men will not only cease to be appointed presidents of universities for the reasons that usually bring men that high privilege, but women will more frequently serve equally with men in such capacities.

On school boards and boards of higher education women already play a distinguished role. Parent-teacher associations throughout the country are almost entirely the doing of American women, and their influence for good in the schools and in the community, and thus throughout the land, has been incalculable.

Women are the cultural torchbearers in America; and even in the darkest parts of the land, wherever a gleam of light is seen it is usually cast from a source upheld by the hand of a woman.

14

WOMAN'S TASK

It was a Victorian saying that the last thing man would civilize would be woman. This was, of course, intended as a criticism of woman's alleged refractoriness. The Victorian male, ensconced in his fortified citadel of infallibility, aware of his own superiority and of the female's inferiority, employed the myth of female inferiority as the explanation of the female's unyieldingness to the blandishments of his conception of civilization. Perhaps it is a fortunate thing for the world that women, prevented from yielding to men's interest in things technological and material, have been able to pay so much more attention to people and their needs, and therefore are better equipped to solve the problems of humanity than most men.

Civilization is the art of being kind, an art at which women excel. Shall I be told that women can be quite as unkind and as bigoted as men? Indeed some can, and a great many other things too; but it is not natural for them to be so, any more than it is natural for men to be so. In general, women tend to retain a sympathy for the other, which so many men seem to lose. Men have done themselves the greatest disservice by comfortably basking in the spurious glow of their traditional attitudes toward women, and by so doing have left themselves out in the cold. In being unfair to women, men have been unfair to themselves, suffered untold losses in innumerable ways, and have crippled the development of their potentialities, for tenderness especially, and for kindness in general. In the Western world tenderness and gentleness have been identified as feminine, denied and unbecoming to men. The truth is, of course, that sensitive feeling and kindly conduct are neither feminine nor masculine traits, *they are human traits*, and like other human behavioral traits, they have to be learned.

One of the primary tasks of women will be to teach their children the meaning of tenderness and gentleness. In an emotionally illiterate society it is largely by the warmth of women's tenderness that the long ice age of man's emotions will be thawed. Machismo, the exaggerated sense of masculinity that stresses such attributes as physical power, virility, domination of women, and aggres-siveness, is a problem, a disaster, the consequences of which hang over us all like an invisible darkness in the sunlight. But we need not despair, for in the days of our darkness there remains a ray of bright hope. It is in the rebirth of our children. In this women will always have the key role to play. Civilization is not just a matter of living together in cities; it is also an attitude of mind. For the larger and more complex the community of which we recognize ourselves as members, the more certainly we are called upon, consciously and willingly, to abrogate our personal sovereignty, and to unite, as a genuine community to assist women, as the principal caregivers, through the family, to do what women are best qualified to do: create healthy, humane beings.

The natural superiority of women is a biological fact and a socially acknowledged reality. The facts have been available for more than half a century, but in a male-dominated world in which the inflation of the male ego has been dependent upon the preservation of the myth of male superiority, and the subordination of women, the significance of those facts has simply been denied attention. When the history of the subject comes to be written, this peculiar omission will no doubt serve as yet another forcible illustration that men see only what and how they want to see.[1]

Male supremacy has been dependent upon the maintenance of the myth of female inferiority, and as long as everyone believed that men were naturally superior to women, neither men nor women were disposed to perceive the facts for what they were. Beliefs and prejudices, especially when they are sanctioned by age and fortified by "experience," are often so much more convincing than facts. But facts, as Mr. Pecksniff said, "is facts"; and the truth does have a way of asserting itself, and eventually, of prevailing. I hope the facts have been made sufficiently clear in this book to cause the reader to reflect upon the possibility that women are naturally, that is, biologically, far better endowed in the viable fundamental respects of their being than has hitherto been generally understood or acknowledged.

Science is not a matter of private whim or personal prejudice; it is a public method of drawing rigorously systematic conclusions from facts that have been confirmed by observation and experiment. The facts cited in this book supporting the thesis of the natural superiority of women will be considered and evaluated by scientists and laymen alike. All that the author can claim to have done is to have set out those facts and offer his interpretation of them; as a scientist I have done my best to ensure their accuracy and to offer a sound interpretation of their meaning. It now remains for readers to evaluate critically what I have done. In the presence of startling ideas, the truly scientific attitude is neither the will to believe nor the will to disbelieve, but the will to investigate. Finally, let us always remember that a scientist is one who believes in proof without certainty, while other people tend to believe in certainty without proof. Furthermore, it should be remembered that facts do not speak for themselves, but are at the mercy of anyone who seeks to juggle them, and that selection of the facts often determines their interpretation.

I consider the theme of this book to be a most important one, for I am convinced, and I hope the reader will agree, that good relations between the sexes are basic to the development of good human relations in all societies. This should be obvious, yet men do not behave as if it were. Is it too much to hope that the claims herein made for the natural superiority of women will shake men out of their complacent acceptance of the myths of sexism? If I had thought that that was too much to expect, I should not have written this book. It is to be hoped that there will be some discussion of my contentions, and that is highly desirable; for the more we talk about the relations between the sexes, and the more informed we are while doing so, the more likely will be our progress toward establishing happier relations between them.

I hope it is clear to every reader that, in stating the case for the natural superiority of women, I have not been trying to demote men by upgrading women—nothing has been further from my mind. Nevertheless, I have been constantly aware that a book with a title such as this, arguing the case as it does, would lead some persons to believe that I am attempting to knock men down by elevating women above them. I cannot state too strongly that this has never been part of my intention. As a scientist, who has spent many years researching and teaching anatomy, physiology, evolution, genetics, child growth and development in medical school; as well as having been a biological and cultural anthropologist at several universities; and as a student of these subjects for some eighty years, I have enjoyed unusual opportunities to separate the facts from the entrenched male supremacist myths.

My intention has been to state the facts about women in order to correct the myths that have for too long served in place of the facts. As we have seen in the preceding pages, the facts prove that woman is biologically the superior organism, superior in the sense of enjoying, by virtue of her biological traits, a higher survival value than the male. These facts should forever dispose of the myth of the female's physical inferiority. Muscular strength should not be confused with constitutional strength. Constitutionally the female is the stronger sex.

It is either a fact or it is not that women are biologically superior to men. The way to deal with such a claim is not to ridicule or dismiss it, however cranky it may at first appear, but instead to attempt to disprove it—by setting out the evidence that accomplishes such disproof. It is quite understandable that there will be many who will argue that we have had more than enough of talk of "superiority" and "inferiority," and, indeed, we *have* when it is a matter of comparing populations and ethnic groups,[2] but in the comparison of the sexes the facts are indisputably in favor of the female. The sensible thing is to consider the meaning of those facts, and the social action they indicate.

With respect to psychological and social qualities, the facts again, it seems to me, have abundantly proven that women are superior to men. The proof here, too, is by the measure of our tests of biological superiority, for women, by their greater loving kindness and humanity, tend to confer survival benefits upon all who come within the orbit of their being more frequently than do men. Women are the bearers, the nurturers of life. Men have tended more often to be the curtailers, the destroyers of life. Clearly, as both men and women are necessary for the creation and continuation of human life, the fundamental pattern of cooperation that is here biologically indicated between the sexes is the one that should prevail.

Though it is a platitude to say that the sexes complement each other, men have not, on the whole, accepted the principle of complementarity of the sexes; most have insisted that women be the inferiors. It has been shown in this book that women are, on the whole, the superior organisms. Perhaps, swallowing this pill, together with their pride, as gracefully as they can, men may more easily hereafter be able to accept the idea that the sexes should complement each other. Each of the sexes has a great deal to learn and unlearn from the other; they can best do so by getting together on an equal though different basis. In other words, the sexes need to learn the truth about each other, to take stock in each other, and know each other's weaknesses and strengths.

The continuation of the human race is contingent upon woman's grace, provided that there is a man to respond to it.

Men will have to give up their belief in masculine superiority and learn that superiority is where it resides, regardless of an individual's gender. Men will have to accept that insofar as biological superiority is concerned, women have the edge on them; but there is not the least reason why this should upset the male ego. On the other hand, men should congratulate themselves that the mothers of their children are so well endowed. It has often been remarked that if men had to have babies, few of them would survive the ordeal. All men should be eternally grateful to women for undertaking the task. How good and pleasing a thought it is that women should be constitutionally, immunologically, stronger than men; that is as it should be, and that is as it is. The natural superiority of women is something for which we should all be grateful. When we recognize it for what it is, the biological safeguard of the species, we shall be all the more ready to cherish and respect it.

Human beings differ greatly in their abilities, but practically not at all along sex lines; that is to say, abilities are not determined by sex. Abilities are functions of the persons, *not* of groups, classes or gender. Hence, so far as abilities are concerned, both sexes should be afforded all the opportunities necessary to realize their potentialities; the judgment of their abilities should never be prejudiced by any bias of sex.

Nor should women ever accept any form of male patronage. They should no longer accept the view that the world be exclusively run by men.

As human beings women have a birthright the right to complete social and political freedom. It is only when this has been achieved that they will be fully able to realize themselves. No one can doubt that such equality will eventually be won by women. The important point is, the sooner it is done, the better; the sooner women accomplish this inevitable change, the sooner will the great contributions that women have to make to humanity become creative realities redounding to the benefit of all.

All human beings should enjoy the rights that are theirs by virtue of their being human, and not one iota of their rights should ever be abridged on the ground of gender.

Gender structures knowledge and power. To secure those rights women will have to labor hard. It cannot be too often repeated that they will have to do most of the work themselves in improving their status. Getting laws passed will not be enough; the long hard pull will be to achieve full recognition and acceptance of their abilities in all phases of national and international life.

It is by becoming actively participating members of their society through their work that women will make greatest progress. The work of the world has for too long been the exclusive preserve of the male, to the great detriment of humanity. There is every reason why it should not continue to be so. The male has sought to keep the management of the world in his own hands because it has satisfied an artificially encultured need within him—the need to feel superior. Women must help men to learn that working in cooperation rather than in opposition is the best support for their egos which they can receive. Men can go no further without women; they need the help of women in balancing the budget of effort and accomplishment; and women need to realize that among their unique contributions to society is what is so often called "the feminine point of view." A full-rounded judgment of most human endeavors is best achieved when it represents the combined wisdom of woman and man. Surely, most people who have made a success of their marriage are aware of this.

Because there is too much technologized economics in our society and not enough understanding of human relations, women can make another major contribution by introducing a greater understanding and practice of human relations in the business world. As one businessman, speaking for many others, remarked to me while showing me around his factory, "You should have seen this place before we employed women. They've civilized it." A scarcely higher tribute could be paid to women's capacity for human relations. Human societies must be based on human relations first, and economic activities must be a secondary function of human relations, not the other way round as they are in the masculine business world. Business is a way of making a living, it should never become the model for a way of life. Humanity comes before five-year plans and blueprints. This is an area in which women have heroic work to do. The genius for humanity that women naturally seem to possess, and develop so highly as mothers, will find material to work upon in every phase of life.

The most important of women's task is the making of human beings, with, or without partners. In this happiest and most rewarding of all labors of love, women bear a great responsibility, for they hold no less than the future in their hands. Because mothers are closer to their children than are fathers, they must of necessity play a more basic role in the growth and development of their children. The importance of mother love for the development of human beings healthy in mind and body is fundamental. Both mothers and fathers must love each other if they are to love their children as they need to be loved, for children learn more from what their parents do than from what they say. Love may not be all, but it is almost all. Women must be free to give their children the love they require, and men must assist them to do so. Here women have a redemptive role to play of the first order of importance, it is no less than the remaking of humanity. As the mothers of humankind women have from the very beginning played a dominant role in the making of human beings. As mothers they hold the basic pattern and patent on, and provide the model for, what humans should be, namely, lovers who love others more than they love themselves. This is clearly observed and defined in that selfless, all-embracing love that the mother has for her baby. Men must understand how much they have to learn from women. Here, indeed, is the great opportunity for mutual aid. The sexes are happiest, and will always be happiest, when they work and play together, creating happy homes and children, helping each other to realize the best that is within them, giving each other the space in which to grow.

Such a mutually creative and enlarging relationship need not be restricted to married life but can be extended to all the relationships between men and women. There is no reason why we cannot be of help to each other in every way, for all relationships between human beings are social and not biologically determined. Men should cease arguing about women and start getting to know them and thinking jointly with them. Toward that end the education of the sexes must receive a thorough reevaluation. The sexes should be educated in the understanding of each other, with opportunities for education that are in every way equal. Alfred North Whitehead, the distinguished philosopher, described education as the guidance of the person toward a comprehension of the art of life. Every person embodies an adventure of existence, and the art of life consists in the guidance of that adventure, an adventure in which men and women must participate equally. The prime business of a democracy, the great democratic task of men and women, is not the making of things, not even the making of money, but the making of humane beings.

The portents are good. During the last fifty years great strides have been made at an accelerating pace. There is every reason to believe that women, together with men, will continue to make progress in the right direction. It has been said that the belief in progress is the wine of the present poured out as a libation to the future. However, the expression of optimistic hopes is not enough. The progress that women have made has been largely of their own doing, and such progress as they achieve in future, it must be repeated, will be the result largely of their own hard work. It is the women who excel as women who will win success for the cause of humanity. As I have already said, the sexes should not compete; they should cooperate and complement each other. When they compete they do themselves and one another a disservice. Women should not try to be like men. Women do not serve the cause of humanity by aping men. This perfectly understandable pitfall must be avoided—namely, accepting the errors of judgment and conduct of so-called superiors who have made one feel inferior, and thereby becoming trapped by the values of one's oppressors. As a wit once remarked, "any woman who wants to be like a man lacks ambition."

Women must realize that they have been and are living in a patriarchal society, that men have tried to make them as they would have them be, and then convince them that as they have made them so it is natural for them to be inferior to men. Women have been more or less deliberately tailored to the pattern preferred by men, custom made, and thus accustomed to thinking of themselves as men's inferiors; women have been deformed and diverted from their true life's course to serve the misconceived needs of the male ego. The male has confused his needs, and he has badly confused women, but not half so badly as he has confused himself. Yet, though not half as confused as men, women are sufficiently so to be caught up in repeating a stereotyped pattern that turns out men as well as women who will uphold the old traditions. It is perfectly true that many men are what they are because they were raised by women but, it should be added, by women who were raised according to masculine standards of what both a woman and a man should be. Such traditional standards are unsound, and women know this better than men because they are less confused than men, and because, as the mothers of humankind, they are its original lovers. A serious and gratifying responsibility is placed upon women.

Women suddenly find themselves in much the same position as the United States finds itself in relation to the rest of the world. Almost too precipitately the United States finds itself the richest and the most powerful nation in the world, and its problem is the recognition of its responsibility to the rest of the world, the proper relation of its strength to the rest of the world's weakness. Similarly, the problem that women will have increasingly to face is the sudden awareness of her strength in relation to man's weakness. Recognition of this problem may prove unbalancing to some women, but when all the sound and fury has died down the question will remain: What can women do to pull humankind through?

Women must cease attempting to define themselves in the image of men and masculine values. Women must learn to respect themselves as women, and not to think of themselves as inadequate men. Respect must be based on self-knowledge and the knowledge of the high privilege of what it means to be a woman. When women understand what it really means, socially and biologically, to be a woman, in terms such as I have set out in this book, they can then confidently move out into the world and assume their rightful place in it. Not having been trusted for so long, many women lost faith in themselves. Women need to recover that faith. Women need confidence in themselves and a fuller awareness of the responsibility that being a woman entails. In the second place, women must assume the obligation of fulfilling their responsibilities, not as subjects of men, but as equally important, if not most important, members of the community of humanity. Women are the mothers of humanity; do not let us ever forget that or underemphasize its importance. What mothers are to their children, and to others, so will men be to men. What man has made of man, he has tried to make of woman, but he has never quite succeeded, for the mother that is in woman will keep declaring herself. Women must assume the full birthright of motherhood. I do not mean that all women must necessarily become the mothers of children—I use the word *mother* in a larger sense than that of the purely biological mother to refer to the woman who extends her love to embrace every person and all humankind, to those qualities that are exemplified by the mother's love for her child but that are also applied to all persons and to all humanity. Women are the carriers of the true spirit of humanity, the love of the mother for her child. The preservation and diffusion of that kind of love is the true function and message of women.

And let me, at this point, endeavor to make it quite clear why I mean the love of a mother for her child and not the love of an equal for an equal, or any other kind of love. Maternal love is the purest and at the same time the most proficient form of love because it is the most compassionate, because it is the most sympathetic, because it is the most understanding and the least censorious. Maternal love does not dispense justice; it neither condemns nor condones; it gives support while endeavoring to understand, and it never forsakes those who are dependent upon that love. Maternal love is much more than just, for it functions as if it were aware that justice without love is not enough. Justice is love digested through rational calcu-lation; love, more important, is justice adapted to the needs of the organism, and the maintenance of the organism then and thereafter in the warm ambience of its support. It is not like the justice that gets lost in the law. It is deep involvement in the other. This, surely, is the kind of love we would wish to see prevail between human beings, rather than the marketing kind of love that limits itself too narrowly and is conditional upon the fulfillment of certain strictly conventional conditions. Why cannot we love our fellow human beings as mothers love their children, unconditionally to love others more than we love ourselves? And why cannot we demonstrate this love without hesitation? Is there, would there be, anything wrong in loving our fellow human beings in this way? Indeed, I believe that there is not only nothing wrong with this way of loving human beings but that unless we learn so to love before much more time has elapsed we may not be able to love at all—we shall cease to exist. It is the way of love in which human beings may live most successfully and happily and in optimum health, and it is the evolutionary destiny of human beings so to love each other. I believe it is the unique function and destiny of women to teach humankind to live as if to live and love were one. Together we need to harness the unique energies of love to no less a task than the rehabilitation of our species.

Perhaps there has never been a time in the history of civilized humankind when all or most humans loved each other as mothers love their children. We can be certain, however, that in the long range of human history humankind has been slowly, painfully, and gropingly finding its way toward discovery of itself; toward a way of life in which human beings will love one another as mothers love their children, to love others more than one loves oneself. Virtually every religious and ethical system testifies to that fact, and as an anthropologist concerned with the study of human nature, I see it as one of the great goals toward which human society is striving. Hence the crucial importance of women in this evolutionary process, and the pressing necessity of becoming consciously aware of what has, for the most part, been attempting unconsciously to realize itself: the love of humans for each other.

True love is not so much self-denying as self-sharing, so suffused with humility and unpretentiousness, but also with strength, that those who exhibit it are not likely to dwell upon its meaning. Women know what love is. Let them not be tempted from their intuitive knowledge by the false idols that men have enthroned for women to worship. Woman must stand firm and be true to her inner nature; to yield to the prevailing false conceptions of love, of unloving love behind the show of love, is to abdicate the great evolutionary mission to keep human beings true to themselves, to keep them from doing violence to their inner nature, to help them realize their potentialities for being loving and cooperative. Were women to fail in this task, all hope for humanity would depart from the world.

> *Some day after mastering the wind,*
> *the waves, the tides and gravity,*
> *we shall harness the energies of love.*
> *And then, for the second time*
> *in the history of the world —*
> *we shall have discovered ourselves.*

Humanity has for too long been sidetracked from the principle of love, of gentleness, of cooperation, by which earlier societies managed to live more closely than modern socially disorganized societies have been able to do. This sidetracking was due, as we have shown in chapter 2, to the destruction of matrism (modeling on a mother-figure), and its replacement with patristic institutions by marauding patriarchal hordes who overran such societies. Every age is an age in transition, and never more so than the age in which we are living. I believe that it is the unique function and destiny of women to teach men to live as if to live and love were one. Not to produce a matriarchal society, but a partnership society.

> *From women's eyes this doctrine I derive:*
> *They sparkle still the right Promethean fire;*
> *They are the books, the arts, the academe*
> *That show, contain, and nourish all the world:*
> *Else, none at all in aught proves excellent.*[3]

Appendix A

United Nations Declaration
on the
Elimination of Discrimination Against Women

Adopted November 7, 1967, in the General Assembly:

The General Assembly,

Considering that the peoples of the United States have, in the Charter, reaffirmed their faith in fundamental human rights, in the dignity and worth of the human person and in the equal rights of men and women,

Considering that the Universal Declaration of Human Rights asserts the principle of nondiscrimination and proclaims that all human beings are born free and equal in dignity and rights and that everyone is entitled to all the rights and freedoms set forth therein, without distinction of any kind, including any distinction as to sex,

Taking into account the resolutions, declarations, conventions, and recommendations of the United Nations and the specialized agencies designed to eliminate all forms of discrimination and to promote equal rights for men and women,

Concerned that, despite the Charter, the Universal Declaration of Human Rights, International Covenants on Human Rights, and other instruments of the United Nations and the specialized agencies and despite the progress made in the matter of equality of rights, there continues to exist considerable discrimination against women,

Considering that discrimination against women is incompatible with human dignity, and with the welfare of the family and of society, prevents their participation on equal terms with men in the political, social, economic, and cultural life of their countries, and is an obstacle to the full development of the potentialities of women in the service of their countries and of humanity,

Bearing in mind the great contribution made by women to social, political, economic, and cultural life and the part they play in the family and particularly in the rearing of children,

Convinced that the full and complete development of a country, the welfare of the world, and the cause of peace require the maximum participation of women as well as men in all fields,

Considering that it is necessary to ensure the universal recognition in law and in fact of the principle of equality of men and women,

Solemnly proclaims this Declaration:

ARTICLE 1

Discrimination against women, denying or limiting as it does their equality of rights with men, is fundamentally unjust and constitutes an offense against human dignity.

ARTICLE 2

All appropriate measures shall be taken to abolish existing laws, customs, regulations, and practices which are discriminatory against women, and to establish adequate legal protection for equal rights of men and women, in particular:

(a)   The principle of equality of rights shall be embodied in the constitution or otherwise guaranteed by law;

(b)   The international instruments of the United Nations and the specialized agencies relating to the elimination of discrimination against women shall be ratified or acceded to and fully implemented as soon a practicable.

ARTICLE 3

All appropriate measures shall be taken to educate public opinion and direct national aspirations toward the eradication of prejudice and the abolition of customary and all other practices which are based on the idea of the inferiority of women.

ARTICLE 4

All appropriate measures shall be taken to ensure to women on equal terms with men without any discrimination:

(a)   The right to vote in all elections and be eligible for election to all publicly elected bodies;

(b)   The right to vote in all public referenda;

(c)   The right to hold public office and to exercise all public functions.

Such rights shall be guaranteed by legislation.

ARTICLE 5

Women shall have the same rights as men to acquire, change, or retain their nationality. Marriage to an alien shall not automatically affect the nationality of the wife either by rendering her stateless or by forcing on her the nationality of her husband.

ARTICLE 6

1.   Without prejudice to the safeguarding of the unity and the harmony of the family which remains the basic unit of any society, all appropriate measures, particularly legislative measures, shall be taken to ensure women, married or unmarried, equal rights with men in the field of civil law, and in particular:

(a)   The right to acquire, administer and enjoy, dispose of and inherit property, including property acquired during the marriage;

(b)   The right to equality in legal capacity and the exercise thereof;

(c)   The same rights as men with regard to the law on the movement of persons.

2.   All appropriate measures shall be taken to ensure the principle of equality of status of the husband and wife, and in particular:

(a)   Women shall have the same right as men to free choice of a spouse and to enter into marriage only with their free and full consent;

(b)   Women shall have equal rights with men during marriage and at its dissolution. In all cases the interest of the child shall be paramount;

(c)   Parents shall have equal rights and duties in matters relating to their children. In all cases the interest of the children shall be paramount;

3.   Child marriage and the betrothal of young girls before puberty shall be prohibited, and effective action, including legislation, shall be taken to specify a minimum age for marriage and to make the registration of marriages in an official registry compulsory.

ARTICLE 7

All provisions of penal codes which constitute discrimination against women shall be repealed.

ARTICLE 8

All appropriate measures, including legislation, shall be taken to combat all forms of traffic in women and exploitation of prostitution of women.

ARTICLE 9

All appropriate measures shall be taken to ensure to girls and women, married or unmarried, equal rights with men in education at all levels, and in particular:
(a)   Equal conditions of access to, and study in, educational institutions of all types, including universities, vocational, technical, and professional schools;
(b)   The same choice of curricula, the same examinations, teaching staff with qualifications of the same standard, and school premises and equipment of the same quality, whether the institutions are coeducational or not;
(c)   Equal opportunities to benefit from scholarships and other study grants;
(d)   Equal opportunities for access to programs of continuing education, including adult literacy programs;
(e)   Access to educational information to help in ensuring the health and well-being of families.

ARTICLE 10

1.   All appropriate measures shall be taken to ensure to women, married or unmarried, equal rights with men in the field of economic and social life, and in particular:
(a)   The right without discrimination, on grounds of marital status or any other grounds, to receive vocational training, to work, to free choice of profession and employment, and to professional and vocational advancement;

(b)   The right to equal remuneration with men and to equality of treatment in respect of work of equal value;

(c)   The right to leave with pay, retirement privileges, and provision for security in respect of unemployment, sickness, old age, or other incapacity to work;

(d)   The right to receive family allowances on equal terms with men.

2.   In order to prevent discrimination against women on account of marriage or maternity and to ensure their effective right to work, measures shall be taken to prevent their dismissal in the event of marriage or maternity and to provide paid maternity leave, and the guarantee of returning to former employment, and to provide the necessary social services, including child-care facilities.

3.   Measures taken to protect women in certain types of work, for reasons inherent in their physical nature, shall not be regarded as discriminatory.

ARTICLE 11

The principle of equality of rights of men and women demands implementation in all states in accordance with the principles of the United Nations Charter and of the Universal Declaration of Human Rights.

Governments, nongovermental organizations, and individuals are urged, therefore, to do all in their power to promote the implementation of the principles contained in this Declaration.

Appendix B

On the Origins of My Views
on the Natural Superiority of Women

The idea of the biological or natural superiority of women has so astonished many people that they have often asked me how I came upon such an "extraordinary" notion. I have attempted to satisfy their curiosity in what follows.

It all began, I suppose, in childhood, when I began to notice, about 1911, when I was six or thereabouts, that women were so much nicer than men. Men customarily greeted me, as they did other boys, would tweak my cheek, muss up my hair, and say, "What a nice boy you are," and then as abruptly go upon the even tenor of their way. I soon realized that this was a perfunctory conventional ritual granting men the liberty to express their hostility toward boys. Women, on the other hand, displayed a genuine and comforting interest in you. Far from tweaking your cheek they would gently caress it, and would warmly and pleasantly enter into conversation with you. Women, I found were kind; men were often cold-fishish, and thoughtless. There were some men who were nice, but when they were not they were horrid. Men seemed to be made of a coarser fiber than women. I heard of men who beat their own children. I never heard that said of a woman. Seated as I was in the land of English male supremacy and inaccessibility, I somehow divined the meaning of a cockney phrase I had occasionally heard, "If yer luvs us, chuck us abaht." I gathered that this was meant to be a cry for attention, even though it were to be at the cost of a physical beating. It was all very puzzling, and led to a great deal of wondering.

As an only child, and rather lonely, I felt uncomfortable, even unwelcome, an intruder in the family, as if I were living in a strange country in which people behaved in inexplicably bizarre ways and had no understanding of children whatever. It was clear to me, from their behavior toward children, that adults could never themselves have been children. And yet they often said things like, "When I was a boy . . ." And then there were photographs of them as children. So something must have occurred between the time when they were children—if they ever were—and the time they became adults, to cause them to forget what it was like to be a child.

And so I became deeply interested in discovering how adults came to be the way they were. It seemed to me a topsy-turvy world, in which children, given the chance, could certainly make better parents than adults, and where women, being so much kinder than men, ought to have been treated more humanely, and given more power in defense of children.

Books offered an answer. A prize book set me off in the right direction. By the time I was fourteen I had read books on anatomy, physiology, neurology, and psychology, but it was not until I had gone to university in 1922, at age seventeen, that I came upon Havelock Ellis's *Man and Woman: A Study of Human Secondary Sexual Characters* that I began to discover the clues for which I had been searching. The book was first published in 1894. It was probably the fifth revised edition issued in 1914 that I read. My major reading at this time was biology, cultural and physical anthropology, logic, philosophy, psychology, and psychoanalysis. The work of Ellis and Freud gave me a compass to steer by; as a result I was able to find my way into all sorts of fascinating subjects in which I read widely.

In 1924–25 I wrote a little book, in which I set out my ideas on the nature of the sexes, showing that the traditionally accepted views concerning that subject were quite unsound, and that, in fact, the differences, significant as they were, were much less than was generally believed. I entitled the book *Androgyne: Or the Future of the Sexes*, and sent it to C. K. Ogden, the editor of *The Today and Tomorrow* series, of which T. S. Eliot wrote, "We are able to peer into the future by means of that brilliant series [which] will constitute a precious document upon the present time." Alas, Ogden returned my manuscript without a single comment. I still have the manuscript, which I never again offered for publication. The few people who have read it say that it was too much before its time. Robert Briffault, author of *The Mothers*, read the manuscript in 1931 and commented on it in his article, "The Evolution of Woman," in that path-breaking symposium, *Woman's Coming of Age.*[1] But that was all.

As a student of physical anthropology I had learned in sexing skeletons (without going into detail here) that those that were delicately made—*gracile* was the term—were more likely to be female, while those that were more coarsely or robustly made were most likely to be male. This was also true in monkeys and apes and was regarded as evidence of greater evolutionary advancement of the female than the male. Ellis and the authorrities he so abundantly quoted confirmed these facts, and it was Ellis who pointed out that the fetuses and young of apes and of human beings are strikingly more alike than are their adult forms. Furthermore, the fetuses and young were much more like adult human beings than they were like adult apes. In short, humans, by retaining many more of their youthful features into adulthood, were so much more advanced than other primates. Finally, since women showed the childlike physical traits to a greater extent than men, women were so much more advanced than men. In setting out the conclusions to which his massive examination of the relevant evidence led, Ellis put it this way,

> [woman] bears the special characteristics of humanity in a higher degree than man . . . simply because she is nearer to the child. . . . She represents more nearly than man the human type to which man is approximating . . . Nature has made women more like children in order that they may better understand and care for children, and in the gift of children Nature has given to women a massive and sustained physiological joy to which there is nothing in men's lives to correspond. Men have had their revenge on Nature and on her protégé. While women have been largely absorbed in that sphere of sexuality which is Nature's, men have roamed the earth, sharpening their aptitudes and energies in perpetual conflict with Nature. It has thus come about that the subjugation of Nature by Man has often practically involved the subjugation, physical and mental, of women by men. The periods of society most favorable for women appear, judging from the experiences of the past, to be somewhat primitive periods in which the militant tendency is not strongly marked.[2]

It well may be imagined what such "revolutionary ideas," as they seemed to me, had upon my mind. Having gone to the references that Ellis so abundantly provided, as well as to other authors, I was fully able to confirm Ellis's conclusions, and that, unfamiliar to Ellis, the phenomenon he referred to had a name: *neoteny*, a term comprised of two Greek words, *neos*, meaning young and *teino*, meaning to stretch out; in other words, evolution or development by prolongation or time extension of fetal or young traits into adulthood.

I have devoted a whole book to this subject, namely, *Growing Young*, and extended the idea of neoteny to the behavioral traits of humans—that as persons we are designed to grow and develop our childlike behavioral traits through all the days of our lives, and not to grow up into fossilized adults who have never developed those early behavioral traits.[3]

But long before *Growing Young*, with the facts of neoteny I felt I was on solid ground in thinking of women as biologically more advanced than men. And so in the course of the years I collected all the evidence I could find bearing on the female's biological superiority, *against* as well as *for*. The evidence garnered from the scientific and medical literature was overwhelmingly in favor of the female's natural biological superiority, while that from my daily experience as an anatomist and biological anthropoligist in medical school and researcher in child growth and development, coupled with my years of everyday observation of the sexes, confirmed the fact that in virtually every respect the female was superior to the male.

From time to time I would talk to people about the superiority of women. Among those to whom I mentioned the idea was Norman Cousins, editor of *The Saturday Review*, and whenever we met he would say to me, "When are you going to write that article on women for us?" Time passed, until one day when I was a bit bored with what I was doing, I sat down at the typewriter and wrote the article from beginning to end without a single correction, and sent it to Cousins with the title "The Superiority of Women." Cousins approved the article and suggested the addition of the word "Natural," a suggestion I readily adopted. The article was published in the issue of March 1, 1952. The reader response to the article was so great (described as "an avalanche") that a number of issues had to be devoted to the publication of selected letters. In the July 4 issue, Dorothy Thompson, the well-known journalist, wrote a splendid commentary entitled "An Enormous Power," in which she underscored the main task of women, as follows:

What women need most of all, if they are to fulfill their social function, is to know themselves, and what they believe in as the result of their most profound and intimate experiences as lovers, wives, mothers and molders and conserves of the family; to trust that experience, and use it as a guide to their social and political decisions; and to find indomitable courage to stand up for their men and their children, in behalf of the power of Life and Love against the forces of Hatred and Death.

Doris Fleischman, a well-known publicist at the time, in her commentary entitled, "Facts Instead of Myths" in a subsequent issue, was highly critical of my article, both of its style and its content.

Observing the excitement generated by the article, the editors of *The Ladies Home Journal* and later *Look* reprinted the article in their pages. The president of the Macmillian Publishing Company got in touch with me and invited me to expand my article into a book. To this I agreed, and in the first week of May 1953 the book was published. I don't know of any book, before or since, which received so much attention from all the media, public and private. There were literally hundreds of reviews, and an immense correspondence initiated by readers of the book. There were many translations. A second edition appeared in 1968, a third in 1974, the fourth in 1991, and this, the fifth. In each edition I have endeavored to bring the book up-to-date while preserving the greater part of the original text.

Of all the reviews, one of my favorites was written by Max Eastman, the delightful writer, humanist, and early feminist.[4] The review was very full, critical, helpful, and concluded with the following words:

> There is a poetic justice in Montagu's book that commands high praise. It must be something above a hundred thousand years now since men began hammering home upon women, and anything that would listen from the rocks at the cave mouth in the surrounding hills, the natural inferiority of the female sex. Faint voices were raised against it, I suppose from the beginning. Bold radicals have occasionally cried out that the sexes are really equal. But this, I believe, is the first time since humanity became articulate that any male has had the hardihood to stand up in public and assert that, tumult and shouting to the contrary notwithstanding, women are the naturally superior sex. It's an overdue revenge, it's a step toward social balance, and it's a good joke on men.[5]

NOTES

FOREWORD

1. Richard J. Herrnstein and Charles Murray, *The Bell Curve* (New York: Free Press, 1994) J. Philippe Rushton, Race, *Evolution, and Behavior* (New York: Transaction Press, 1994).

2. For examples of this perspective in evolutionary psychology see Robert Wright's, *The Moral Animal* (New York: Pantheon Press, 1994) and John Townsend's, *What Women Want, What Men Want* (New York: Oxford University Press, 1998).

3. Aldous Huxley, "Forward" to the First Edition, 1942, in Ashley Montagu, *Man's Most Dangerous Myth*, 6ᵗʰ ed. (Walnut Creek, Ca.: AltaMira Press, 1997), 11–12.

4. Ashley Montagu, *The Natural Superiority of Women*, 4ᵗʰ ed. (New York: Collier Books [Macmillan], 1992), 8.

5. Montagu, *Man's Most Dangerous Myth*, 6ᵗʰ ed., 32.

6. Franz Boas, *Race, Language, and Culture* (New York: Macmillan, 1940).

7. Stephen Jay Gould, *The Mismeasure of Man* (New York: Norton, 1981).

8. Sir Arthur Keith in a famous rectoral address at the University of Aberdeen, as quoted by Boas in *Race, Language, and Culture*, 8.

9. Ibid.

10. United Nations Educational, Scientific, and Cultural Organization, *The Race Concept: Results of an Inquiry* (Paris: UNESCO, 1952).

11. Ibid.

12. Donna Haraway refers to the UNESCO statements on race as "sacred texts of mid-century biological humanism" in her magnum opus about the history of primatology, *Primate Visions: Gender, Race and Nature in the World of Modern Science* (New York: Routledge, 1989).

13. Boas, *Race, Language, and Culture*, 60–75.

14. Montagu, *Man's Most Dangerous Myth*, 35.

15. UNESCO, *The Race Concept: Results of an Inquiry*, 12–13.

16. Haraway, *Primate Visions*, 202.

17. See Chapter 9 of Pat Shipman's *The Evolution of Racism* (New York: Simon and Schuster, 1994). Shipman criticizes Montagu and others responsible for the UNESCO statements as motivated by political concerns rather than sound science. Her approach is sometimes oddly personal and antagonistic, as when she writes of Montagu that he has "a heightened sensitivity to possible racism that drives his professional life" (p. 160), one which she says he "projects onto others." Also see my review of Shipman's book ("Racist Science," *The Nation*, vol. 259 (28 Nov. 1994): 18.

18. For a discussion of the cultural context of Darwin's ideas regarding human gender, see Ruth Hubbard, *The Politics of Women's Biology* (New Brunswick: Rutgers University Press, 1990), chapter 7 "Have Only Men Evolved?," 87–106.

19. Charles Darwin, *On the Origin of Species by Means of Natural Selection*. London: John Murray, 1859.

20. Charles Darwin, *The Descent of Man* vol. 2. (London: John Murray, 1871), 327–28.

21. For further historical context, see Hubbard, *Politics of Women's Biology*, 87–106.

22. Patrick Geddes and J. Arthur Thomson, *The Evolution of Sex* (London: Walter Scott, 1889).

23. Wolfgang Wickler, *The Sexual Code: The Social Behavior of Animals and Men* (Garden City, New York: Doubleday, Anchor Books, 1973); Valerius Geist, *Mountain Sheep* (Chicago: University of Chicago Press, 1971); George C. Williams, *Sex and Evolution* (Princeton: Princeton University Press, 1975).

24. See Hubbard's *Politics of Womens Biology*, pp. 87–106; and Susan Sperling's "Baboons with Briefcases vs. Langurs with Lipstick: Feminism and Functionalism in Primate Studies" in R. N. Lancaster and M. di Leonardo, eds., *The Gender/Sexuality Reader*, edited by (New York: Routledge, 1997), 176–204.

25. For a discussion of some of the "contradictions, tensions, and paradoxes" from which patterns emerge in the historical context of Western gender ideology see L. J. Jordanova "Natural Facts: A Historical Perspective on Science and Sexuality," in Carol

MacCormack and Marilyn Strathern, eds., *Nature, Culture, and Gender* (Cambridge University Press, 1980).

26. "Biological humanism" is Haraway's term for these perpectives. For further discussion see chapter 8 of *Primate Visions*, 186–230.

27. For an able statement of this model see Sherwood L. Washburn and C. S. Lancaster, "The Evolution of Hunting" in Richard Lee and Irven DeVore, eds., *Man the Hunter* (Chicago: Aldine, 1968), 293–303.

28. Haraway limns the ideological and human engineering goals of Yerkes work with primates in "Animal Sociology and a Natural Economy of the Body Politic, Part I, A Political Physiology of Dominance" in *Signs* 4 (1978): 21–36.

29. The Japanese have undertaken important primate studies since 1948, including longitudinal studies of habituated groups of Japanese macaques (*Macaca fuscata*) as well as naturalistic field studies of other species in Africa and Asia. Many of these studies have only been made recently available through translation to English speakers. For a discussion of contrasting visions of primates cross-culturally see Pamela Asquith, *Some Aspects of Anthropomorphism in the Terminology and Philosophy Underlying Western and Japanese Studies of the Social Behaviour of Nonhuman Primates*, Ph.D. Thesis, Oxford University, 1981.

30. Linda Marie Fedigan *Primate Paradigms: Sex Roles and Social Bonds* (Montreal: Eden Press, 1982).

31. For a good summary of the genetic and behavioral evidence for a close relationship between humans and chimpanzees, see Richard Wrangham's "Ape Cultures and Missing Links" in *Symbols* (Spring 1995), 2–20. For a summary of revisionist data critiquing the "savanna hypothesis" for human origins see James Shreeve's "Sunset on the Savanna," *Discover Magazine* (July 1996), 116–25.

32. Jane Goodall, *Chimpanzees of the Gombe* (Cambridge: Harvard University Press, 1986).

33. Nancey Tanner and Adrienne Zihlman "Women in Human Evolution, Part 1. Innovation and Selection in Human Origins." *Signs* 1 (1976): 585–608; Adrienne Zihlman "Women and Evolution, Part 2. Subsistence and Social Organization among Early Hominids." *Signs* 4 (1978): 4–20.

34. Thelma Rowell "The Concept of Dominance," *Behavioral Biology* 11 (1974): 131–54.

35. Sandra Harding, *The Science Question in Feminism* (Ithaca: Cornell University Press, 1986); Haraway, *Primate Visions.*

36. For a discussion of Harding and Haraway's perspectives on feminism in science generally and primatology specifically, see Sperling "Baboons with Briefcases."

37. Haraway *Primate Visions*, 126–27.

38. Robert Ardrey, *African Genesis* (London: Collins, 1961), *The Territorial Imperative* (New York: Athenium, 1966), *The Social Contract* (New York: Athenium, 1970); *The Hunting Hypothesis* (New York: Athenium) 1976; Lionel Tiger and Robin Fox, *The Imperial Animal* (New York: Holt, Rinehart, and Winston, 1971); Desmond Morris, *The Naked Ape* (New York: McGraw Hill, 1967); Konrad Lorenz, *On Aggression* (New York: Harcourt, Brace, and World, 1966).

39. Jane Goodall, *In the Shadow of Man* (Boston: Houghton Mifflin, 1971); Elaine Morgan, *The Descent of Woman* (New York: Stein and Day, 1972); Evelyn Reed, *Woman's Evolution* (New York: Pathfinder, 1975).

40. Francis Dalhlberg, ed. *Woman the Gatherer* (New Haven: Yale University Press, 1981); Nancey Tanner, *On Becoming Human* (Cambridge: Cambridge University Press, 1981); Richard Lee, *The !Kung San: Men, Women, and Work in a Foraging Society* (New York: Cambridge University Press, 1979).

41. T. T. Bachofen, *Das Mutterecht* (Stuttgart, 1861).

42. Di Leonardo, *Gender at the Crossroads,* 4.

43. Thomas Kuhn, *The Structure of Scientific Revolutions* (Chicago: University of Chicago Press 1962).

44. Micaela di Leonardo, *Exotics at Home: Anthropologies, Others, American Modernity* (Chicago: University of Chicago Press, 1998).

45. Elizabeth Fernea, *Guests of the Sheik* (New York: Doubleday, 1969).

46. Rayna Rapp Reiter, ed., *Toward an Anthropology of Women* (New York: Monthly Review Press, 1975).

47. Michelle Rosaldo and Louise Lamphere, eds., *Women, Culture, and Society* (Palo Alto: Stanford University Press, 1974).

48. See the discussion of this material in di Leonardo's *Gender at the Crossroads,* 9.

49. Eleanor Burke Leacock, *Myths of Male Dominance: Collected Articles* (New York: Monthly Review Press, 1981).

50. See Marija Gimbutas, *The Gods and Goddesses of Old Europe: 7000–3500 B.C.* (Berkeley: University of California Press, 1974), and *The Language of the Goddess* (San Francisco: Harper and Row, 1989).

51. See di Leonardo's historical and theoretical contextualization of these works in *Gender at the Crossroads*, 1–48.

52. Gayle Rubin "The Traffic in Women: Notes on a 'Political Economy of Sex,'" in Rayna Rapp Reiter, ed., *Toward an Anthropology of Women* (New York: Monthly Review Press, 1975), 157–210.

53. See di Leonardo, *Gender at the Crossroads*, 10–17.

54. Frederick Engels (1884) *The Origin of the Family, Private Property and the State*, ed. By Eleanor Leacock (New York: International Publishers, 1972).

55. See di Leonardo's *Gender at the Crossroads*, 10–12.

56. Sherry Ortner, "Is Female to Male as Nature is to Culture?" in Michelle Rosaldo and Louise Lamphere, eds., *Women, Culture, and Society* (Stanford: Stanford University Press, 1972), 67–88.

57. MacCormack and Strathern, *Nature, Cutlure and Gender*.

58. Michelle Rosaldo," Women, Culture, and Society: a Theoretical Overview," in Rosaldo and Lamphere, *Women, Culture and Society*, 67–88.

59. Nancy Chodorow, *The Reproduction of Mothering: Psychoanalysis and the Sociology of Gender* (Berkely: University of California Press 1978).

60. Margery Wolf, *The House of Lim: a Study of a Chinese Farm Family* (New York: Appleton-Century-Crofts); Liz Crihfield Dalby, *Geisha* (Berkeley: University of California Press 1983).

61. Rayna Rapp, "Anthropology: Review Essay," *Signs* 4 (1978): 497–513. See also Maurice and Jean Bloch, "Women and the Dialectics of Nature in Eighteenth-Century French Thought," in MacCormack and Strathern, *Nature, Culture and Gender,* 25–41; L. J. Jordanova, "Natural Facts: A Historical Perspective on Science and Sexuality," in MacCormack and Strathern, *Nature, Culture and Gender,* 42–69.

62. Edwin Wilmsen quoted in Micaela di Leonardo, *Exotics at Home* (Chicago: Chicago University Press, 1998), 287. Also see Edwin Wilmsen, *Land Filled with Flies: A Political Economy of the Kalahari* (Chicago: University of Chicago Press, 1989).

63. Melford Spiro, *Gender Ideology and Psychological Reality* (New Haven: Yale University Press, 1998).

64. Jane Collier, Michelle Rosaldo, and Silvia Yanagisako "Is There a Family?" in Roger Lancaster, Micaela di Leonardo, eds., *The Gender/Sexuality Reader* (New York: Routledge, 1997).

65. Ibid., p. 74.

66. Ibid., p. 79.

67. Montagu, *The Natural Superiority of Women* 5th ed. (New York: Collier/Macmillan, 1992), 149.

68. Gould, *Mismeasure of Man.*

69. Janet Shibley Hyde, "Meta-Analysis and the Psychology of Gender Differences," in Barbara Laslett, Sally G. Kohlstedt, and Evelynn Hammonds, eds., *Gender and Scientific Authority* (Chicago: University of Chicago Press 1996), 302–22.

70. Ibid.

71. See Anne Anastasi, *Differential Psychology: Individual and Group Differences in Behavior*, 3rd Edition (New York: Macmillan, 1958); and Leona E. Tyler, *The Psychology of Human Differences*, 3d ed. (New York: Appleton, Century, Crofts, 1965).

72. Eleanor E. Maccoby and Carol N. Jacklin,eds., *The Psychology of Sex Differences* (Stanford: Stanford University Press, 1974).

73. See Janet Shibley Hyde's discussion of Block's critique and those of others on these issues in "Meta-Analysis of Gender Differences," 307–308.

74. Ibid., pp. 319–20.

75. See Adolph Reed, Jr.'s critical review of *The Bell Curve* in *The Nation* (28 Nov. 1994): 654–62. Reed examines the linkages between right-wing funding and the *Bell Curve* authors, as well as the history of the race and I.Q. issue in America.

76. See Daniel Kevles *In the Name of Eugenics: Eugenics and the Uses of Human Heredity* (New York: Knopf, 1985) for a comprehensive history of American and British eugenics movements and their effects.

77. See Reed's discussion of Gardner's points in *The Nation* (29 Nov. 1994): 657–59.

78. Quote by Reed in *The Nation*, 656.

79. This epigenetic perspective vs. the reductionist view of genetic determinism has been expressed by many modern developmental biologists and geneticists. See Susan Oyama, *The Ontogeny of*

Information: Developmental Systems and Evolution (Cambridge: Cambridge University Press, 1985).

80. Ashley Montagu, *Man's Most Dangerous Myth*, 6ᵗʰ ed.

81. Hernnstein and Murray, *The Bell Curve*.

82. Geddes and Thomson *Evolution of Sex*; Havelock Ellis, *Man and Woman* [1898] (London: A. & C. Black, 1934).

83. Carol Gilligan *In a Different Voice* (Cambridge: Harvard University Press, 1982).

84. See Susan Sperling and Yewoubdar Beyene " A Pound of Biology and a Pinch of Culture or a Pinch of Biology and a Pound of Culture: The Necessity of Integrating Biology and Culture in Reproductive Studies," in Lori D. Hager, ed., *Women in Human Evolution* (London: Routledge, 1997).

85. See di Leonardo's discussion of feminist postmodernism in *Gender at The Crossroads*, 17–27.

86. For a number of discussions of gay/lesbian studies, Lancaster and di Leonardo, *The Gender/Sexuality Reader*.

87. Sperling "Baboons with Briefcases," 204–34.

88. Quoted in Sperling, ibid., p. 215.

89. Ibid.

90. This perspective may be found in John Townsend, *What Women Want—What Men Want: Why the Sexes Still See Love and Commitment so Differently* (New York: Oxford University Press 1998).

91. Thomas Lacqueur, *Making Sex: Body and Gender from the Greeks to Freud* (Cambridge: Harvard University Press, 1990).

92. Susan Oyama, *The Ontogeny of Information* (Cambridge: Cambridge University Press, 1985).

PROLOGUE

1. Mary Cohart, ed., *Unsung Champions of Women* (Albequeque: University of New Mexico); Michael S. Kimmel & Thomas E. Mosmiller, eds., *Against the Tide: Pro-Feminist Men in the United States* 1776–1990 (Boston: Beacon Press, 1992); Anna Quindlen, "Life in the 30s," *New York Times* (10 September 1985); Katha Pollitt, "Are Women Morally Superior to Men?," *The Nation* (28 December 1992): 799–807.

CHAPTER 1

1. Germaine Greer, *The Obstacle Race: The Fortunes of Women Painters and Their Work* (New York: Farrar Straus Giroux, 1979). For women's achievements in a variety of fields, see Dale Spender, *Women of Ideas and What Men Have Done to Them* (London and Boston: Routledge & Kegan Paul, 1982); Debra R. Kaufman and Barbara L. Richardson, *Achievement and Women: Challenging the Assumptions* (New York: Free Press, 1982); Martha Tamara Shuch Mednick, Sandra Schwartz Tangri, and Lois Wiadis Hoffman, eds., *Women and Achievement: Social Motivational Analyses* (New York: John Wiley & Sons, 1975); M. Kay Martin and Barbara Voorhies, *Female of the Species* (New York; Columbia University Press, 1975); John Benditt (d.), "Women in Science," *Science* 255 (13 March 1972): 1365–73.

2. Cynthia E. Russett, *Sexual Science: The Victorian Construction of Womanhood* (Cambridge: Harvard University Press, 1989).

3. Ashley Montagu, *Man's Most Dangerous Myth: The Fallacy of Race*, 1st ed. (New York: Columbia University Press, 1942); 6th ed. (Walnut Creek, Ca.: AltaMira Press, 1998). For an excellent brief account of the influences that entered into the construction of the Nazi myth of race, see Henry Hatfield, "The Myth of Nazism," in Henry Murray, ed., *Myth and Mythmaking* (New York: Braziller, 1960), 220; Michael Demiaskleevich, *The National Mind: English, French, German* (New York: American Book Co, 1938).

4. Ruth Adam, *A Woman's Place: 1910–1975* (New York: W. W. Norton & Co., 1975); Kim Chernin, *Reinventing Eve* (New York: Times Books, 1987).

5. For the development of these views, see Ashley Montagu, *Growing Young*, 2nd ed. (Westport, Ct.: Greenwood Press, 1989).

6. There is an English translation with a superb introduction by Montague Summers: *Malleus Maleficarum* (London: John Rodker, 1928); Karen Sacks, *Sisters and Wives: The Past and Future of Sexual Equality* (Westport, Ct.: Greenwood Press, 1979); G. J. Barker-Benfield, *The Horrors of the Half-Known Life: Male Attitudes Towards Women and Sexuality in Nineteenth Century America* (New York: Harper & Row, 1976); Stephen Kern, *Anatomy and Destiny: A Cultural History of the Human Body* (Indianapolis and New York: University of Indiana Press, 1974); Sheila Rowbotham, *A Century of Women: A History of Women in Britain and the United States* (New York: Viking, 1997); Carol Camden, *The Elizabethan Woman* (Houston, New York, and London: Elsevier,

1972) Suzanne W. Hull, *Women According to Men; The World of Tudor-Stuart Women* (Walnut Creek, Ca.: AltaMira Press, 1996); Rosalind Rosenberg, *Intellectual roots of Modern Feminism* (New Haven: Yale University Press, 1982); Julia O'Faolain and Laura Martines, *Not in God's Image—Women in History from the Greeks to the Victorians* (New York: Harper & Row, 1973).

CHAPTER 2

1. Ashley Montagu, ed., *The Concept of the Primitive* (New York: Free Press, 1968).

2. John Pfeiffer, "Did Woman Make Man?" *New York Times Book Review*, (30 August 1981), 12; David F. Noble, *A World Without Women* (New York: Knopf, 1992).

3. Frances Dahlberg, ed., *Woman the Gatherer* (New Haven: Yale University Press, 1981), Riane Eisler, *Sacred Pleasure: Sex, Myth, and the Politics of the Body* (San Francisco: Harper, 1995); Tanner, *On Becoming Human.*

4. Agnes Estioko-Griffin and P. Bion Griffin, "Woman the Hunter: The Agta," in Dahlberg, *Woman the Gatherer,* 121–51; Tim Inglod, David Riches, and James Woodburn, eds., *Hunters and Gatherers,* 2 vols. (New York: St. Martin's Press, 1988).

5. Richard Borshay Lee, *The Kung San: Men, Women and Work in a Foraging Society* (New York: Cambridge University Press, 1979).

6. Richard Borshay Lee, "Male-Female Residence Arrangements and Political Power in Human Hunter-Gatherers," *Archives of Sexual Behavior* 3 (2:1974): 167–72; Susan Kent, ed., *Gender in African Prehistory* (Walnut Creek, Ca.: AltaMira Press, 1998).

7. C. Hutt, *Males and Females* (New York: Penguin Books, 1979). See also Carol R. Ember, "Cross-Cultural Perspective on Sex Differences," in Ruth H. Munroe, Robert L. Munroe, and Beatrice B. Whiting, eds., *Handbook of Cross-Cultural Human Development* (New York and London: Garland STPM Press, 1981), 531–80; Cynthia F. Epstein, *Deceptive Distinctions: Sex, Gender, and the Social Order* (New Haven: Yale Press, 1988); Beth B. Hess and Myra M. Feree, eds., *Analyzing Gender, A Handbook of Social Science Research* (Newbury Park, Ca: Sage Publications, 1987); Rhoda K. Unger, *Female and Male* (New York: Harper & Row, 1979); G. Rattray Taylor, *Sex in History* (New York: Thames & Hudson, 1954).

8. Ember, "Cross-Cultural Perspective on Sex Differences."

9.   Some early approaches were made by Gertrude R. Levy, *The Gate of Horn: A Study of the Religious Conceptions of the Stone Age and Their Influence upon European Thought* (London: Faber & Faber, 1948); Herbert G. Spearing, *The Childhood of Art* (London: Ernest Benn, 1930); André Leroi-Gourhan, *Treasures of Prehistoric Art* (New York: Abrams, 1967); H. Frankfort and H. A. Frankfort, eds., *The Intellectual Adventure of Ancient Man* (Chicago: University of Chicago, 1946); Otis T. Mason, *Woman's Share in Primitive Culture* (London and New York: Macmillan, 1985); Robert Briffault, *The Mothers*, 3 vols. (London: Allen & Unwin, 1929); Johannes Maringer, *The Gods of Prehistoric Man* (New York: Alfred A. Knopf, 1960); Sharon W. Tiffany, ed., *Women and Society* (St. Albans, Vt.: Eden Press, 1979).

10. Erich Neumann, *The Great Mother* (New York: Pantheon Books, 1955); Briffault, *The Mothers*; David Bakan, *And They Took Themselves Wives: The Emergence of Patriarchy in Western Civilization* (New York: Harper & Row, 1971); Marija Gimbutas, *The Gods and Goddesses of Old Europe: 7000–3500 B.C.* (Berkeley and Los Angeles: University of California Press, 1974).

11. Gimbutas, *Gods and Goddesses;* and *The Language of the Goddess* (San Francisco: Harper & Row, 1989). See also Eleanor Gadun, *The Once and Future Goddess* (San Francisco: Harper & Row, 1989); Margaret Ehrenberg, *Women in Prehistory* (Norman & London; University of Oklahoma Press, 1989); Gerda Lerner, *The Creation of Patriarchy* (New York: Oxford University Press, 1986); Merlin Stone, *Ancient Mirrors of Womanhood* (Boston: Beacon Press, 1991).

12. Gimbutas, *Language of the Goddess*, xx; Rattray Taylor, *Sex in History*.

13. *Gylany*, a term coined by Riane Eisler in her book, *The Chalice and the Blade* (San Francisco: Harper & Row, 1987), combining prefixes taken from Greek, *gy* "woman" and *an* "man," and the letter *l* standing for the linking of both halves of humanity in which both are equal. See also Eisler, *Sacred Pleasure*.

14. Gimbutas, *Language of the Goddess*, xx.

15. Davaid Bakan, *And They Took Themselves Wives;* Lerner, *Creation of Patriarchy*.

16. The Archaeological Institute of America, *Archeaological Discoveries in the Holy Land* (New York: Thomas Y. Crowell, 1967); Ralph Patai, *The Hebrew Goddess* (New York: KTAV Publishing House, 1967); Emmanuel Anati, *Palestine Before the Hebrews* (New York: Alfred A. Knopf, 1963).

17. Anati, 115.

18. Ralph Linton, *The Study of Man* (New York: Appleton-Century, 1936), 116.

19. Charles P. Mountford, *Aboriginal Conception Beliefs* (Melbourne: Hyland House, 1981); Ashley Montagu, *Coming into Being Among the Australian Aborigines,* 2d ed. (London & Boston: Routledge and Kegan Paul, 1974).

20. Agnes C. Vaughan, "The Genesis of Human Offspring: A Study in Early Greek Culture," *Smith College Classical Studies* 12 (June 1945): viii–117.

21. For an extraordinary and original early examination of this subject, including a magnificent discussion of the qualities of women and their denigration by men, see M. A. R. Tuker's wonderful book, *Past & Future of Ethics* (London: Oxford University Press, 1938). It is a book that will always be worth reading; it is a work which, as the Scottish philosopher David Hume said of his own great work, *A Treatise of Human Nature* (1739), "fell stillborn from the press."

22. Ashley Montagu, "The Origins of Subincision in Australia," *Oceana* 8 (1937): 107–207; Montagu, *Coming into Being.*

23. Over the last twenty years Fran Hosken of Lexington, Mass., has been performing the herculean task of producing a world survey of sexual mutilations and the status of women, *Women's International Network News.* See also the field work inquiry by Hanny Lightfoot-Klein, *Prisoners of Ritual: An Odyssey into Female Genital Circumcision in Africa* (New York: The Haworth Press, 1989); Ashley Montagu, "Mutilated Humanity," *The Humanist* 55 (July/August 1995): 12–15.

24. June Ehrlich, Mildred A. Moorehead, and Ray E. Trussell, *The Quantity, Cost of Medical and Hospital Care Secured by a Sample of Teamster Families in the New York Area* (New York: Columbia University, School of Public Health and Administrative Medicine, 1962), 3.

25. Edith Jacobson, "The Development of the Wish for a Child in Boys," *The Psychoanalytic Study of the Child,* V (New York: Free Press, 1954); Leon Salzman, "Psychology of the Female," *Archives of General Psychiatry* 17 (1967): 195–203; Francis Cerra, "Before Surgery, Second Opinion Urged," *New York Times* (8 August 1975), 28.

26. Ashley Montagu, "Physiology and the Origins of the Menstrual Prohibitions," *Quarterly Review of Biology* 15 (1940): 211–20; W.

N. Stephens, "A Cross-Cultural Study of Menstrual Taboos," *Genetic Psychology Monographs* 74 (1961): 385.

27. Sharon Lebell, *Naming Ourselves, Naming Our Children* (Freedom, Ca.: The Crossing Press, 1988), 9.

CHAPTER 3

1. Margarete Mitscherlich, *The Peaceable Sex: On Aggression in Women and Men* (New York: Fromm International Publishing, 1987).

2. N. J. Berrill, "Women Should Run the World," *Maclean's Magazine* 15 (February 1958), 8.

3. Thomas Jefferson, "Notes on the State of Virginia 1781–1785," Paris, 1785, in Saul Padover, ed., *The Complete Jefferson* (New York: Tudor Publishing Co., 1943), 607.

4. James Ritchie, "The Father's Role in Family-Centered Childbirth," *Midwife and Health Visitor* (1970), 305.

5. Susan Brownmiller, *Against Our Will: Men, Women, and Rape* (New York: Simon & Schuster, 1975); Diana Russell, *The Politics of Rape: The Victim's Perspective* (New York: Stein & Day, 1955); Duncan Chappell, et al., eds., *Forcible Rape: The Crime, the Victim, the Offender* (New York: Columbia University Press, 1977).

6. H. R. Hays, *The Dangerous Sex* (New York: G. P. Putnam's Sons, 1964).

7. H. H. Remmers and D. H. Radler, *The American Teenager* (Indianapolis: Bobbs-Merrill Co., 1957).

8. Naomi Wolf, *The Beauty Myth: How Images of Beauty Are Used Against Women* (New York: Morrow, 1991).

9. Rhoda K. Unger, *Female and Male* (New York: Harper & Row, 1979).

10. Ashley Montagu, *The Reproductive Development of the Female* 2nd ed. (Littleton, Ma.: PSG Publishing Co., 1979).

CHAPTER 4

1. Peter L. Berger and Thomas Luckmann, *The Social Construction of Reality: A Treatise in the Sociology of Knowledge* (New York: Penguin Books, 1971).

2. Ashley Montagu and Edward Darling, *The Prevalence of Nonsense* (New York: Harper & Row, 1967) and *The Ignorance of Certainty*

(New York: Harper & Row, 1970). Bergen Evans, *The Natural History of Nonsense* (New York: Alfred A. Knopf, 1946).

3. For many other accounts of similar female records see Marjorie P. K. Weiser and Jean S. Arbeiter, *Womanlist* (New York: Atheneum, 1981); Ann S. Harris and Linda Nochlin, *Women Artists 1550–1950* (New York: Knopf, 1976).

4. For an exhaustive list of cranial capacities of apes and prehistoric and contemporary humans, see Ashley Montagu, *An Introduction to Physical Anthropology*, 3d ed. (Springfield, IL: C. C. Thomas, 1960), 458–59.

5. Ellis, *Man and Woman* (1934), 119ff; Mathilde Vaerting and Mathias Vaerting, *The Dominant Sex* (London: Allen & Unwin, 1923). The great classic on the sexes: Hermann H. Ploss, Max Bartels, and Paul Bartels, *Woman: An Historical, Gynaeocological, & Anthropological Compendium*, 3 vols. (London: William Heinemann, 1935). See also Deborah , *Sex on the Brain: The Biological Differences Between Men and Women* (New York: Penguin, 1997).

6. M. Benedikt, *Kraniometric und Kephalometrie* (Vienna: 1888), 125.

7. Ellis, *Man and Woman*, 141.

8. I have dealt with this important subject in my book, *Growing Young*. See also Stephen Jay Gould, *Ontogeny and Phylogeny* (Cambridge, Ma.: Harvard University Press, 1977).

9. Arthur Keith, *A New Theory of Human Evolution* (London: Watts, 1948), 198.

10. Ellis, *Man and Woman*, 519.

11. Ashley Montagu, *The Human Revolution* (New York: Bantam Books, 1967).

CHAPTER 5

1. Alfred Hoet, personal communication.

2. N. J. Berrill, *Worlds Without End* (New York: Macmillan, 1964), 155–56.

3. Victor A. McKusick, *On the X Chromosome of Man* (Washington, D.C.: American Institute of Biological Sciences, 1964), 66.

4. J. H. Tjio, and T. T. Puck, "The Somatic Chromosomes of Man," *Proceedings of the National Academy of Sciences*, 44 (1958): 1229–37.

5. David T. Portilo and John L. Sullivan, "Immunological Basis for Superior Survival of Females," *American Journal of Diseases of Childhood* 133 (1980): 1251–53; Blum, *Sex on the Brain.*

6. Ernest B. Hook, "A Method for the Detection of the Contributioin of X Heterosis to Female Surivival," *American Journal of Human Genetics* 21 (1969): 290–92.

CHAPTER 6

1. Alfred Kinsey and Paul Hebhard, *Sexual Behavior in the Human Female* (Philadelphia: W. B. Saunders, 1953), 649–50.

2. William Masters and Virginia Johnson, *Human Sexual Response* (New York: Little, Brown, & Co, 1966).

3. Kinsey and Hebhard, *Sexual Behavior,* 649–50.

4. Geddes and Thomson, *The Evolution of Sex,* 270; Heather Remoff, *Sexual Choice: Woman's Decision* (New York: Dutton/Lewis Publishing, 1984).

5. N. Tinbergen, *Social Behavior in Animals* (New York: John Wiley & Sons, 1953), 22.

6. Kinsey and Hebhard, *Sexual Behavior,* 684.

7. Charles Wagley, *Amazon Town* (New York: Columbia University Press, 1965), 169.

8. Kinsey and Hebhard, *Sexual Behavior,* 353.

CHAPTER 7

1. M. Weissman and G. Klerman, "Sex Differences and the Epidemiology of Depression," *Archives of General Psychiatry* 37 (1977): 98–111; Robert J. Campbell, *Psychiatric Dictionary,* 5th ed. (New York: Oxford University Press, 1981).

2. Maggie Scarf, "The Moore Sorrowful Sex," *Psychology Today* (April 1979), 52. Also see her book, *Unfinished Business: Pressure Points in Women* (New York: Doubleday, 1980).

3. J. L. Evans, "Psychiatric Illness in the Physician's Wife," *American Journal of Psychiatry* 122 (1965): 159–63; Cuthbert Watts, "Depression—the Root Causes," *New Scientist* (4 Sept. 1975), 531–35.

4. Kathryn Lasky Knight, *Atlantic Circle* (New York: Norton, 1985), 14.

5. Mary Ann Mason, *The Equality Trap* (New York: Simon & Schuster, 1990).

6. Amram Scheinfeld, *Women and Men* (New York: Harcourt, Brace & Co., 1944), 214.

7. Ibid.

8. Ashley Montagu, *The Nature of Human Aggression* (New York: Oxford University Press, 1976).

9. Ashley Montagu, *Touching*, 3rd ed. (New York: Harper & Row, 1986).

10. W. B. Johnson and L. W. Terman, "Some Highlights in the Literature of Psychological Sex Differences Since 1920," *Journal of Psychology* 9 (1940): 327–36.

11. Scheinfeld, *Women and Men*, 214.

12. For a series of studies of these two groups see Donald C. Grayson, Differential Mortality and the Donner Party Disaster," *Evolutionary Anthropology*, vol. 2 (1993): 151–59; and "Human Mortality in a Natural Disaster: The Willie Handcart Company," *Journal of Anthropological Research*, vol. 52 (1996): 185–205.

13. J. Doyle, "Going to the Chair," *Buffalo Evening News*, (24 March 1971).

14. David Lester and Michele Alexander, "More than One Execution: Who Goes First?" *Journal of the American Medical Association* 217 (1971): 215.

15. E. Roberts, M. E. Cohen, J. J. Purtell, "Hysteria in Men," *New England Journal of Medicine* 246 (1952): 678–85. See also Ilza Veith, *Hysteria: The History of a Disease* (Chicago: University of Chicago Press, 1965).

16. For an illuminating discussion of these matters, see J. M. Masson, *A Dark Science* (New York: Noonday Press, 1986); J. M. Masson, *Final Analysis: The Making and Unmaking of a Psychoanalyst* (New York: Pocket Books, 1990); Veith, *Hysteria;* Alex Comfort, *The Anxiety Makers* (New York: Dell Publishing Co, 1970).

17. Rosamond Lehmann, "Three Giants: Charolotte Brontë, Mrs. Gaskell, and George Eliot," *New York Times Book Review*, (21 Dec. 1952), 5.

18. This is a subject which has been ably dealt with by Grace Shulman in her article, "Women the Inventors," *The Nation* (11 Dec. 1972), 594–96.

19. Mary Ellmann, *Thinking About Women* (New York: Harcourt, Brace & World, 1968).

20. Roger Fry, *Vision and Design* (London: Chatto & Windus, 1920), 96.

21. Scheinfeld, *Women and Men,* 223.

22. Nathan Masor, "The Relation of Age and Sex to Telling Lies," *Journal of the American Geriatric Society* 7 (1959): 859–61.

23. Helen Deutsch, *The Psychology of Women* (New York: Grune & Stratton, 1944), 136–37.

Chapter 8

1. Janet Lewis, "The Rise of Woman Power," *Institutional Investor* 23 (1989): 176–82.

2. Factsheet for the *1977 Catalyst Census of Women Board Directors of the* Fortune *500.* (1-212-777-8900).

3. *1996 Statistics on Women Business Ownership.* U.S. Small Business Administration.

Chapter 9

1. Helen Thompson Woolley, "Psychological Literature: A Review of the Recent Literature on the Psychology of Sex," *Psychological Bulletin* 7 (1910): 340.

2. For critical evaluations of IQ tests, see Harry Mensh and Elaine Mensh, *The IQ Mythology: Class, Race, and Inequality* (Carbondale: Southern Illinois University Press, 1991); Ashley Montagu, ed., *Race and IQ* (New York: Oxford University Press, 1975); Stephanie A. Shields, "Functionalism, Darwinism, and the Psychology of Women: A Study in Social Myth," *American Psychologist* (July 1975): 739–54.

3. George Stoddard, *The Meaning of Intelligence* (New York: Macmillan, 1943), 4.

4. Mensh and Mensh, *IQ Mythology.*

5. Montagu, *Man's Most Dangerous Myth.*

6. Howard Gardner, *Frames of Mind* (New York: Basic Books, 1983) and. *To Open Minds* (New York: Basic Books, 1989).

7. Anne Anastasi, *Differential Psychology,* 3rd ed. (New York: Macmillan, 1958).

8. Stoddard, *Meaning of Intelligence,* 274.

9. John E. Gibson, "Are Women Smarter than Men?" *McCall's,* April 1953, 56ff.

10. David Mines, "Life's Odds Are Against Women Mathematicians," *New Scientist* 26 (August 1962): 561.

11. John Ernest, "Mathematics and Sex," *New York Times* (27 July 1976); Blum, *Sex on the Brain*.

CHAPTER 10

1. Susan M. Ervin–Tripp, "Women with Ph. D's," *Science* 174 (1971): 1281.

2. Philip H. Abelson, "Women in Academia," *Science* 175 (1971): 127. See also Arie Y. Lewin and Linda Duchan, "Women in Academia," *Science* 173 (1972): 892–95; Grace Rubin–Rabson, "Women and the Professions," *Science* 176 (1972): 184; Florence Moog, "Women, Students, Tenure," *Science* 174 (1971): 983; Deborah Shapley, "University Women's Rights: Whose Feet Are Dragging?" *Science* 175 (1971): 151; Rita J. Simo, Shirley M. Clark, and Kathleen Galway, "The Woman Ph.D: A Recent Profile," in Martha T. Mednick, Sandra S. Tangri, and Lois W. Hoffman, eds., *Women and Achievement* (New York: John Wiley, 1975), 355–71; Helen S. Astin and Alan E. Bayer, "Sex Discrimination in Academe," in Mednick et al., *Women and Acheivemnt*, 372–95.

3. Sophie Drinker, *Music and Women* (New York: Coward-McCann, 1948).

4. Ibid., 295.

5. George Upton, *Women and Music* (Boston: James R. Osgood, 1888), 16.

6. Ibid., 21–22.

7. See "Women Discuss Striving for Status as Composers," *New York Times*, (1 Dec. 1987), p. C19. See also Aaron I. Chen, ed., *The International Encylopedia of Women Composers* (New York: R. R. Bowker, 1987).

8. Harris and Nochlin, *Women Artists: 1550–1950*.

9. Greer, *Obstacle Race*, 327.

10. See Reine–Marie Paris, *Camille: The Life of Camille Claudel* (New York: Arcade, 1988); Robert Wernick, "Camille Claudel's Tempestuous Life of Art and Passion," *Smithsonian* (September 1985), 57–64.

11. Natalie Angier, "Women Swell Ranks of Science, but Remain Invisible at the Top," *New York Times* (21 May 1991), p. C1, C12;

Londa Schienbinger, *The Mind Has No Sex: Women in the Origins of Modern Science* (Cambridge: Harvard University Press, 1989).

12. National Science Foundation. *Women, Minorities, and Persons with Disabilities in Science and Engineering,* Arlington, VA: NSF 96–311.

13. Sy Montgomery, *Walking with Apes* (New York: Houghton Mifflin, 1991).

14. Shirley Strum, *Almost Human: A Journey Into the World of Baboons* (New York: Random House, 1987)

15. Margaret Power, *The Egalitarians* (Cambridge: Cambridge University Press, 1991)

16. Patricia Braus, How Women Will Change Medicine, *American Demographics,* November 1994.

17. Ibid.

CHAPTER 11

1. Leo Frobenius, *Der Kopf als Schicksal* (Munich, 1924), 88, translated by R. F. C. Hull, in C. G. Jung and Ce. Kerényi, *Essays on a Science of Mythology,* Bollingen series 22 (New York: Pantheon Books, 1949), 141–42.

2. Marguerite Mitscherlich, *The Peaceable Sex: On Aggression in Women and Men* (New York: Fromm International Publishing, 1987).

3. See Ashley Montagu, *On Being Human* (New York: Dutton, 1976); Montagu, *Growing Young.*

4. The cradle, the best mother's aid and baby's comfort ever invented, and physiologically and psychologically most beneficial to the baby, was discarded on the recommendation of (male) pediatricians in the 1920s; by the end of the 1930s it had virtually disappeared and was replaced by the utterly unsatisfactory crib. On this subject and the importance of rocking, see Montagu, *Touching.*

5. William E. Ritter, *Darwin and the Golden Rule* (New York: Storm Publishers, 1954), 203.

6. Ashley Montagu, *The Direction of Human Development* 2nd ed. (New York: Hawthorn Books, 1970); also in Montagu, *On Being Human.* See also John Bowlby, *Attachment and Loss,* vol. 1, *Attachment* (New York: Basic Books, 1969); Harry F. Harlow and M. K. Harlow, "Learning to Love," *American Scientist* 54 (1966):

244–72; H. F. Harlow, "Primary Affectional Patterns in Primates," *American Journal of Orthopsychiatry* 30 (1960): 676–84.

7. On of the gest books on the subject is Ian Suttie, *The Origins of Love and Hate* (Baltimore: Penguin Books, 1960), 207.

8. For a full development of this subject see Montagu, *Direction of Human Development*, and Montagu, *Growing Young*.

CHAPTER 12

1. Chauncey D. Leake, "Ethicogenesis," *Scientific Monthly* 60 (1945): 245–25. See Robert Augros and George Stanciu, *The New Biology* (Boston: Shambhala Publications, 1987), particularly the chapter on cooperation; Ashley Montagu, *Darwin, Competition and Cooperation* (New York: Schuman, 1952); Peter Kropotkin, *Mutual Aid* (Boston: Porter Sargent, 1955). (Kropotkin's book was first published as a series of articles in *The Fortnightly Review* [London] in 1888, and first published in book form in 1902).

2. Steven Locke, et al., eds., *Foundations of Psychoneuroimmunology* (New York: Aldine Publishing Co., 1985). Norman Cousins, *Head First: The Biology of Hope* (New York: Dutton, 1990).

3. Montagu, *Nature of Human Aggression*.

4. For detailed discussions see Ann Fausto-Sterling, *Myths of Gender: Biological Theoeries About Women and Men* (New York: Basic Books, 1985); Alice S. Rossi, ed., *Gender and the Life Course* (New York: Aldine Publishing Co., 1985); Holly Devor, *Gender Blending: Con-fronting the Limits of Duality* (Bloomington: Indiana University Press, 1989); Michael S. Kimmel, ed., *Changing Men: New Dimensions in Research on Men and Masculinity* (Newbury Park, CA: Sage Publications, 1987); Robert J. Stoller, *Sex and Gender* (New York: Harper & Row, 1972); Ann Oakley, *Sex, Gender and Society* (New York: Harper & Row 1972); John Money and Anke E. Ehrhardt, *Man and Woman—Boy and Girl* (Baltimore: Johns Hopkins University Press, 1972); Joseph Zubin and John Mahoney, eds., *Contemporary Sexual Behavior* (Baltimore: Johns Hopkins University Press, 1973); Patrick C. Lee and Robert S. Stewart, *Sex Differences* (New York: Urizen Books, 1976); Judith Lorber and Susan A. Farrell, *The Social Construction of Gender* (Newbury Park, Ca.: Sage Publications, 1989); Richard Schickel, "Gender Bender," *Time,* 24 June 1991, p. 52–56; Margaret Carlson, "Is This What Feminism Is All About?" *Time* (24 June 1991), 57; Helen Silverberg, *Gender and American Social Science*

(Princeton: Princeton University Press, 1998); Marc F. Fasteau, *The Male Machine* (New York: Delta, 1975).

5.   Carolyn Heilbrun, *Toward a Recognition of Androgny* (New York: Knopf, 1973); June Singer, *Androgeny: Toward a New Theory of Sexuality* (New York: Anchor Books: 1977).

CHAPTER 13

1.   Ashley Montagu, *Culture and Human Development* (Englewood Cliffs N. J.: Prentice Hall, 1974); and Montagu, *Direction of Human Development.* For the evidence see John Bowlby, *Child Care and the Growth of Love* (New York: Penguin Books, 1953); Robert G. Patton and Lytt I. Gardner, *Growth and Failure in Maternal Deprivation* (Springfield, IL: C. C. Thomas, 1963); Yvonne Brackbill, ed., *Infancy and Early Childhood* (New York: The Free Press, 1967); Grant Newton and Seymour Levine, eds., *Early Experience and Behavior: The Psychobiology of Development* (Springfield, Il: C. C. Thomas, 1968); Eda J. LeShan, *The Conspiracy Against Childhood* (New York: Atheneum, 1967); Harry F. Harlow, *Learning to Love* (New York: Ballantine Books, 1971); Montagu, *On Being Human;* Ashley Montagu and Floyd Matson, *The Human Connection* (New York: McGraw–Hill, 1979).

2.   See Ashley Montagu, "Breastfeeding and Its Relation to Morphological, Behavioral, and Psychocultural Development," in Dana Raphael, ed., *Breastfeeding and Food Policy in a Hungry World* (New York: Academic Press, 1979), 189–97.

3.   Pearl Buck, *Of Men and Women* (New York: John Day Company, 1941), 55–56.

CHAPTER 14

1.   Peter L. Berger and Thomas Luckmann, *The Social Construction of Reality* (New York: Doubleday, 1966). Bernice A. Carroll, ed., *Liberating Women's History* (Urbana: University of Illinois Press, 1976); Gerda Lerner, *The Majority Finds Its Past* (New York: Oxford University Press, 1979); Andrea Dworkin, *Woman Hating* (New York: Dutton, 1974); Marielouise Janssen–Jurreit, *Sexism: The Male Monopoly on History and Thought* (New York: Farrar Straus Giroux, 1982); Londa Schiebinger, *The Mind Has No Sex? Women in the Origins of Modern Science* (Cambridge: Harvard University Press, 1989).

2. Montagu, *Man's Most Dangerous Myth*. See also Montagu, *On Being Human*.

3. Shakespeare, *Love's Labour's Lost*, iv–3.

APPENDIX B

1. S. D. Schmalhausen and V. F. Calverton, eds., *Woman's Coming of Age* (New York: Horace Liveright, 1931), 4.

2. Ellis, *Man and Woman*, 522.

3. See Montagu, *Growing Young*.

4. See William O'Neill's biography of Eastman, *The Last Romantic* (New York: Oxford University Press, 1978).

5. *The Freeman* (15 June 1953), 674–65.

Index